Concepts and Methods of Social Work

Concepts and Methods of Social Work

Dr. Poonam Rani

RANDOM

RANDOM PUBLICATIONS

NEW DELHI (INDIA)

Concepts and Methods of Social Work

ISBN 978-93-5111-624-0

Published in 2015 in India by

RANDOM PUBLICATIONS

4376-A/4B, Gali Murari Lal, Ansari Road
New Delhi-110 002
Phone : +9111-43580356, 011-23289044, 011-43142548
e-mail: sales@randompublications.com,
info@randompublications.com, randomexports@gmail.com

Reprinted 2021

Type Setting by : Friends Media, Delhi-110089
Digitally Printed at: Replika Press Pvt. Ltd.

Preface

Social work practice is also strengths-based. Social workers help people or groups identify their problems, determine their skills and capacities, what they are doing well, and how that was accomplished, and then analyze ways that those strengths might be applied to the identified problems. Many social workers work directly with clients who are individuals, families or small groups. These social workers help clients cope with problems such as poverty, abuse, addiction, and mental illness by providing counseling, connecting clients with service providers, and empowering clients to meet their own needs.

Social work is a helping profession which fundamentally and radically aims to assist the individuals, groups and community to cope with their complex socio-economic psychological problems through enabling themselves so that they can solve their problem by helping themselves. According to one of the great pioneer

Many social workers specialize in serving a particular population or working in a specific setting. In all settings, these workers may also be called licensed clinical social workers, if they hold the appropriate State mandated license. Child, family, and school social workers provide social services and assistance to improve the social and psychological functioning of children and their families. Workers in this field assess their client's needs and offer assistance to improve their situation. This often includes coordinating available services to assist a child or family. They may assist single parents in finding day care, arrange adoptions, or help find foster homes for neglected, abandoned, or abused children.

This book presents a comprehensive coverage of all important methods of social work. It provides readers an opportunity to develop knowledge of the principles, values and methods of social work.

I would like to thank my team for standing beside me throughout my career and writing this book. My special thanks go to "Random Publications" who have published the book.

– Dr. Poonam Rani

Contents

1

Meaning and Concepts of Social Work

INTRODUCTION

Social work is a profession for those with a strong desire to help improve people's lives. *Social workers* assist people by helping them cope with and solve issues in their everyday lives, such as family and personal problems and dealing with relationships. Some social workers help clients who face a disability, life-threatening disease, social problem, such as inadequate housing, unemployment, or substance abuse. Social workers also assist families that have serious domestic conflicts, sometimes involving child or spousal abuse. Additionally, they may conduct research, advocate for improved services, or become involved in planning or policy development.

Many social workers specialize in serving a particular population or working in a specific setting. In all settings, these workers may also be called *licensed clinical social workers*, if they hold the appropriate State mandated license. *Child, family, and school social workers* provide social services and assistance to improve the social and psychological functioning of children and their families. Workers in this field assess their client's needs and offer assistance to improve their situation. This often includes coordinating available services to assist a child or family. They may assist single parents in finding day care, arrange adoptions, or help find foster homes for neglected, abandoned, or abused children.

These workers may specialize in working with a particular problem, population or setting, such as child protective services, adoption, homelessness, domestic violence, or foster care. In schools, social workers often serve as the link between students' families and the school, working with parents, guardians, teachers, and other school officials to ensure that students reach their academic and personal potential. They also assist students in dealing with stress or emotional problems. Many school social workers work directly with children with disabilities and their families. In addition, they address problems such as misbehaviour, truancy, teenage pregnancy, and drug and alcohol problems and advise teachers on how to cope with difficult students.

School social workers may teach workshops to entire classes on topics like conflict resolution. Child, family, and school social workers may be known as child welfare social workers, family services social workers, or child protective services social workers. These workers often work for individual and family services agencies, schools, or State or local governments. *Medical and public health social workers* provide psychosocial support to individuals, families, or vulnerable populations so they can cope with chronic, acute, or terminal illnesses, such as Alzheimer's disease, cancer, or AIDS. They also advise family caregivers, counsel patients, and help plan for patients' needs after discharge from hospitals. They may arrange for at-home services, such as meals-on-wheels or home care.

Some work on interdisciplinary teams that evaluate certain kinds of patients, such as geriatric or organ transplant patients. Some specialize in services for senior citizens and their families. These social workers may run support groups for the adult children of aging parents. Also, they may assess, coordinate, and monitor services such as housing, transportation, and long-term care.

These workers may be known as gerontological social workers. Medical and public health social workers may work for hospitals, nursing and personal care facilities, individual and family services agencies, or local governments. *Mental health and substance abuse social workers* assess and treat individuals with mental illness or substance abuse problems. Such services include individual and group therapy, outreach, crisis intervention, social rehabilitation, and teaching skills needed for everyday living.

They also may help plan for supportive services to ease clients' return to the community when leaving in-patient facilities. They may provide services to assist family members of those who suffer from addiction or other mental health issues. These workers may work in outpatient facilities, where clients come in for treatment and then leave, or in inpatient Programmes, where patients reside at the facility.

Some mental health and substance social workers may work in employee-assistance Programmes. In this setting, they may help people cope with job-related pressures or with personal problems that affect the quality of their work. Other social workers work in private practice, where they are employed directly by the client. These social workers may be known as clinical social workers, occupational social workers, or substance abuse social workers. Other types of social workers include social work administrators, researchers, planners and policymakers, who develop and implement Programmes to address issues such as child abuse, homelessness, substance abuse, poverty, and violence. These workers research and analyse policies, Programmes, and regulations. They identify social problems and suggest legislative and other solutions. They may help raise funds or write grants to support these programmes.

SCOPE OF SOCIAL WORK

One Discipline, borrowed from America, taught in India at the university level is the discipline of Social Work. We have graduate, post-graduate, MPhil and PhD degrees awarded in this discipline, as is in the case of most other disciplines. But Social Work is a professional course. It can earn a living directly. Starting with one institute offering a programme in Social Work in 1946, we have today a hoard of such institutes functioning from all across the country. The earliest graduates in Social Work migrated to the United States of America or Europe because Social Work is a recognised profession there. A degree in Social Work offered good employment opportunities as well as scope for private practice.

In India Social Work never got established as an independent profession. The government social welfare departments, hospitals largely employed trained social workers against lower middle rung posts. When Indian labour laws made it compulsory to appoint welfare officers in the factories, Social Work degree became a passport to appointment against these posts. With time, welfare officers saw themselves becoming personnel officers and later human resource development managers. People with Social Work background thus got higher status in society. When management education came to India, HRD became a preferred area of specialisation and management graduates soon replaced Social Work graduates from HRD jobs.

A new attractive field opened for the Social Work graduates when some non-government organisations adopted corporate culture under the influence of its foreign donors. But these employment opportunities were limited in numbers because how many NGOs in India would find foreign funds? High profile jobs for Social Work graduates were therefore ruled out. The scope for practicing Social Work as private profession in India is next to nil. Petty political party workers who also call themselves social workers appear to be doing better. The image of a social worker amongst the general public is such that if a trained social worker were to introduce himself/herself the response coming from the opposite person most likely is to be: I am a social worker too. It is difficult for the Indian people to conceive that there could be professionals around called social workers to be approached when facing personal or family problems. The reason is not far to see. Helping each other in the Indian traditions is a noble cause. Every body therefore shows eagerness to help every body else. Why in that case someone pay a social worker?

Since the very concept of professional social work is missing from the Indian minds, trained social workers are going to find it very difficult to establish roots in this country. It is also to remember that profession wise it is the clients who approach the professionals and not the other way round. If we look at the methods of professional social work, they talk of helping people individually helping people in groups and helping people's communities. It may be seen that of these, the last two methods can not be practiced by trained social workers in private practice since these require a larger setting. Only organised bodies such government, corporate houses, NGOs can afford it. Trained social workers therefore have to be necessarily employed to be able to practice these two methods. This leaves Social Casework method as the only method that can be employed by trained social workers to earn an independent living. In Social Casework method, the trained social worker interviews his/her client, in private and takes down the personal history.

Through this he/she makes an assessment of the likely cause for the problem faced by the client. The process of interviewing is simple chit-chatting. The client may not even know if he/she is being helped or having a street corner talk. One interview with the client is not sufficient; more have to be arranged. Some clients may not be prepared for repeat visits. Even if the cause is discovered successfully, the solution that is offered to the client may not be out of the ordinary.

It consists of plain suggestions and motivational talks. Unlike doctors and psychiatrists who prescribe medicines, professional social workers prescribe no such thing. This leaves the clients a bit disappointed. In fact, many people have been giving advises to them. Experience shows that people in India are happier discussing their personal problems with astrologers, tantrics, priests and saddhus for they offer mantras, tabeej, bhasma, flowers, *etc.* said to be containing charismatic powers or ask to perform certain rituals such as feeding the fish, donating mustard oil, performing puja etc that heal all the problems. People have no hesitation in paying them; sometimes even paying big money.

It appears that people are more interested in purchasing hope than getting rid of the problem. From the discussion so far it is clear that professional Social Work is a big failure in India; it can neither provide you decent employment nor earn an independent living. Students of Social Work at the universities, colleges and departments are therefore heading for a disaster. The government should take steps to weed out such unnecessary disciplines from our education system or consider modifying these to suit our conditions. Employing trained social workers in rural areas where community organisation is a big challenge also appears to be an attractive option. Is any body listening?

MODERN SOCIAL WORK

Modern social work is to focus on the modern world values. It is about the present world issues. It may count a couple of issues from simple to complex. It may count family welfare, which is to make good things for a family. It is about giving benefits to single families. It is about child welfare where different organisations are working for the welfare of children round the global. Their focus is children. It is about criminal justice in which they are supposed to do justice with those who are accountable for a crime in the society. It is about mental health and cares where they take care of people and work on the grooming of their mental status. It is about leisure and youth services where they work on the youngsters and focus on their participation for the national growth. It is also about physical health which is to make good health of the people who comprise a society. It is all about things that are accountable for development of a social system.

ASSUMPTIONS AND VALUES OF SOCIAL WORK

ASSUMPTIONS

- Personal familial and communal problems are the result of human interactions with others
- Problems can facilitated and enrich human life
- The centrality of the human being

VALUES

It is impossible to venture far into discussions about social work values without a passing nod in the direction of Father Biestek's work.

He defined seven principles necessary for a good relationship between the social worker and client:

1. *Acceptance*: to be recognised as a person of worth.
2. *Client self-determination*: to make choices and decisions.
3. *Confidentiality*: to keep personal information secret.
4. *Controlled emotional involvement*: to get a sympathetic response from a an interested professional who adopts a certain level of emotional involvement.
5. *Individualisation*: to be treated as an individual.
6. *None judgmental attitude*: not to be judged.
7. *Purposeful expression of feelings*: to have the opportunity as a client to express one's feelings.

Through these immutable principles, Biestek offered us a certainty, grounded in his religious convictions, about how social workers and clients ought to behave. A certainty not perhaps reflected in the world of today, if indeed it was ever present. Ultimately his list has done social work a disservice. The very existence of such a list promotes a false sense of security among some in the social work profession who cling with unthinking na‹vet, to the supposedly unambiguous principles enshrined in Biestek's tablet.

How often do we hear consideration of values reduced to slogans such as 'confidentiality' which are bandied around by colleagues as if that word were all there were to say on the subject. Keeping confidences is an important part of good social work practice. Yet what does it really mean to adopt and adhere to a principle of 'confidentiality'? Social workers tell managers what clients tell them; social workers reveal what they know in court; social workers do not have a protected position as between client and lawyer or the priest and the penitent; social workers contend with the stipulations of the data protection act and the requirements of open records: social workers speak to the press about injustice at their peril.

Yet resonating m each of these issues is the lack of clarity about whether social workers' primary duty is to client or state as employer. Each of Biestek's principles could be examined in detail to reveal similar substantial deficiencies in form and content. Turning to professional associations, such as the British Association of Social Workers for advice about values what do we find? A code of ethics prescribing and requiring various types of behaviour. To understand much of the content of BASWs code requires a return to the heady days of the early 1970s. In the immediate post Seebohm world, when social services departments were created on 1 April 1971, there were promises of future glory. Social workers confidently expected to banish poverty and delinquency.

Amid the euphoria, debates about the nature of social work were rife. The social worker's claim to professional status, and equivalence with teachers, lawyers and doctors, was firmly asserted through the code of practice, first adopted in 1975. Perhaps the most significant statement is the opening sentence: Social work is a professional activity.' The word 'professional' occurs no less than nine times in the first 150 words of the code! 'The 12 principles of practice enumerated in the code vary from the highly desirable requirement not to act towards clients on the basis of any form of prejudice to the gratuitous exhortation to collaborate with others in the interests of clients —all in all something of a pastiche of various characteristics supposedly defining a profession.

Finally, what is perhaps most remarkable about the BASW code of practice is its lack of influence—the reasons for this state of affairs provide a subject for endless speculation. Such codes of practice are rooted in the historical epoch and ideological clutter that generated them. Compare the National Association of Social Workers code of ethics, in the USA, which has a distinct part of six items for social workers engaged in research and a requirement not to solicit the clients of one's own agency for private practice. To which the retort of many a hard pressed and under paid British social worker might be chance would be a fine thing. There is one other repository of wisdom where one might expect to find guidance about the nature of social work values, the Central Council for Education and Training in Social Work.

Given its responsibilities for regulating and validating social work training, CCETSW has grappled with this question at various times. In 1987, CCETSW stipulated that social workers must be able to articulate a coherent value system and to demonstrate an understanding of its application to the professional activity of social work, placing on social workers a requirement that would have taxed a professor of philosophy or indeed a saint. Fortunately this requirement has been eased so that now a newly qualified social worker is only required to be committed to social justice and social welfare, to enhancing the quality of life of individuals, families and groups within communities, and to a repudiation of all forms of negative discrimination. These with some elaboration are described as the values of social work, indicating a confidence, perhaps misplaced, in CCETSW's recent writing on values. In earlier writings CCETSW expressed somewhat more diffidence in defining values in social work.

The working party, set up to examine the teaching of values, abandoned the attempt to define values —very sensibly, in the light of almost 200 different definitions for the term values. Instead CCETSW chose to use the term in the following way: A value determines what a person thinks he ought to do, which may or may not be the same as what he wants to do, or what is in his interest to do, or in fact what he actually does. Values in this sense give rise to general standards and ideals by which we judge our own and others conduct: they also give rise to specific obligations. This is a helpful statement which delineates one dimension of what values might mean. It does not reduce the notion of values to an immutable list.

Also it allows for the possibility that individuals will have differing values just as to the social, political, racial and economic grouping to which they belong. Something we know to be the case from our everyday experience. So to ask continually, 'what are the values of social work', is to miss the point. Even though, phrases such as the 'value base' suggest that there is something firm and fundamental upon which to build the edifice of social work, there is no single set of values that commands universal assent among practitioners, educators or clients. Any list of values that we night construct would be an elaboration of our personal/political/religious/ideological beliefs. As indeed are the accounts of values considered so far. CCETSWs 1976 statement is helpful because it does not attempt to describe a list but rather suggests a relationship between values and action. We often talk as if there were a common and universal set of values. This may have rather more to do with the need for affirmation as a part of a very diverse social work profession than the existence of consensus at the level of meaning.

Noel Timms described social work values in the following way:

- Almost any kind of belief and obligation, anything preferred for any reason or for no apparent reason at all, any objective in the short or long run, any ideal or rule, is heaped into a large pantechnicon carrying the device 'Social Work Values - will travel anywhere'.

We should do well to heed this view and all that it implies for the practice of social work. This confusion and lack of agreement about the nature and content of values in social work might imply that they are of little use. However there are at least two important sessions to be drawn.

Firstly that if we wish to make use of any of the concepts that fall within the broad notion of social work values we must learn to be precise in the way we talk about them. Given the plethora of possible meanings is it not better to speak of terms such as moral judgements, fundamental principles of practice, the ideology or philosophy of social work *etc.* to name but a few?

Secondly, if we are seeing firm prescriptions which require no further thought then indeed talk of social work values will not be of any great help. Yet, if we shift the nature of enquiry from searching out definitive answers to promoting a greater understanding through striving for meaning, clarification and illumination, values in social work have much to offer to us.

HISTORY OF SOCIAL WORK IN U.K., U.S.A., AND INDIA

In the 1850s, Elizabeth Blackwell introduced "visitors" into the homes of New York's sick. Immigration accompanied by rapid urbanization and industrialization, increased city social problems. Poverty and its accompanying difficulties forced society to address needed services. As a result, new charities, both public and private, responded to the challenge. Many of the new relief efforts were inefficient and poorly organised. As charity resources expanded, experienced workers saw the need for improved organisation and management and they began to apply order to the problems in their communities. The hardship and slow economy of the 1870s threw millions of men out of work and sparked riots and strikes. The strikes shut down most of the nation's railroad traffic and, as a result, commerce came to a halt.

Elected officials, shocked and frightened by the poverty, destitution and general unrest, expanded local relief efforts hoping to moderate the depression's severity and to re-establish social order.

During this time, a new movement of charitable organisations began to appear that we now associate more directly with the evolution of early social work. The Charity Organisations were created to reorganise the public and private resources that had proliferated during the 1870s. In 1877, the first American Charity Organisation society was established in Buffalo, New York. Over the next two decades the movement spread rapidly.

At the turn of the century, virtually every major urban area in America hosted some form of Charity Organisation society. Leaders believed poverty could be eradicated through planned intervention or treatment rather than by direct relief alone. Many were disturbed by what they saw as an inefficient and chaotic array of urban philanthropy. Therefore, a central record keeping system was created to track those who received assistance and prevented the indigent from receiving relief from more than one agency.

Someone, though, had to perform the crucial tasks of investigation and treatment, and that someone was the "friendly visitor", and yielded the birth of what would be the social work profession was born. In the early 1890s, Mary Richmond, then director of the Baltimore Charity Organisation, began developing training Programmes. In 1898, the New York Charity Organisation started the first school for social workers. The original curriculum was designed as a six week set of summer classes and included formal lectures and field-work.

THE BIRTH OF SOCIAL WORK

The friendly visitors were women who were volunteers or missionaries and most from the upper class society. They strived to lessen the burden of the poor through direct service and prayer. The friendly visitors would first study and investigate relief applications, separate the recipients into deserving or undeserving classes and then treat them by making referrals and providing them with friendship. Friendly visiting put many members of the upper classes in close proximity with the other classes. This familiarity often forced them to confront situations where such broad factors as exploitive working conditions and industrial injury were more often to blame for poverty than character flaws or lack of morals among the poor.

Some visitors began to see that poverty was a far more complex problem than they had been led to believe. As the attitudes and policies of the charity Organisations began to change, so, too, did the character of friendly visiting. As friendly visitors became more systematic and professional, a consensus spread that visitors needed training. In 1891, the charity Organisation movement in New York began publishing a journal to disseminate new ideas in the field. Training Programmes under the leadership of new professionals such as Mary Richmond sprang up around the country. In 1898 these activities culminated with the establishment of the New York Summer School For Applied Philanthropy. Soon the friendly visitors were replaced by, or became, "professional" social workers.

Early on the now educated/trained friendly visitors began to refer to themselves as "caseworkers". It wasn't until the 1890's that they began to use the term "social workers. The early professional social workers also broadened the application of their new skills to include other types of charity work through expanding "casework" practice into child welfare institutions and juvenile courts. By the beginning of the 20th century, the volunteer friendly visitor of the early Charity Organisations had evolved into what we now identify as social casework.

THE DEPRESSION

The 1890s economic slump was even more severe than the one that had occurred in the 1870s. Banks closed, unemployment soared, and three million men were idle due to unemployment. Racism, so often a symptom of class tensions, rose to disturbing levels. Traditional agencies such as the Children's Aid Society and the Salvation Army were overwhelmed, incapable of meeting the demands placed on their services. Faced with the grim realities of the depression, many Charity Organisation leaders began to change and suggested the need for new thinking about poverty. Even the Charity Organisations stance to not simply provide direct financial assistance had to change. As a result, by turn of the century, two-thirds of all Charity Organisation societies were directly involved with relief efforts.

SETTLEMENTS—A NEW IDEA

In London, a new idea was formed that was focused on improving the circumstances and causes of poverty than the flaws of the poor. From this idea emerged the first settlement house, Toynbee Hall, which was established in 1884. It was located in the slums of London and was established to help bridge the gap between London's rich and poor. The Toynbee model provided a residence where university men settled. This provided an outpost of culture and education in the poverty driven neighbourhood. The premise was that university students could learn as much from the poor as the poor could learn from the university students.

In the mid-1880s, a group of college-educated Americans visited Toynbee Hall. Upon their return to America, some of these students were so impressed by what they saw at Toynbee Hall that they created similar establishments in American cities. In 1886, Stanton Coit established a settlement house in New York. In 1889, Vida Scudder opened another New York settlement staffed with recently graduated college women. In that same year, Jane Addams and Ellen Gates Starr opened Hull House in Chicago. These successes were quickly followed by others. Soon settlements were spread throughout urban America. By the mid-1890s there were fifty, and by 1900 there were more than a hundred recognized settlements. The efforts of the settlement worker were different from those of the friendly visitors who focused mostly on the so-called indigent population or those we refer to today as the chronically poor. The settlement movement, in contrast, devoted most of its energies in working with what we would today regard as the poorer segments of the working class, particularly immigrants. They sought to reform aspects of American society that they identified as problematic.

Instead of focusing their efforts on changing the individual behaviours and values of the poor, settlement workers tried to change the neighbourhoods and expand opportunities for working class people who were poor, but not indigent. The entry of the settlements and their residents in low-income immigrant neighbourhoods brought new attitudes and perspectives to the charity field. Settlement workers researched and surveyed the problems of the poor through studies that documented the systemic nature of the problem. They argued that the social problems were the result of structural circumstances based on the general situations in which the poor lived, rather than individual deficiencies. The studies had national impact that described the conditions and trials of a variety of groups including immigrants, working women, children, and the unemployed.

Public education, juvenile courts, public playgrounds, citizenship, daycare, and cultural awareness Programmes are just a few examples of the reform activities adopted by settlement workers. Many found themselves pulled into union organising and local politics as they searched for strategies to improve the lives of their neighbours. In 1906, several New York settlements sponsored the friendly visitor concept for three school districts to deal with those whom neither the attendance officer, school nurse, or classroom teacher were equipped. The teacher or principal refereed children whose educational experience was obstructed by deficient scholarship, demoralizing home conditions, misconduct, physical defect and similar handicaps. After an examination into the background and personality of each child, the visitor used whatever personal influence or social adjustments were necessary to insure efficient performance. Hull House was one of the most famous settlement sites. Many who lived there were immigrants from countries such as Italy, Russia, Poland, Germany, Ireland, and Greece. For these working poor, Hull House provided a day care centre for children of working mothers, a community kitchen, and visiting nurses. Jane Addams and her staff gave classes in English literacy, art, and other subjects.

Hull House also became a meeting place for clubs and labour unions. Most of the people who worked with Addams in Hull House were well educated, middle-class women. Hull House gave them an opportunity to use their education and it provided a training ground for careers in social work. Led by young Hull House resident, Mary Kenny O'Sullivan, the settlement served as a hub for organising shirtwaist workers and pushed for the passage of the Illinois Factory Act, a bill that provided protective policies for working women and children. As reform issues emerged from their work in the community, settlement workers would then take on broader issues. Their crusade expanded to include creating basic services such as kindergartens, playgrounds, nurseries, child labour and eventually, under the adept leadership of Florence Kelly, led to the establishment of The Women's Trade Union League and The Children's Bureau.

Many groups had hope that government could be an instrument for improvement. This school of thought eventually led to the formation of the Progressive Party during Teddy Roosevelt's 3rd party campaign for the Presidency in 1916. Many of them, such as Lillian Wald, Florence Kelly, Jane Adams, and Paul Kellogg, rose to national prominence. Such leaders continued their commitment to social change and reform. Until 1920, American women could not vote. Addams joined in the movement for women's suffrage. Jane Addams also became involved in wider efforts for social reform, including housing and sanitation issues, factory inspection, rights of immigrants, women and children, creating kindergarten, playgrounds, child labour laws, anti-drug enforcement, pacifism, and the 8-hour day. In Chicago, Mary McDowall helped create the National Consumer's League and hundreds of settlement workers joined the crusade for improving conditions of women and children workers led by Frances Kelly. Mrs. Kelly also became a leader in the early women's labour movement. In New York, settlement leaders such as Lillian Wald and Robert Hunter put social workers into public schools and promoted the idea of school-provided lunches. In some cities, leaders sought better housing for the poor. They gave keynote addresses at national conferences, wrote articles in national magazines and were commonly quoted in the nation's leading newspapers. Some of the more influential leaders developed interests in issues that extended beyond the neighbourhood.

An example of this type of national activity was the crusade to improve the circumstances of women and children which led to the creation of the Children's Bureau. The Country's infant and maternal mortality rates were the highest of any industrial country, the growing number of orphans was overwhelming local resources, both the public and private foster homes and orphanage networks were overcome by the sheer number of new wards, and millions of children were working instead of attending school. The same leaders who fought so prodigiously for maternal and infant health Programmes and widows' pensions were also prominent in the crusade against child labour. That problem proved to be more recalcitrant than either widow's pensions or health Programmes. Both industry and many poor families opposed laws that limited or prohibited young children from working. Industry for the obvious reason, were recruiting children to work, as they could pay child workers at a cheap rate.

Poor families often needed the paltry contributions of their working children just to survive. Leaders soon became involved in many issues. They included advocacy of labour, civil rights, suffrage and peace. Seeking change, Florence Kelly called for the creation of a national Children's Bureau in 1900. In 1906, they created the National Committee on Child Labour which sponsored investigations and lobbied for legislation protecting children. Child labour was not eliminated until new legislation was passed as part of the NEW DEAL. After bringing her concerns before President Theodoure Roosevelt, Kelly along with Lillian Wald, Edward Devine, James West, and Homer Folks brought together more leaders from communities throughout America to address such issues. With the support of President Roosevelt, a White House Conference On Children was held in 1909. Reformers began the campaign for what was then known as a widow's pension.

These leaders felt that most children should be cared for in their own home as opposed to the all too common practice of removing children from the homes of poor single parents. They felt that the government was paying more for a child's care in an asylum or orphanage than it would cost to pay the mother to take care of her children at home. The resulting publicity put child welfare on the national agenda and generated enough political pressure to force the creation of the Children's Bureau in 1912. Julia Lathrop from Chicago's Hull House was named to head the U.S. Children's Bureau in 1912. Initially, the Children's Bureau's role was limited to conducting research and collecting data on children's issues.

One of the first studies undertaken by the new organisation was of maternal and infant mortality. Armed with statistics showing a shockingly high rate of maternal deaths, bureau workers began a campaign for Programmes to directly address the problem. The Sheppard-Towner bill was introduced in 1918 by Congresswoman Jeanette Rankin. Ms. Rankin was the first congresswoman in the U.S. Congress and a social worker.

The proposed legislation provided funds to local health departments for maternal and infant health services and after considerable opposition from conservative legislators was finally signed by the president in 1921. This legislation was so successful that funding, initially due to expire in 1927 was extended for an additional two years. When the act finally expired in 1929, there were more than 3,000 local Programmes and maternal and infant mortality rates were significantly improved. In 1911, Missouri enacted the first widow's pension. By 1919, 39 states had similar Programmes.

CHARLOTTE AND MECKLENBURG COUTY,S DEPARTMENT

On August 4, 1919, The Mecklenburg Board of County Commissioners and the Board of Education organised the County's Department of Public Welfare. The department was located in the Charlotte City Hall. The staff included the superintendent, Mr. Lucius H.Ranson and a secretary. The budget for the first fiscal year was $2,239.76. Public Welfare activities included enforcement of school attendance laws, child labour laws, and supervision of Juvenile Court. On October 29, 1919, The Commissioners appointed a 3-member Board of Public Welfare which held their inaugural Board of Public Welfare meeting on November 17, 1919. Nationally, leaders also played an important part in combating racism and civil inequality.

Plans were made for the creation of a permanent organisation which then evolved into the National Association For The Advancement Of Coloured People. The NAACP's first central committee included William Walling, Jane Adams, and W.E.B. Du Bois. Adams also founded the American Civil Liberties. CASEWORK-By the time America became involved in the First World War, casework had developed as a major force in the new field of social work. No longer regarded as a technique only suitable for private charities serving the poor, casework was identified as a broad skill applicable in a wide variety of arenas including mental hygiene, schools, hospitals, and juvenile courts. Dr.

Richard Cabot introduced a medical social services department at Massachusetts General Hospital in 1905.

Seven years after founding the service, a specialty in medical social work was offered by the Boston School of Social Work. A number of hospitals, mainly in the Northeast, established medical social work departments. Mental institutes also began to see the benefit of social services. Adolf Meyer, a prominent leader in the mental hygiene movement, believed that psychiatry needed to focus more of its efforts outside the asylum. He identified the social worker as a primary agent in providing a better understanding of the patient's social environment. By 1920, Social workers addressed mental hygiene problems in mental hospitals, outpatient clinics and juvenile courts. In 1917 the National Social Workers' Exchange was formed. The Exchange dealt with a number of issues including employment, working conditions, and salaries. The success of the exchange provided evidence that there was a need for a national organisation. By 1920, school social service Programmes were functioning Iowa, Massachusetts, and New York.

In 1921 a group from the Social Workers' Exchange met at the National Conference and voted to change their name to the American Association of Social Workers. They opened their membership to accept everyone, trained or volunteer, who identified themselves as social worker. By 1919 this Programme had grown and changed its name to the New York School of Social Work, later to become the Columbia University School of Social Work. The University of Chicago was offering extension courses on social work which grew into a full curriculum known as the Chicago School of Civics and Philanthropy. In 1920 it officially became the University of Chicago, School of Social Work. By 1920 there were 17 schools of social work that formed the Association of Training Schools of Professional Schools Of Social Work. The organisation was the predecessor to what is now known as the Council On Social Work Education. The new field of social work was now ready to begin creating a true and widely recognized profession. By the end of the 1920s, most of the states and larger cities used an executive based system of administration for supervising public charities. This shift reflected the growing role state and local governments were playing in the field of relief. Social casework's began to increase shortly before the 1920s.

NORTH CAROLINA

In 1921, the NC General Assembly enacted the first Welfare Law, which proscribes the duties of the Superintendent, including:

- Assist the State board in finding employment for the unemployed
- Care and supervision of the poor, and administration of the poor funds
- Creation of a 3-member Black Advisory Board to study welfare problems of Blacks and requested that the Counties assist in serving them

- Monitor the condition of persons discharged from hospitals for the insane and other State institutions
- Oversight of all dependent and delinquent children, especially those on parole or probation
- Oversight of all prisoners in the County on parole and probation
- Promote wholesome recreation in the County and enforce laws regulating commercial amusement

World War I provided unique opportunities for social caseworkers to prove the utility of their skills on non-poverty populations. Mary Richmond's *Social Diagnosis* was the first definitive text on casework. *Social Diagnosis*, propelled casework from one of a number of approaches used by charity workers into a major form of practice. In 1925, no longer would the social worker be viewed solely as a charity worker delivering relief and moral uplift, but rather employ new skills in aiding poor, middle class or even affluent clients. By 1926, the Red Cross had organised social service departments in federal hospitals. This in turn led to the establishment of a nationwide system of social services attached to Veterans Administration clinics, outpatient departments and hospitals.

THE GREAT DEPRESSION

The trauma created by the depression produced a new kind of government and a new way of thinking about poverty. The depression, with its high unemployment rates among willing workers, shattered the dominant view that poverty was the result of personal failure. Before the depression, most people thought of welfare as something poor people received from mostly private charities. After the depression, welfare became a widely recognized responsibility of the federal government, and poverty was better understood as a situation caused by forces beyond individual control. Before the depression, relief Programmes were relatively simple arrangements. After the depression, welfare Programmes became a complex array of services, benefits, and taxes that affect virtually everyone.

The Great Depression left important marks on the social work profession. Largely due to the leadership of individuals who began their careers in settlements and moved into public service in the twenties, social work took its place on the national stage. Protégés of such early settlement leaders as Florence Kelly, Jane Addams, and Lillian Wald were major architects of what is now recognized as watershed public welfare policies. Harry Hopkins, Frances Perkins, Molly Dewson and Aubrey Williams not only led social work's advance into public welfare. President Herbert Hoover, along with most American leaders, assumed that the depression would be of short duration.

Hoover refused to do anything until unemployment rates were inordinately high. By the early 1930s the nation was in crisis. Unemployment in some cities was over 40 per cent and bankruptcy was a common occurrence. Thousands of unemployed males, called hobos or simply "Bo's", roamed the country in a fruitless search for work.

Farmers from all over the heartland were losing their land. Farm prices were so low that farmers were selling their produce for less than it cost them to transport the goods to market. Meanwhile, New York's Governor Franklin D. Roosevelt was not afraid to act. FDR had a number of very gifted social workers on his staff, largely refugees from the settlement movement. Some, such as Frances Perkins, his state secretary of labour, he had inherited from previous governor Al Smith. Others, such as Harry Hopkins, he had recruited from private charities.

Governor Roosevelt, with the help and encouragement of his social workers, crafted both unemployment and public works Programmes that were quickly imitated in other states. Social workers realised the seriousness of the depression before most other professionals. Their work put them in a unique vantage point where they had an all too clear a picture of the people's plight. Social workers were also among the Great Depression's earliest victims. Faced with the dual hardships of increased demand and decreased donations, a third of all private agencies were forced to close their doors.

THE NEW DEAL

The nation was in crisis when FDR became president in 1933. Millions were unemployed. Farms were abandoned, banks were failing, industrial output was a trickle, and most public and private relief Programmes were out of money. The president wasted little time. In his first 100 days in office, he and congress passed an unparalleled number of bills designed to do something about the depression. Taken as a whole, these Programmes became collectively known as the New Deal. The Federal Emergency Relief Act was designed to pump new money into state welfare Programmes; the Civilian Conservation Corps put thousands of young men to work in national forests and parks; the Public Works Administration started public works such as schools, courthouses and bridges, employing thousands of construction workers. The National Recovery Administration, dubbed the *BLUE EAGLE*, created a network of policies and Programmes to help small businesses, and the Agriculture Adjustment ACT promoted policies to help farmers.

THE SECOND NEW DEAL

By 1935, the nation had regained some of its confidence and economic indicators were improved. However, for much of the nation the depression continued to be a grim reality. Payrolls were still less than half of 1925 levels. Millions of the unemployed continued their fruitless search for work. It became obvious that the depression was going to be more stubborn than many hoped.

In this context, Roosevelt and his inside group of planners put together a set of Programmes designed to be more permanent than the prior emergency measures. Those Programmes, taken as a group, quickly became known as the Second New Deal. Arguably, the most prominent of the new Programmes was the Works Progress Administration, headed by the social worker Harry Hopkins. The WPA was a work-relief Programme designed to replace the FERA. It reflected the strong bias of both FDR and Hopkins that work Programmes were a much superior solution to the problems associated with poverty than did welfare. The WPA eventually employed more than 8 million Americans. Throughout the early years of the depression many in FDR's administration had advocated for a youth Programme.

First Lady Eleanor Roosevelt was especially concerned about the plight of what she termed "America's unwanted youth". The CCC responded to this group in a small way but there were still millions of teens out of school, out of work, and out of luck. FDR issued the executive order creating a *works* Programme for these youths in the summer of 1935. The National Youth Administration was headed by a young woman, Aubrey Williams, who was a protégé of Harry Hopkins and had been a staunch advocate for Programmes for women and children.

THE BIRTH OF SOCIAL SECURITY

The real keystone of the second New Deal was an ambitious set of social insurances and permanent relief Programmes. These Programmes were welded into the 1935 Social Security Act. Certainly, the most important single piece of domestic legislation in the 20th century, the Social Security Act was far more encompassing than the Programme which now bears its name.

Created by the Committee On Economic Security, this legislation was largely the product of social workers Harry Hopkins and Frances Perkins who worked closely with FDR throughout the process. Eventually a number of policy experts and legislators were involved in creating a broad set of Programmes that put the national government permanently in the business of welfare. The major components of the Social Security Act were the Social Insurance and the Public Assistance Programmes.

SOCIAL INSURANCE

The Social Security Act provided federal support for two social insurance Programmes that had been already initiated in many states. Unemployment Insurance and Workers' Compensation were crucial components in this set of provisions. However, the most ambitious part of the social insurance provisions was the creation of a federally administered Programme that provided limited insurance to workers in their old age. Officially this Programme was the Old Age Survivors and Disability Insurance but is now known generally as Social

Security. Together this set of social insurances was conceived as a matrix of Programmes offering working people some guarantees against economic and social problems beyond their individual control.

The Social Security Act created two major elements. One provided aid to people with disabilities and the other granted aid for widows and their children. The New Deal marginalized African Americans, Women, Hispanics and Asian-Americans. While the two New Deals were able to temporize some of the Great Depression's worst effects and created a welfare infrastructure that would serve the nation for the rest of the century, they failed to solve the economic problems that created the crisis. In retrospect, we now recognize that the various emergency measures, deemed so dramatic and radical in their time, were too meagre to pull the country out of the depression.

It took the enormous deficits created by World War II finally put an end to the depression. The emergency relief Programmes and the later creation of the Social Security system had a profound impact on the social work profession. First, it pushed the profession into the arena of public welfare. The crisis pulled thousands of social workers out of private agencies and into administrative and supervisory roles in the new public Programmes.

Another important impact created by the proliferation of public Programmes, was the increased number of people practicing social work. Thousands were recruited into social work through the gates of public Programmes. Many of these new social workers came from backgrounds quite different from their more experienced cohorts from established private charity Programmes. Most came from working class rather than upper class families. As the 1930s came to a close, social work had been transformed and had taken its place as an essential component of society.

THE CONTEXT OF SOCIAL WORK

The diverse nature of social work has been made more complex since the 1980s because of the changes that social work has had to embrace, some of which have given rise to confusions and uncertainties. The election of the Labour government in 1997 has given rise to other changes. Devolution has resulted in different policies being implemented in England, Wales and Scotland. For example, the Social Work Council envisaged for England is different from the one planned for Scotland.

Again, changes put forward for probation services in England and Wales are different from those planned for offender services in Scotland. One philosophy behind some of these changes is a commitment to reduce health and social inequalities through the establishment of national standards and objectives in relation to health and social services and a framework for assessing performance and effectiveness. These objectives can be seen in initiatives stemming from Quality Protects and Modernising Health and Social Services and in the government's commitment to a 'what works is what counts' approach to service delivery. Improvements in the quality of care will be overseen through the establishment of a proposed regulatory body, the General Social Care Council, which is due to be established in 2001. To achieve these aims, a collaboration between health and social services and interdisciplinary approaches to social care are seen as essential, although this may take different forms in various parts of the United Kingdom.

Although the current framework of social work education and training was only established in 1995, it is about to be changed again. The introduction of changes will be linked to the setting up of the Social Work Council and development of the new Code of Conduct for social workers. These changes and proposals, together with the linking of Quality Protects grants with quality of services, will continue to have a profound impact on social work and the range and quality of services provided. If the crisis in recruiting and retaining social workers continues, it is difficult to see how these changes can be implemented without incentives to improve staff morale and performance.

CHANGES IN THE LAW

Since the late 1980s, there have been three major pieces of leglisation affecting social work practice, namely the National Health Service and Community Care Act 1990; the Children Act, England, 1989 and the Criminal Justice Act 1991. The last has been substantially amended and superseded by subsequent legislation. In addition, there is now a considerable amount of case law emanating from interpretations of the Children Act 1989. The introduction of the Family Law Act 1996, particularly its provisions for addressing domestic violence, is an important development for social workers and probation officers.

(Legislation closely modelled on the Children Act, England 1989 includes the Children Act, Scotland, 1995 and the Children (Northern Ireland) Order 1997). In support of legislation codes of practice and guidance are drawn up by the government. These are important because they state government's expectations of local authorities in relation to good practice. For example, guidance issued under section 7(1) of the Local Authority Social Services Act 1970 means that, should local authorities fail to act in accordance with the guidance, a complaint can be made to the ombudsman or it may count as evidence against them in legal proceedings.

The difference between regulations, codes and guidance is described as follows:

- One might sum up the differences between the requirements of these various official documents like this: Regulations say 'You must/shall'; codes say 'You ought/should'. When guidance explains regulations, it reaffirms the 'You must' messages. However when it goes beyond regulation setting out good practice, it conveys the message that 'It is highly desirable to...' or 'Unless there is good reason not to, you should...' rather than, 'You must'.

We have described these differences in some detail because familiarity with the requirements of government, including the law, could be an important basis from which to argue for certain services to be provided and to 'endorse anti-discriminatory practice'. Some commentators have suggested that the European legislation when implemented, such as the Human Rights Act, may help service users to secure relevant services.

OUTLINE OF THE TEXT

We look at the theoretical underpinnings to practice. We look at how we can use theory and research to enhance our practice skills. In particular we explore what we mean when we use different theoretical terms and identify ten practice choices, giving a case example of their use in practice. These provide a framework to help us understand other theories and human behaviour. We bring theory and practice into closer dialogue by looking at communication, listening and assessment skills, and how we can evidence effectiveness. We explore how these theoretical concepts relate in practice. We describe 50 skills used within social work on a regular basis, giving a name to many of the skills practitioners already use but may not have categorized. Other core skills are included, but not described separately. These include communication, interviewing, observation, listening, assessment and decision-making skills, bringing the total number to roughly 56 skills.

We have encountered other skills worthy of mention but it was not possible to include them all without changing the nature of the book. Some readers may be disappointed not to find certain skills included, such as those associated with particular practice approaches like cognitive-behavioural or client-centred approaches. However, whenever possible we have tried to give references to further reading. Every skill has a theoretical underpinning but the emphasis in this text is on the use of skills in practice, rather than explaining the theoretical root of each skill.

That would require a book in its own right, which, hopefully, will one day be written. The perspective we stress throughout this part, and the text as a whole, is that every intervention should have a purpose and, as much as possible, that purpose should be identified clearly and openly as part of the agreement we establish with service users and other key individuals and professionals involved. If we fail at the outset to find agreement or to identify a common purpose this omission is likely to emerge as a difficulty later on.

This emphasis on being clear and specific in areas makes our contact with service users more purposeful and also allows us to assess the appropriateness of specific social work methods, approaches, perspectives, interventions and skills in terms of their effectiveness in bringing about desired and agreed outcomes. The focus of this book is on work with individuals, because the individual is located in other social formations, namely the family, group and community. However, the skills described are transferable and can be related to other practice orientations, and to work with service users in different settings. Some points of clarification about the text are worth noting. Throughout, we have described people who come within the remit of social work as service users. This term is not ideal, but nor are others. This dilemma is made more complicated because, in my experience, none of the terms used – service users, consumers, recipients of services or clients – draw on a language commonly used by people in receipt of social work services. The suggestion that the word client should refer to 'those who have social work imposed upon them' and service users to denote 'recipients of social work intervention voluntarily entered into' is an interesting differentiation but not always an easy distinction to draw. Nevertheless, Wise's conceptualization is helpful because it highlights the importance of language, and its limitations. Changing the words we use, while introducing a climate of hope and the chance for a fresh start, cannot in itself ensure that we have fundamentally altered the stigma and oppression that travels with certain oppressed groups. Nor can it ensure that those people are treated better, both within social work and outside.

Also on the subject of language, it is remarkable to note, given the historic and present day dominance of women in social work, both as service users and practitioners, how many authors use the male pronoun he. On occasion we have chosen to highlight how inappropriately this pronoun is used by adding the adverb sic. The interventions identified do not solely refer to work with service users, but can include any other people we encounter during the course of our work. Sometimes our colleagues, managers or other professionals need to be supported and challenged in ways that are similar to our interactions with service users.

Indeed, Wootton suggests that rather than focusing our attention on service users, many of whom lack the power and resources to change their lives, 'would not caseworkers do better to get their hands on some of our world's rulers?' The pronoun we refers to the fact that we have written this text as a practitioner. As a result, most case examples tend to describe my experience of working with children and families, which may not feel satisfactory for practitioners working in other fields of social work. We apologize for this. In the case examples all names and other identifiable characteristics have been changed to protect service users' identities. In relation to this text, unless stated to the contrary the reader can assume that the situations described refer to service users who have sought our help on a voluntary basis.

2

Methods of Social Work

INTRODUCTION

Social work as a profession is a product of this century. Although its roots are well established in history from the time when people 1st began to take responsibility for their neighbours through activities which were called charity, poor relief, philanthropy and social reform.

Social work is to fight against Five Evils as:

1. Physical want
2. Disease
3. Ignorance
4. Squalor
5. Idleness

Objective:

- To remove social injustice
- To relieve social injustice
- To reduce redress
- To prevent suffering
- To assist the weaker parts
- To rehabilitate the distress class people

All social work activities are classified into six major categories:

1. Social Casework
2. Social group work
3. Community organisation
4. Social action
5. Social welfare research
6. Social welfare administration

SOCIAL CASEWORK

Social Casework is a method which helps by counseling the individual client to effect better social relationships and a social adjustment that makes it possible him to lead a satisfying and useful life. Gordon Hamilton points out that, "The objective of Casework is to administer practical services and offer counseling in such a way as to arouse and conserve psychological energies of the client activity to involve him in the use of the service towards the solution of her/his dilemma."

SOCIAL GROUP WORK

Social group work is an activity which helps to participate in the activities of a group for their intellectual, emotional and physical growth and for the attainment of desirable goals of the groups. Group work as such as a method by which the group worker enables various types of groups to function in such a manner that both group interaction and programme activities contribute to the growth of the individual and the programme activities contribute to the growth of the individual and the achievement of desirable social goals.

Community Organisation

Community organisation is the process of planning and developing social services in order to meet the health and welfare needs of a community or larger unit. Mildred Barry says, "Community organisation in social work is the process of creating and maintaining a progressively more effective adjustment between community resources and commuity welfare needs."

Social Action

It s an organised group process solving general social problems and furthering social welfare objectives by legislative, social, health or economic progress. The term social action refers to organised and legally permitted activities designed to mobiles public opinion, legislation and public administration in favour of objectives believed to be socially desirable.

Social Welfare Research

Social welfare research systematic critically investigation of questions in the social welfare field with the purpose of yielding answares to problems of social work and of extending generally social work concept. The methods applied in social work research have been to a large extent derived grom those used in sociology and social psychology as well as in history and Anthropology.

Social Welfare Administration

Social welfare administration process is to organise and to direct a social agency. The administrative aspects of social work have to do with the organisation and management of social agencies public and private, including in those terms general administrative relationships among units of the same

SCOPE

In the factory setting one meets the working men with different economic, political and socio cultural back ground and tradition, with different physical capacities, mental abilities, emotional qualities and institutional moves they have came together to make their living through work. When they come with a social mind set, which is inadequate to become an industrial man, he find himself maladjusted and his behaviour turn to become abnormal to work and work organisation. An organisation more concentrate to business surplus and in the acute state of competition and business changes there is little time to spend some time with the worker to resolve the personal crisis.

Remove the maladjusted personnel from the payroll and appoint another who is competent enough to perform the functions may be the organisational solution. They don't have the knowledge or skill to intervene into personal problems of the employees. Mistreated by the management and neglected by labour unions he is always anxious to know about his job and how he fits in the total scheme of things, what his status in the organisation is and where he stands in the hierarchy of relationship, how he is respected by his fellow workers and what role he plays in promoting prosperity of the entire enterprise from where he seeks his own satisfaction. Thus he works under condition, which is more open than not, results in indiscipline and low morale.

He thinks that the existing pattern of labour management relations hardly provides proper machinery for amicable settlement of differences and creates conditions of industrial peace. All the worker is under the greatest handicap of the paucity proper referral agencies. In many organisations service conditions are often intolerable. There is high task orientation and less relationship orientation managerial approach in addition to capital incentive approaches. Here the management neglects the greatest asset, human resources, and it affect the morale and motivation of employees at work.

A worker may be good in his skill and knowledge to contribute best to the organisation. But because of lack of experience in handling human problems at work, the managers in the organisation have to leave those worker problems aside. His service conditions are often intolerable the climate of human relations at the work places is hopelessly impaired and the personnel organisation where he works to rarely knit.

The organisational climate, prevalent practices and the managerial approaches thus affect the worker adjustment of the members in their work situation. Lack of integration of the personal and organisational goal is the main factor that leads to maladjustment of the workers in the organisation. Organisational stress is one of the major intervention areas of the industrial casework process.

Many stress inducing factors like lack of supervisory support, lack of acceptance of the innovative suggestions, feeling of inequality, inadequate authority, lack of group cohesiveness, job requirement capability mismatch, role conflict role ambiguity etc are all directly affecting the individual worker at the personal level and develop maladjustments.

In the day-to-day work relationships he often comes in clash with the supervisor, strains his relation with him and he is charge sheeted for insubordination. A feeling enter his mind that he is misunderstood by the management that they are prejudiced against him.

Due to the lack of adequate proper training accounts keeping he commits a clerical error and is unfortunately charged for the misappropriation of companies fund.

He may be exposed to many disciplinary actions. The disciplinary actions affect the reputation of the worker in the industry. The single way to cope up with this problem is to quit the employment to protect his self-esteem. Organisation may not take effort to correct the individual worker and help him to identify his mistake.

A proper guidance and better support itself can lead employees to better performance and high integrity. Absenteeism and the labour turnover are the best examples of the individual workers maladjustment in the organisational setting. Indian organisations are facing these problems in its acute level.

The problems at the organisational level and the psychosocial level of employees in the labour setting have better opportunity to resolve those crisis thorough Industrial casework process.

PRINCIPLE OF INDIVIDUALIZATION

"Individualization is the recognition and understanding of each client's unique qualities and the differential use of principles and methods in assisting each towards a better adjustment."

- Individualization is based upon the right of human beings to be individuals.
- And to be treated not just as human being but as a human being with his personal differences.
- Client–Caseworker enter into a close relationship.
- Problems may be similar but factors involved in their causation are entirely different from each other.
  - Lack of material resources
  - Lack of appropriate information
  - Health related handicap
  - Stressful situations
  - Personality features

Theories of Psychology, Sociology, Medicine applies to all the persons, same time he has some character which are unique to him only.

- Different background/heredity/environment.
- Minute and subtle psychological and constitutional factors
- Inter-play between bio-psycho-social factors and environment
- Situation of the client

- His problems of social functioning
- Dominant mode of adjustments
- Life-style/activities
- His ego-strength
- Intellectual level
- Socio-economic situation
- Co-operation

Each person has different internal and external stimuli. His emotions and memories influence his thinking, feelings and behaviour in an individual manner.

- Individual capacity differs.
- Client requires a differential treatment.
- Select technique just as to the intellectual level, socio-economic situation, ego-strength, *etc.* of the client.
- Pay attention to a specific needs, problems, situation, resources and capacities of each client.
- SCW is to help as individual live a socially productive and individually satisfying life limited to his capacities and social realities.
- *Role of* Casework*er*:
  - Free from bias and prejudice
  - Knowledge of human behaviour
  - Ability to listen and observe
  - Ability to move at the client's pace
  - Ability to enter the feelings of the client
  - Ability to keep perspective
- *Essentials of Individualization*:
  - Thoughtfulness in details—comfortable room, chair, water, fan, lighting, no interruption.
  - Keeping appointments.
  - Privacy in interviews.
  - Language.
  - Encouraging the client
  - Flexibility
  - Preparation for interviews

PRINCIPLE OF ACCEPTANCE

"Acceptance is a principle of action where in the Case worker perceives and deals with the client as he really is, including his strengths and weakness, his congenial and uncongenial qualities, his positive and negative feelings, his constructive and destructive attitude and behaviour, maintaining all the while a sense of the client's innate dignity and personal worth."

- Unconditional acceptance of the client.
- Acceptance and approval.

- Acceptance implies liking the client irrespective of his negative qualities and conduct.
- An expression of goodwill towards the client.
- Conveying deep concern and active understanding to the client who is liked by the worker in spite of his problem-behaviour.
- Principle of Acceptance is based on the assumptions of humanitarianism.
- The purpose of acceptance is therapeutic.
- Respect for their capacity and worth, beliefs in their capacity to grow and change and cope with situations.
- If disliked by us, we may behave to keep him off from ourselves and no positive relationship will be possible.
- Acceptance involves observance of common courtesies, respect for his ideas, and treat him as equal to self, eg: leaving chair, wishing him, receiving, sending off, respecting appointments, *etc.*
- Purpose of Acceptance—to respect, to help, to add, to comfort, therapeutic understanding, acknowledging, receiving, *etc.*
- Quality of Acceptance—warmth, courtesy, listening, respect, concern, interest, consistent, maturity, fairness, willingness to enter and share life exp., *etc.*
- *Roles of* Casework*er*:
  - Attention should be focused on the needs of client and not of the CWer.
  - CWer should recognize the client's potential for self-help.
  - CWer must have a clear awareness of the purpose for which help is required.
  - CWer must possess self awareness.
- *Obstacles to Acceptance*:
  - Insufficient knowledge of patterns of human behaviour.
  - Non-acceptance of something in self.
  - Imputing to the client one's own feelings.
  - Bias and prejudice.
  - Loss of respect for others.
  - Over-identification.
- *Kubler–Ross's Five Stages of Dying*:
  - *Denial*: "No, not me.":
  - (a) Clients perceive themselves as weak, sinful or irresponsible.
  - (b) Clients often mourn the loss of that which must be changed.
  - (c) Constructive changes are not apt to occur for people in denial.
  - (d) Case workers need to focus on the denial and explore why the person believes there is no problem.
  - (c) *E.g.*: Drinking problem–denial for 20 years–1st and 2nd marriage–road accident–excuses for everything.
    - *Rage and anger*: "Why me?"

(a) Client resents the fact that they have to change while others do not.
(b) Anyone can be the target of their anger.
(c) Use anger to avoid discussing the issue at hand.
(d) Anger can be directed at the Case worker for confronting the reality.
(e) Case worker allows the client to ventilate his anger–reduces his intensity, empathize, emotional support.
(f) *E.g.*: teenager who is pregnant.
 – *Bargaining*: "Yes, me, but..."
(a) Clients begin to accept the problem, but will bargain for 'just one more time'.
(b) Promise to be good, do something in exchange, try to change a few circumstances and believe that few changes will allow them to continue in their old ways.
(c) Case worker confronts clients with the reality of their circumstances and their bargaining efforts.
(d) *E.g.*: smoking when tense, social drinking.
 – *Depression*: "Yes, me."
(a) Become very quiet.
(b) Stop denying their problem.
(c) Anger has subsided, and they no longer try to bargain.
(d) Gain insight onto their particular problem and realise they must change.
(e) However, alternatives are nit yet perceived as viable solutions.
(f) Blame themselves for their problems and frequently mourn what they will have to give up.
(g) Case worker needs to convey empathy and help clients see that their problems are not overwhelming.
(f) They need hope; frequently this can be accomplished by helping them develop resolution strategies.
 – *Acceptance*: "I have a problem, but it's all right."
(a) Clients make a concrete effort at this stage to work out alternatives, not only those suggested, but also some of their own.
(b) Attitude will be of "I can do it!" and of hope.
(c) Fear is still present but much reduced.

PRINCIPLE OF NON-JUDGMENTAL ATTITUDE

- "Non-judgmental attitude is the recognition that the caseworker's role is to understand and help the client rather than judge or condemn them."
- The principle is based on the conviction that the casework function excludes assigning guilt or innocence or degree of client responsibility for causation of the problems and needs.

- But includes making evaluative judgements about the attitudes, standards or actions of the client.
- *E.g.*: Criminal, though the society has already has already judged the criminal through its legal machinery, the social worker assumes a posture of a non-condemnatory acceptance and helpfulness, affirming the individual as a person worthy of attention.
- *Role of* Casework*er*:
  - Caseworker must help the client understand the values and standards laid down by society and the law.
  - Caseworker must be sensitive to client's feelings.
  - Caseworker must herself be sensitive be aware/clear of the value systems that exist in her community.
- *Obstacles*:
  - Any element of bias or prejudice prevents the case worker from being objective.
  - A premature assurance that the problem has been understood has to be avoided.
  - No reference to other people with similar problems and no comparisons.
  - Avoid transference.

PRINCIPLE OF PURPOSEFUL EXPRESSION OF FEELINGS

- "Purposeful expression of feelings is the recognition of the client's need to express his feelings freely, especially his negative feelings. It is the client's need for expression at a time when his problem is partially or predominantly emotional."
- Need to express feelings especially the negative feelings.
- Frustration can result, if the basic psychological needs for expression are deprived.
- Case worker listens purposefully neither discouragingly nor condemning.
- Sometimes they can be actively stimulated.
- Purposes for Expression of feelings:
  - Relieves pressure and tension, help client see the problem more adequately.
  - Helps case worker understand what the problem means to the client.
  - Listening is a good form of psychological support.
  - Sometimes the negative feelings may be the real problem.
  - It depends on the Caseworker–Client relationship.
- *Limitations*:
  - Agency function limits–time factor and case load of the case worker may make it impossible for case worker to spend more time with client.

- Client may over dependent on the case worker.
- Care must be taken to prevent the client from putting too much burden on the worker.
- At times hostility shown might be an unhealthy attention-seeking device.
- Transference/counter-transference.

- *Role of* Casework*er*:
  - Allow for communication, stimulate client to talk.
  - Show a genuine desire to help.
  - Case worker must create a congenial atmosphere in which the client feels comfortable to talk to.
  - Should also participate in the conversation actively.
- *Transference*: Dewald-"Transference is a form of displacement in which the individual unconsciously displaces onto a current object those drives defences, attitudes, feelings and responses which were experienced or developed in relationship with earlier objects in the individual's life."
  - Unconscious attitudes and associated feelings transferred from the past onto the present relationship, usually irrational.
  - The client transfers these into the present interaction because of some similarity of the actors in the current situation with those he has encountered earlier in life.
  - May be positive or negative.
  - Can be tackled by clarification, interpretation, spacing the interview, *etc.*
- *Counter–transference*:
  - Social worker also has unconscious tendency to transfer on the client.
  - The job of the caseworker to recognize his feelings and must control them.
- *Types of Transference*:
  - *Positive*: *E.g.* Parents have shown to be friendly and helpful, the client will transfer a desire to help, friendship, guidance, emotional support and interest.
  - *Negative*: *E.g.* Parents not shown interest and indifferent, the client will have feelings of unfriendliness, suspicion and distrust.
- *Uses of Transference*:
  - Understanding the transference–his behaviour, unconscious need of the client.
  - Utilizing the transference–integrate past and present experiences and earlier relationships.
  - Interpreting the transference–careful analysis of his unconscious defences.

PRINCIPLE OF CONTROLLED EMOTIONAL INVOLVEMENT

- "Controlled emotional involvement is the case worker's sensitivity to the client's feelings, an understanding of their meaning, and a purposeful and appropriate response to the client's feelings."
- Need for communication–caseworker should not be emotionally involved with the client during the case work process.
- Response to the client on the feeling level is the most important psychological element in the case work relationship and most difficult of the case work skills.
- Communication is a two-way process.
- One person speaks directly and he expects response, need to maintain a certain degree of detachment.
- Communication should be a combination of ideas and feelings.
- *Purpose of controlled emotional involvement*:
  - Case worker's sensitivity to the client's feelings.
  - Understand the meaning of clients' feelings.
  - Purposeful and appropriate response to the client's feelings.
  - Psychological support and to encourage.
  - For clarification, to stop further expression.
- *Three components of CEI*:
  1. *Sensitivity*: seeing and listening to the feelings of the client.
  2. *Understanding*: to understand the meaning of the feelings in relation to the client.
  3. *Response*: verbal and non verbal.
- Communicate to the client through some form of words, facial expression, and tone of speech or of action.

PRINCIPLE OF CLIENT SELF-DETERMINATION

- "Client self-determination is the recognition of the right and need of the client to have freedom in making his own choice and decision in the case work process."
- Conviction that every individual has the innate ability to make his own choices, decisions under normal circumstances.
- Any case worker who prevents a client from taking decisions is unethical and unprofessional.
- Case worker is only an enabler who helps the client through his expertise, to take the best possible decision and action in the circumstances.
- *Three basic assumptions*:
  1. Fundamental right to make his own decisions.
  2. Concept of democratic living.
  3. For effective treatment.

- *Role of* Casework*er*:
  - DO–help the client see the problem clearly/with perspective.
  - DO–should activate the client's own dormant resources.
  - DO–create a favourable environment in which the client feels free to grow and work out a solution to his problem.
  - DO–make them aware of the resources available in the community.
  - DON'T–not assume the principle decision-making role and allow the client to play a subordinate role.
  - DON'T–not probe unnecessarily unless it is relevant to the problem.
  - DON'T–not manipulate any decision directly/indirectly.
  - DON'T–not urge the clients to accept his decision.
- *Limitations*:
  - It is relative, not absolute.
  - Arising out of civil law. *E.g.* criminals.
  - Arising out of moral law.
  - Arising out of agency function.
  - Client's capacity for making positive and constructive decision-making. *E.g.* children, immature adults, psychotics, MR, adolescents with personality problems.

PRINCIPLE OF CONFIDENTIALITY

- "Confidentiality is the preservation of secret information concerning the client which is disclosed in the professional relationship."
- It is basic right of the client
- Ethical obligation of the caseworker.
- Necessary for effective casework service.
- Client must have a firm faith that the facts disclosed by him will remain confidential.
- Information is shared with professionals within/outside agency with client's permission.
- Obligation binds all equally to preserve the information.
- *Limitations*:
  - Duty to self.
  - Right of other.
  - Right of the social worker.
  - Right of Agency.
  - Right of Society as a whole

PURPOSE OF SOCIAL CASEWORK

- Basic purpose is to enable the client to enjoy with some degree of permanence. More satisfying, effective and acceptable experiences in the social situation in which he finds himself.

- Essential task is the facilitation of the social relationship.
- Chief aim is to help them mobilize their capacities for the solution of their problems.
- Help them so that they will be better able to meet future difficulties with a more effectively organised personal strength.
- A Bring about a better adjustment between individual clients and his situation or environment.
- Better adjustment in the social relationships of the individual and the development of individual personality.
- In general, the purpose of social case work is to help an individual client to solve his psycho-social problems in such a way so that he finds himself capable of dealing with these problems at present and also may solve in future if such problems arise.

OBJECTIVES OF SOCIAL CASEWORK

- To understand and solve the internal problems of the individual.
- To strengthen his ego power.
- Remediation of problems in social functioning.
- Prevention of problems in social functioning.
- Development of resources to enhance social functioning.

SOCIAL CASEWORK VALUES

Social casework values have roots in the democratic social system.

They are:

- Every man has inherent worth and dignity.
- Every individual has the right to self-determination.
- Every individual is the primary concern of society, has potential for and the right to growth.
- Every individual, in turn, has to contribute to the society's development by assuming his social responsibility.
- The individual and society in which one lives are interdependent.
- Basic human needs have to be met by services which are not dependent upon in accord either to moral behaviour or to race, nationality, caste, *etc.*

BASIC ASSUMPTIONS OF SOCIAL CASEWORK

- Man is a bio-psycho-social being who is in constant interaction with his environment.
- All problems in social functioning are psycho-social in nature and most are interpersonal as well.
- Within certain limits, man can be understood and helped.
- Man can grow and change limited only by his inherent capacities and potentials.

HISTORICAL DEVELOPMENT OF SOCIAL CASEWORK

- Ancient times–individuals in every society have been helped by others to solve their problems.
- Late 19th and early 20th century–it took professional shape.
- 1869–Origin of Charity Organisation Society in London.
- The main aim of the society was to find out ways and means of helping the poor and needy and thus to organise used 'volunteers', called 'friendly visitors'.
- They visited the homes of the poor for the purpose of assessing their need, for rendering material assistance and for giving them guidance and advice.
- These friendly visitors were subsequently called 'paid agents'.
- These paid helpers gradually developed systematic procedures in performing their tasks; they collected data, helped them after assessing and also maintained records.
- Case work gradually developed into a professional method.
- 1877–Organised efforts were taken by the American Charity Organisation Society in U.S.A., similar to that in London.
- The 'paid agents' received training in investigation, diagnosis and treatment for which the New York School of Philanthropy was established towards the end of the 19th century.th
- 1895–End of 19th century in England, a concept called 'Almoners' was introduced. Sir Charles Loch appointed Almoners to help hospitals to serve patients effectively. Almoners were similar to friendly visitors and paid agents.
- 1898–The first School of Social Work was established in New York.
- 1911–Case work had emerged in USA as an accepted formal technique. Since the early social workers handled cases of families in need, they were called caseworkers in USA.
- 1914–1917–The first training programme for casework started at this time, based more on the medical model–Summer training–started by many schools of social work–recognized by professionals.
- 1917–Mary Richmond wrote; 'Social Diagnosis' which set forth a methodology of helping clients through systematic ways of assessing their problems and handling them. It is also introduced the principle of individualization and client's right to self-determination.
- Impact of I World War–The First World War made a wide impact on social case work. Psychiatry in this period became more important. The contribution of Freud and his followers influenced the method employed by the caseworkers in dealing with the individuals. CGC movement and treatment, prevention of mental problems and delinquency strengthened the psychological orientation of this approach.

- 1920s–Various definitions of case work under the influence of Freudian theory. Caseworkers realised that ore responsibilities should be given to individuals to make decisions of their life. Professionals also began to move into other fields like prisons, schools, *etc.*
- 1930–Economic depression–Case workers had to consider the economic factors which were causing distress to clients, leading to emotional distress and breakdown. Focus shifted from individual to modification and manipulation of the client's environment to enable him to adapt to his situations satisfactorily.
- After World War II, with the problems of morale, leadership, propaganda, separation, communication, *etc.*, social workers found social sciences more useful. There was increase in personal problems on the part of clients due to financial crises.
- 1950s–This was an era of private practice. Professional agencies started growing in this field. Casework started going into the community. Richmond, Hamilton and Pearlman also emphasized on the problems of social functioning.
- 1960s–Lot of importance was given to research and social action. Heredity vs. environment–casework method adopted new techniques and principles.
- *Social* Casework *in India*: American case work had its influence in India, as the first professional social workers who did case work in the Indian setting were trained in the American Schools of Social work.
- 1911–N.M. Joshi, one of the founders of the Trade Union Movement established an organisation called the Social Service League. The League conducted training programmes foe volunteers, whose services were later utilized for relief work among people suffering form famines, epidemics, floods and other disasters, and also for welfare programmes among the poor and the destitute.
- 1936–The Sir Dorabji Tata Graduate School of Social Work was started in Bombay, the training for social work changed into a full time career oriented, educational programme. 1946–Casework figured, both as a theoretical course and also as a method of practice in the academic programme.
- Social work as a profession and as an academic programme has been enlarged and enriched by new perspective, ideas and theories.

LIMITATIONS OF SOCIAL CASEWORK IN INDIA

- Borrowed the methodology from the West.
- Lack of indigenous literature.
- Lack of recognition to the field of social work.

- More focus on urban settings and silent on its relevance to the rural areas.
- It is time consuming.

DEMOCRACY IN SOCIAL WORK

Democracy is a political form of government in which governing power is derived from the people, either by direct referendum or by means of elected representatives of the people. The term comes from the Greek: "rule of the people", which was coined from dêmos "people" and Kratos "power", in the middle of the 5th-4th century B.C to denote the political systems then existing in some Greek city-states, notably Athens following a popular uprising in 508 B.C. Even though there is no specific, universally accepted definition of 'democracy', equality and freedom have been identified as important characteristics of democracy since ancient times. These principles are reflected in all citizens being equal before the law and having equal access to power.

For example, in a representative democracy, every vote has equal weight, no restrictions can apply to anyone wanting to become a representative, and the freedom of its citizens is secured by legitimized rights and liberties which are generally protected by a constitution. There are several varieties of democracy, some of which provide better representation and more freedoms for their citizens than others. However, if any democracy is not carefully legislated—through the use of balances—to avoid an uneven distribution of political power, such as the separation of powers, then a branch of the system of rule could accumulate power thus become undemocratic.

The "majority rule" is often described as a characteristic feature of democracy, but without governmental or constitutional protections of individual liberties, it is possible for a minority of individuals to be oppressed by the "tyranny of the majority". An essential process in representative democracies is competitive elections that are fair both substantively and procedurally. Furthermore, freedom of political expression, freedom of speech, and freedom of the press are essential so that citizens are informed and able to vote in their personal interests.

Popular sovereignty is common but not a universal motivating subject for establishing a democracy. In some countries, democracy is based on the philosophical principle of equal rights. Many people use the term "democracy" as shorthand for liberal democracy, which may include additional elements such as political pluralism; equality before the law; the right to petition elected officials for redress of grievances; due process; civil liberties; human rights; and elements of civil society outside the government. In the United States, separation of powers is often cited as a supporting attribute, but in other countries, such as the United Kingdom, the dominant philosophy is parliamentary sovereignty. In other cases, "democracy" is used to mean direct democracy. Though the term "democracy" is typically used in the context of a political state, the principles are applicable to private organisations and other groups also.

Democracy has its origins in Ancient Greece. However other cultures have significantly contributed to the evolution of democracy such as Ancient Rome, Europe, and North and South America. The concept of representative democracy arose largely from ideas and institutions that developed during the European Middle Ages and the Age of Enlightenment and in the American and French Revolutions. Democracy has been called the "last form of government" and has spread considerably across the globe. The right to vote has been expanded in many Jurisdictions over time from relatively narrow groups with New Zealand the first nation to grant universal suffrage for all its citizens in 1893.

HISTORY OF DEMOCRACY

Ancient Origins

The term democracy first appeared in ancient Greek political and philosophical thought. The philosopher Plato contrasted democracy, the system of "rule by the governed", with the alternative systems of monarchy, oligarchy and timocracy. Although Athenian democracy is today considered by many to have been a form of direct democracy, originally it had two distinguishing features: first the allotment of ordinary citizens to government offices and courts, and secondarily the assembly of all the citizens. All citizens were eligible to speak and vote in the Assembly, which set the laws of the city-state. However, the Athenian citizenship was only for males born from a father who was citizen and who had been doing their "military service" between 18 and 20 years old; this excluded women, slaves, foreigners and males under 20 years old.

Of the 250,000 inhabitants only some 30,000 on average were citizens. Of those 30,000 perhaps 5,000 might regularly attend one or more meetings of the popular Assembly. Most of the officers and magistrates of Athenian government were allotted; only the generals and a few other officers were elected. A possible example of primitive democracy may have been the early Sumerian city-states.

A similar proto-democracy or oligarchy existed temporarily among the Medes in the 6th century B.C., but which came to an end after the Achaemenid Emperor Darius the Great declared that the best monarchy was better than the best oligarchy or best democracy. A serious claim for early democratic institutions comes from the independent "republics" of India, sanghas and ganas, which existed as early as the 6th century B.C. and persisted in some areas until the 4th century A.D. The evidence is scattered and no pure historical source exists for that period. In addition, mentions that independent and democratic states existed in India. However, modern scholars note that the word democracy at the 3rd century B.C. and later had been degraded and could mean any autonomous state no matter how oligarchic it was. The lack of the concept of citizen equality across caste system boundaries lead many scholars to believe that the true nature of ganas and sanghas would not be comparable to that of truly democratic institutions.

Even though the Roman Republic contributed significantly to certain aspects of democracy, only a minority of Romans were citizens. As such, having votes in elections for choosing representatives and then the votes of the powerful were given more weight through a system of Gerrymandering. For that reason, almost all high officials, including members of the Senate, came from a few wealthy and noble families. However, many notable exceptions did occur.

Middle Ages

During the Middle Ages, there were various systems involving elections or assemblies, although often only involving a small amount of the population, the election of Gopala in Bengal, the Polish-Lithuanian Commonwealth, the Althing in Iceland, the Løgting in the Faroe Islands certain medieval Italian city-states such as Venice, the tuatha system in early medieval Ireland, the Veche in Novgorod and Pskov Republics of medieval Russia, Scandinavian Things, The States in Tirol and Switzerland and the autonomous merchant city of Sakai in the 16th century in Japan.

However, participation was often restricted to a minority, and so may be better classified as oligarchy. Most regions in medieval Europe were ruled by clergy or feudal lords. A little closer to modern democracy were the Cossack republics of Ukraine in the 16th–17th centuries: Cossack Hetmanate and Zaporizhian Sich. The highest post—the Hetman—was elected by the representatives from the country's districts. Because these states were very militarised, the right to participate in Hetman's elections was largely restricted to those who served in the Cossack Army and over time was curtailed effectively limiting these rights to higher army ranks. The Parliament of England had its roots in the restrictions on the power of kings written into Magna Carta, explicitly protected certain rights of the King's subjects, whether free or fettered — and implicitly supported what became English writ of habeas corpus, safeguarding individual freedom against unlawful imprisonment with right to appeal. The first elected parliament was De Montfort's Parliament in England in 1265. However only a small minority actually had a voice; Parliament was elected by only a few per cent of the population, and the power to call parliament was at the pleasure of the monarch.

The power of Parliament increased in stages over the succeeding centuries. After the Glorious Revolution of 1688, the English Bill of Rights of 1689 was enacted, which codified certain rights and increased the influence of Parliament. The franchise was slowly increased and Parliament gradually gained more power until the monarch became largely a figurehead. As the franchise was increased, it also was made more uniform, as many so-called rotten boroughs, with a handful of voters electing a Member of Parliament, were eliminated in the Reform Act of 1832. Democracy was also seen to a certain extent in bands and tribes such as the Iroquois Confederacy. However, in the Iroquois Confederacy only the males of certain clans could be leaders and some clans were excluded. Only the oldest females from the same clans could choose and remove the leaders. This excluded most of the population.

An interesting element is that there should be consensus among the leaders, not majority support decided by voting, when making decisions. Band societies, such as the Bushmen, which usually number 20-50 people in the band often do not have leaders and make decisions based on consensus among the majority. In Melanesia, farming village communities have traditionally been egalitarian and lacking in a rigid, authoritarian hierarchy.

Although a "Big man" or "Big woman" could gain influence, that influence was conditional on a continued demonstration of leadership skills, and on the willingness of the community. Every person was expected to share in communal duties, and entitled to participate in communal decisions. However, strong social pressure encouraged conformity and discouraged individualism.

18th and 19th Centuries

Although not described as a democracy by the founding fathers, the United States founders shared a determination to root the American experiment in the principle of natural freedom and equality. The United States Constitution, adopted in 1788, provided for an elected government and protected civil rights and liberties for some. In the colonial period before 1776, and for some time after, only adult white male property owners could vote; enslaved Africans, free black people and women were not extended the franchise. On the American frontier, democracy became a way of life, with widespread social, economic and political equality. However, slavery was a social and economic institution, particularly in eleven states in the American South, that a variety of organisations were established advocating the movement of black people from the United States to locations where they would enjoy greater freedom and equality.

During the 1820s and 1830s the American Colonization Society was the primary vehicle for proposals to return black Americans to freedom in Africa, and in 1821 the A.C.S. established the colony of Liberia, assisting thousands of former African-American slaves and free black people to move there from the

United States. By the 1840s almost all property restrictions were ended and nearly all white adult male citizens could vote; and turnout averaged 60–80 per cent in frequent elections for local, state and national officials. The system gradually evolved, from Jeffersonian Democracy to Jacksonian Democracy and beyond. In the 1860 United States Census the slave population in the United States had grown to four million, and in Reconstruction after the Civil War the newly freed slaves became citizens with a nominal right to vote.

Full enfranchisement of citizens was not secured until after the African-American Civil Rights Movement gained passage by the United States Congress of the Voting Rights Act of 1965. In 1789, Revolutionary France adopted the Declaration of the Rights of Man and of the Citizen and, although short-lived, the National Convention was elected by all males in 1792. Universal male suffrage was definitely established in France in March 1848 in the wake of the French Revolution of 1848. In 1848, several revolutions broke out in Europe as rulers were confronted with popular demands for liberal constitutions and more democratic government.

The Australian colonies became democratic during the mid-19th century, with South Australia being the first government in the world to introduce women's suffrage in 1861. New Zealand granted suffrage to Mâori men in 1867, white men in 1879, and women in 1893, thus becoming the first major nation to achieve universal suffrage. However, women were not eligible to stand for parliament until 1919. Liberal democracies were few and often short-lived before the late 19th century, and various nations and territories have also claimed to be the first with universal suffrage.

20th Century

20th century transitions to liberal democracy have come in successive "waves of democracy," variously resulting from wars, revolutions, decolonization, religious and economic circumstances. World War I and the dissolution of the Ottoman and Austro-Hungarian empires resulted in the creation of new nation-states from Europe, most of them at least nominally democratic. In the 1920s democracy flourished, but the Great Depression brought disenchantment, and most of the countries of Europe, Latin America, and Asia turned to strong-man rule or dictatorships. Fascism and dictatorships flourished in Nazi Germany, Italy, Spain and Portugal, as well as non-democratic regimes in the Baltics, the Balkans, Brazil, Cuba, China, and Japan, among others.

World War II brought a definitive reversal of this trend in western Europe. The successful democratization of the American, British, and French sectors of occupied Germany, Austria, Italy, and the occupied Japan served as a model for the later theory of regime change. However, most of Eastern Europe, including the Soviet sector of Germany was forced into the non-democratic

Soviet bloc. The war was followed by decolonization, and again most of the new independent states had nominally democratic constitutions. India emerged as the world's largest democracy and continues to be so.

In the decades following World War II, most western democratic nations had mixed economies and developed a welfare state, reflecting a consensus among their electorates and political parties. In the 1950s and 1960s, economic growth was high in both the western and Communist countries; it later declined in the state-controlled economies. By 1960, the vast majority of country-states were nominally democracies, although the majority of the world's populations lived in nations that experienced sham elections, and other forms of subterfuge A subsequent wave of democratization brought substantial gains towards true liberal democracy for many nations. Spain, Portugal and several of the military dictatorships in South America returned to civilian rule in the late 1970s and early 1980s. This was followed by nations in East and South Asia by the mid-to-late 1980s.

Economic malaise in the 1980s, along with resentment of communist oppression, contributed to the collapse of the Soviet Union, the associated end of the Cold War, and the democratization and liberalization of the former Eastern bloc countries. The most successful of the new democracies were those geographically and culturally closest to western Europe, and they are now members or candidate members of the European Union. Some researchers consider that in contemporary Russia there is no real democracy and one of forms of dictatorship takes place. The liberal trend spread to some nations in Africa in the 1990s, most prominently in South Africa.

Some recent examples of attempts of liberalization include the Indonesian Revolution of 1998, the Bulldozer Revolution in Yugoslavia, the Rose Revolution in Georgia, the Orange Revolution in Ukraine, the Cedar Revolution in Lebanon, and the Tulip Revolution in Kyrgyzstan. Currently, there are 123 countries that are democratic. As such, it has been speculated that this trend may continue in the future to the point where liberal democratic nation-states become the universal standard form of human society. This prediction forms the core of Francis Fukayama's "End of History" controversial theory. These theories are criticized by those who fear an evolution of liberal democracies to post-democracy, and other who points out the high number of illiberal democracies.

DEVELOPMENT OF DEMOCRACY

Several philosophers and researchers outlined historical and social factors supporting the evolution of democracy. Cultural factors like Protestantism influenced the development of democracy, rule of law, human rights and political liberty. Others declared the influence of wealth. In a related theory, Ronald Inglehart suggests that the increase in living standards has convinced people that they can take their basic survival for granted, and led to increased emphasis on self-expression values, which is highly correlated to democracy. Recently established theories stress the relevance of education and human capital and within them of cognitive ability. They increase tolerance, rationality, political literacy and participation. Two effects of education and cognitive ability are distinguished: a cognitive effect and an ethical effect, which itself depends on intelligence. Evidence that is consistent with conventional theories of why democracy emerges and is sustained has been hard to come by.

Recent statistical analyses have challenged modernization theory by demonstrating that there is no reliable evidence for the claim that democracy is more likely to emerge when countries become wealthier, more educated, or less unequal.

Neither is there convincing evidence that increased reliance on oil revenues prevents democratization, despite a vast theoretical literature called "The Resource Curse" that asserts that oil revenues sever the link between citizen taxation and government accountability, the key to representative democracy. The lack of evidence for these conventional theories of democratization have led researchers to search for the "deep" determinants of contemporary political institutions, be they geographical or demographic.

Facts

In practice it may not pay the incumbents to conduct fair elections in countries that have no history of democracy. A study showed that incumbents who rig elections stay in office 2.5 times as long as those who permit fair elections. Above $2,700 *per capita* democracies have been found to be less prone to violence, but below that threshold, more violence. The same study shows that election misconduct is more likely in countries with low per capita incomes, small populations, rich in natural resources, and a lack of institutional checks and balances. Sub-Saharan countries, as well as Afghanistan, all tend to fall into that category. Governments that have frequent elections averaged over the political cycle have significantly better economic policies than those who don't. This does not apply to governments with fraudulent elections, however.

Opposition to Democracy

Democracy in modern times has almost always faced opposition from the existing government. The implementation of a democratic government within a non-democratic state is typically brought about by democratic revolution. Monarchy had traditionally been opposed to democracy, and to this day remains opposed to its abolition, although often political compromise has been reached in the form of shared government. Currently, opposition to democracy exists most notably in communist states, and absolute monarchies which appear to have various reasons for opposing the implementation of democracy or democratic reforms.

Criticism of Democracy

Economists since Milton Friedman have strongly criticized the efficiency of democracy. They base this on their premise of the irrational voter. Their argument is that voters are highly uninformed about many political issues, especially relating to economics, and have a strong bias about the few issues on which they are fairly knowledgeable.

Mob Rule

Plato's The Republic presents a critical view of democracy through the narration of Socrates: "Democracy, which is a charming form of government, full of variety and disorder, and dispensing a sort of equality to equals and unequaled alike." In his work, Plato lists 5 forms of government from best to worst. Assuming that the Republic was intended to be a serious critique of the political thought in Athens, Plato argues that only Kallipolis, an aristocracy led by the unwilling philosopher-kings is a just form of government.

Moral Decay

Traditional Asian cultures, in particular that of Confucian and Islamic thought, believe that democracy results in the people's distrust and disrespect of governments or religious sanctity. The distrust and disrespect pervades to all parts of society whenever and wherever there is seniority and juniority, for example between a parent and a child, a teacher and a student.

Political Instability

More recently, democracy is criticised for not offering enough political stability. As governments are frequently elected on and off there tends to be frequent changes in the policies of democratic countries both domestically and internationally. Even if a political party maintains power, vociferous, headline grabbing protests and harsh criticism from the mass media are often enough to force sudden, unexpected political change. Frequent policy changes with regard to business and immigration are likely to deter investment and so hinder economic growth. For this reason, many people have put forward the idea that democracy is undesirable for a developing country in which economic growth and the reduction of poverty are top priority.

Short-termism

Democracy is also criticised for frequent elections due to the instability of coalition governments. Coalitions are frequently formed after the elections in many countries and the basis of alliance is predominantly to enable a viable majority, not an ideological concurrence. This opportunist alliance not only has the handicap of having to cater to too many ideologically opposing factions, but it is usually short lived since any perceived or actual imbalance in the treatment of coalition partners, or changes to leadership in the coalition partners themselves, can very easily result in the coalition partner withdrawing its support from the government.

Slow Governmental Response

Democratic institutions work on consensus to decide an issue, which usually takes longer than a unilateral decision.

Vote Buying

This is a simple form of appealing to the short term interests of the voters. This tactic has been known to be heavily used in north and north-east region of Thailand. The same tactic is widespread in the southern part of Italy, where also the local mafias take active part into the process. Another form is commonly called pork barrel where local areas or political sectors are given special benefits but whose costs are spread among all taxpayers.

Volatility/Unsustainability

The new establishment of democratic institutions in countries! where the associated practices have as yet been uncommon or deemed culturally unacceptable, can result in institutions, that are not sustainable in the long term. One circumstance supporting this outcome may be when it is part of the common perception among the populace that the institutions were established as a direct result of foreign pressure.

Popular Rule as a Facade

The 20th Century Italian thinkers Vilfredo Pareto and Gaetano Mosca argued that democracy was illusory, and served only to mask the reality of elite rule. Indeed, they argued that elite oligarchy is the unbendable law of human nature, due largely to the apathy and division of the masses and that democratic institutions would do no more than shift the exercise of power from oppression to manipulation.

EQUALITY

Social equality is a social state of affairs in which all people within a specific society or isolated group have the same status in a certain respect. At the very least, social equality includes equal rights under the law, such as security, voting rights, freedom of speech and assembly, and the extent of property rights. However, it also includes access to education, health care and other social securities. It also includes equal opportunities and obligations, and so involves the whole society. Social equality requires the lack of legally enforced social class or caste boundaries and the lack of unjustified discrimination motivated by an inalienable part of a person's identity.

For example, gender, age, sexual orientation, origin, caste or class, income or property, language, religion, convictions, opinions, health or disability must not result in unequal treatment under the law and should not reduce opportunities unjustifiably. Social equality refers to social, rather than economic, or income equality. "Equal opportunities" is interpreted as being judged by ability, which is compatible with a free-market economy. A problem is horizontal inequality, the inequality of two persons of same origin and ability. Perfect social equality is an ideal situation that, for various reasons, does not exist in any society in the world today.

The reasons for this are widely debated. Reasons cited for social inequality include commonly economics, immigration/emigration, foreign politics and national politics. Also, in complexity economics, it has been found that horizontal inequality arises in complex systems. A counter example to social equality was the social inequality of medieval Europe, where a person's estate, which was usually inherited, determined the legal and social rights the person had. For example, clergy could claim the benefit of clergy to receive a more lenient punishment for a crime.

Likewise, women have historically been and still are in some countries formally denied access to higher education—even if they could pay the tuition. In 19th century Europe, if female enrollment was even permitted, women had to apply for an "exemption from gender" to enroll in a university. In apartheid-era South Africa, both blacks and whites had formal access to health care and similar public services. However, the segregated health care arranged for blacks did not meet the same standards as those for whites. That is, there was enforced social inequality. Currently, in North Korea, certain groups are officially considered "disloyal" to the regime; the "disloyalty" is inherited, prevents advancement in society, and results in harsher punishments for crimes.

FORMS OF SOCIAL WORK

Democracy has taken a number of forms, both in theory and practice. The following kinds are not exclusive of one another: many specify details of aspects that are independent of one another and can co-exist in a single system.

REPRESENTATIVE

Representative democracy involves the selection of government officials by the people being represented. If the head of state is also democratically elected then it is called a democratic republic. The most common mechanisms involve election of the candidate with a majority or a plurality of the votes. Representatives may be elected or become diplomatic representatives by a particular district or represent the entire electorate proportionally proportional systems, with some using a combination of the two. Some representative democracies also incorporate elements of direct democracy, such as referendums. A characteristic of representative democracy is that while the representatives are elected by the people to act in their interest, they retain the freedom to exercise their own judgement as how best to do so.

Parliamentary

Parliamentary democracy is a representative democracy where government is appointed by parliamentary representatives as opposed to a 'presidential rule' wherein the President is both head of state and the head of government and is elected by the voters. Under a parliamentary democracy, government is exercised by delegation to an executive ministry and subject to ongoing review, checks and balances by the legislative parliament elected by the people.

Liberal

A Liberal democracy is a representative democracy in which the ability of the elected representatives to exercise decision-making power is subject to the rule of law, and usually moderated by a constitution that emphasizes the protection of the rights and freedoms of individuals, and which places constraints on the leaders and on the extent to which the will of the majority can be exercised against the rights of minorities.

Direct

Direct democracy is a political system where the citizens participate in the decision-making personally, contrary to relying on intermediaries or representatives. The supporters of direct democracy argue that democracy is more than merely a procedural issue.

A direct democracy gives the voting population the power to:

- Change constitutional laws,
- Put forth initiatives, referenda and suggestions for laws,
- Give binding orders to elective officials, such as revoking them before the end of their elected term, or initiating a lawsuit for breaking a campaign promise.

Of the three measures declared, most operate in developed democracies today. This is part of a gradual shift towards direct democracies. Examples of this include the extensive use of referenda in California with more than 20 million voters, and. in Switzerland, where five million voters decide on national referenda and initiatives two to four times a year; direct democratic instruments are also well established at the cantonal and communal level.

Vermont towns have been known for their yearly town meetings, held every March to decide on local issues. No direct democracy is in existence outside the framework of a different overarching form of government. Most direct democracies to date have been weak forms, relatively small communities, usually city-states. The world is yet to see a large, fundamental, working example of direct democracy as of yet, with most examples being small and weak forms.

Participatory

A Parpolity or Participatory Polity is a theoretical form of democracy that is ruled by a Nested Council structure. The guiding philosophy is that people should have decision making power in proportion to how much they are affected by the decision. Local councils of 25–50 people are completely autonomous on issues that affect only them, and these councils send delegates to higher level councils who are again autonomous regarding issues that affect only the population affected by that council.

A council court of randomly chosen citizens serves as a check on the tyranny of the majority, and rules on which body gets to vote on which issue. Delegates can vote differently than their sending council might wish, but are mandated to communicate the wishes of their sending council. Delegates are recallable at any time. Referenda are possible at any time via votes of the majority of lower level councils, however, not everything is a referendum as this is most likely a waste of time.

Socialist

Socialist thought has several different views on democracy. Social democracy, democratic socialism, and the dictatorship of the proletariat are some examples. Many democratic socialists and social democrats believe in a form of participatory democracy and workplace democracy combined with a representative democracy.

Within Marxist orthodoxy there is a hostility to what is commonly called "liberal democracy", which they simply refer to as parliamentary democracy because of its often centralized nature. Because of their desire to eliminate the political elitism they see in capitalism, Marxists, Leninists and Trotskyists believe in direct democracy implemented though a system of communes. This system ultimately manifests itself as council democracy and begins with workplace democracy.

Anarchist

Anarchists are split in this domain, depending on whether they believe that a majority-rule is tyrannic or not. The only form of democracy considered acceptable to many anarchists is direct democracy. Pierre-Joseph Proudhon argued that the only acceptable form of direct democracy is one in which it is recognized that majority decisions are not binding on the minority, even when unanimous. However, anarcho-communist Murray Bookchin criticized individualist anarchists for opposing democracy, and says "majority rule" is consistent with anarchism.

Some anarcho-communists oppose the majoritarian nature of direct democracy, feeling that it can impede individual liberty and opt in favour of a non-majoritarian form of consensus democracy, similar to Proudhon's position on direct democracy. Henry David Thoreau, who did not self-identify as an anarchist but argued for "a better government" and is cited as an inspiration by some anarchists, argued that people should not be in the position of ruling others or being ruled when there is no consent.

Iroquois

Iroquois society had a form of participatory democracy and representative democracy. Iroquois government and law was discussed by Benjamin Franklin and Thomas Jefferson. Though some others disagree, some scholars regard it to have influenced the formation of American representative democracy.

Sortition

Sometimes called "democracy without elections", sortition is the process of choosing decision makers via a random process.

The intention is that those chosen will be representative of the opinions and interests of the people at large, and be more fair and impartial than an elected official. The technique was in widespread use in Athenian Democracy and is still used in modern jury selection.

Consensus

Consensus democracy requires varying degrees of consensus rather than just a mere democratic majority. It typically attempts to protect minority rights from domination by majority rule.

Supranational

Qualified majority voting is designed by the Treaty of Rome to be the principal method of reaching decisions in the European Council of Ministers. This system allocates votes to member states in part just as to their population, but heavily weighted in favour of the smaller states. This might be seen as a form of representative democracy, but representatives to the Council might be appointed rather than directly elected. Some might consider the "individuals" being democratically represented to be states rather than people, as with many other international organisations. European Parliament members are democratically directly elected on the basis of universal suffrage, may be seen as an example of a supranational democratic institution.

Cosmopolitan

Cosmopolitan democracy, also known as Global democracy or World Federalism is a political system in which democracy is implemented on a global scale, either directly or through representatives. The supporters of cosmopolitan democracy argue that it is fundamentally different from any form of national or regional democracy, because in a Cosmopolitan Democracy, decisions are made by people influenced by them, while in Regional and National Federal Democracies, decisions often influence people outside the constituency, which by-definition can not vote. In a globalised world, argue the supporters of Cosmopolitan Democracy, any attempt to solve global problems would either be undemocratic or have to implement cosmopolitan democracy. The challenge of cosmopolitan democracy is to apply some of the values and norms of democracy, including the rule of law, the non-violent resolutions of conflicts, and the equality among citizens, also beyond the state. This requires to reform international organisations, first of all the United Nations, and to create new institutions, such as a World Parliament, which could increase the degree of public control and accountability on international politics. Cosmopolitan Democracy was promoted, among others, by physicist Albert Einstein, writer Kurt Vonnegut, columnist George Monbiot, and David Held and Daniele Archibugi.

Non-governmental

Aside from the public sphere, similar democratic principles and mechanisms of voting and representation have been used to govern other kinds of communities and organisations.

- Many non-governmental organisations decide policy and leadership by voting.
- Most trade unions choose their leadership through democratic elections.
- Cooperatives are enterprises owned and democratically controlled by their customers or workers.

THEORY OF SOCIAL WORK

ARISTOTLE

Aristotle contrasted rule by the many with rule by the few and with rule by a single person. He also thought that there was a good and a bad variant of each system. For Aristotle the underlying principle of democracy is freedom, since only in a democracy the citizens can have a share in freedom. In essence, he argues that this is what every democracy should make its aim. There are two main aspects of freedom: being ruled and ruling in turn, since everyone is equal just as to number, not merit, and to be able to live as one pleases. Now a fundamental principle of the democratic form of constitution is liberty—that is what is usually asserted, implying that only under this constitution do men participate in liberty, for they assert this as the aim of every democracy.

But one factor of liberty is to govern and be governed in turn; for the popular principle of justice is to have equality just as to number, not worth, and if this is the principle of justice prevailing, the multitude must of necessity be sovereign and the decision of the majority must be final and must constitute justice, for they say that each of the citizens ought to have an equal share; so that it results that in democracies the poor are more powerful than the rich, because there are more of them and whatever is decided by the majority is sovereign.

This then is one mark of liberty which all democrats set down as a principle of the constitution. And one is for a man to live as he likes; for they say that this is the function of liberty, inasmuch as to live not as one likes is the life of a man that is a slave. This is the second principle of democracy, and from it has come the claim not to be governed, preferably not by anybody, or failing that, to govern and be governed in turns; and this is the way in which the second principle contributes to equalitarian liberty.

Conceptions

Among political theorists, there are many contending conceptions of democracy.

- Aggregative democracy uses democratic processes to solicit citizens' preferences and then aggregate them together to determine what social policies society should adopt. Therefore, proponents of this view hold that democratic participation should primarily focus on voting, where the policy with the most votes gets implemented. There are different variants of this:
  - Under minimalism, democracy is a system of government in which citizens give teams of political leaders the right to rule in periodic elections. This minimalist conception, citizens cannot and should not "rule" because, for example, on most issues, most of the time, they have no clear views or their views are not well-founded. Joseph Schumpeter articulated this view most famously; Capitalism, Socialism, and Democracy. Contemporary proponents of minimalism include William H. Riker, Adam Przeworski, Richard Posner.
  - Direct democracy, on the other hand, holds that citizens should participate directly, not through their representatives, in making laws and policies. Proponents of direct democracy offer varied reasons to support this view. Political activity can be valuable in itself, it socializes and educates citizens, and popular participation can check powerful elites. Most importantly, citizens do not really rule themselves unless they directly decide laws and policies.
  - Governments will tend to produce laws and policies that are close to the views of the median voter–with half to his left and the

other half to his right. This is not actually a desirable outcome as it represents the action of self-interested and somewhat unaccountable political elites competing for votes. Downs suggests that ideological political parties are necessary to act as a mediating broker between individual and governments.

- Robert A. Dahl argues that the fundamental democratic principle is that, when it comes to binding collective decisions, each person in a political community is entitled to have his/her interests be given equal consideration. He uses the term polyarchy to refer to societies in which there exists a certain set of institutions and procedures which are perceived as leading to such democracy. First and foremost among these institutions is the regular occurrence of free and open elections which are used to select representatives who then manage all or most of the public policy of the society. However, these polyarchic procedures may not create a full democracy if, for example, poverty prevents political participation. Some see a problem with the wealthy having more influence and therefore argue for reforms like campaign finance reform. Some may see it as a problem that the majority of the voters decide policy, as opposed to majority rule of the entire population. This can be used as an argument for making political participation mandatory, like compulsory voting or for making it more patient by simply refusing power to the government until the full majority feels inclined to speak their minds.

- Deliberative democracy is based on the notion that democracy is government by discussion. Deliberative democrats contend that laws and policies should be based upon reasons that all citizens can accept. The political arena should be one in which leaders and citizens make arguments, listen, and change their minds.
- Radical democracy is based on the idea that there are hierarchical and oppressive power relations that exist in society. Democracy's role is to make visible and challenge those relations by allowing for difference, dissent and antagonisms in decision making processes.

Republic

In contemporary usage, the term democracy refers to a government chosen by the people, whether it is direct or representative. The term republic has many different meanings, but today often refers to a representative democracy with an elected head of state, such as a president, serving for a limited term, in contrast to states with a hereditary monarch as a head of state, even if these states also are representative democracies with an elected or appointed head of government such as a prime minister. The Founding Fathers of the United

States rarely praised and often criticized democracy, which in their time tended to specifically mean direct democracy; James Madison argued, especially in The Federalist No. 10, that what distinguished a democracy from a republic was that the former became weaker as it got larger and suffered more violently from the effects of faction, whereas a republic could get stronger as it got larger and combats faction by its very structure. What was critical to American values, John Adams insisted, was that the government be "bound by fixed laws, which the people have a voice in making, and a right to defend." As Benjamin Franklin was exiting after writing the U.S. constitution, a woman asked him "Well, Doctor, what have we got—a republic or a monarchy?". He replied "A republic—if you can keep it."

Constitutional Monarchs and Upper Chambers

Initially after the American and French revolutions the question was open whether a democracy, in order to restrain unchecked majority rule, should have an elitist upper chamber, the members perhaps appointed meritorious experts or having lifetime tenures, or should have a constitutional monarch with limited but real powers. Some countries turned powerful monarchs into constitutional monarchs with limited or, often gradually, merely symbolic roles. Often the monarchy was abolished along with the aristocratic system. Many nations had elite upper houses of legislatures which often had lifetime tenure, but eventually these lost power or else became elective and remained powerful.

LIBERTY AND JUSTICE

Brother and sister they are the children of major supporting character Superpatriot. The twins are deliberately total opposites of each other. Liberty is fierce, strong-willed, outspoken and temperamental but gullible while Justice is subservient, keen, polite and rather un-intelligent. Neither of them has any powers but is both in top physical condition.

FICTIONAL CHARACTER HISTORY

Original Earth

Until issue 75 the Savage Dragon series was set on another Earth to one it is current set on. This Earth was destroyed and with few exceptions all of the characters on that world were killed when it was including Liberty and Justice. The twins were the product of the union between Superpatriot and a girl named Rebecca who met at a peace rally in 1971 but were raised by her and Jake Farrell, an old 'acquaintance' of Superpatriot's who works for the US government and had a supporting role in the Freak Force ongoing series who they call 'Uncle Jake'.

It is later revealed that Rebecca abandoned the children in the end and joined the underground organisation The Covenant of the Sword, eventually becoming a techno-organic lifeform. Coincidentally her daughter Liberty would become a Covenant member years later. Justice first appeared solo in Savage Dragon #12 in 1994. He was given no origin or story and was confused with Superpatriot by two thugs selling micro-chips because he was wearing the character's old costume. Justice followed the trail of the stolen micro-chips and stumbled upon Openface and Octopus, who would become major villains in later stories, and a case of mistaken identity lead to a fight between him and She-Dragon. Dragon refused to let them help him look for the criminals whom he apprehended singlehandedly.

The character did not appear again for another year in the first issue of Superpatriot: Liberty and Justice. Now working in Milwaukee rather than Chicago, he was now working with his sister Liberty, trying to carve out a reputation for themselves there. Liberty is a member of the Covenant of the Sword, erroneously believing that the organisation really does good work and the villainous Covenant are 'rogue cells'. She also hates her father abandoning her, which he, in fact, did not do. After the two are rescued by their father, Liberty is keen to hunt down another 'rogue cell' and Justice is keen for a team-up with his dad, so Superpatriot gives in and allows them to come to Japan. Their battle with Covenant members leads to their arrest and Liberty's flippancy about her 'being Covenant' leads to the sibling's capture by them. Superpatriot rescues the two and the two begin to appear regularly in the main Savage Dragon series where it seems they, particularly Libby, have a better relationship with their father.

The two helped out during the Super-Freak Gang War that resulted from The Dragon killing Overlord, the head of the Super-Freak Mafia The Vicious Circle, which ended after a huge battle in the Super-villain prison. In the aftermath of this battle, Justice met Dart and shortly after, the two began to date. This made Killcat, a delusional vigilante from Detroit who was convinced he and Dart had a relationship, to get so jealous he assaulted Justice and hospitalized him, which in turn made Dart so angry she hospitalized Killcat and the two ended up next to each other in the same ward. Dart then came and had sex with Justice in full view of Killcat. The duo attempt to assist in a reality disruption threatening to turn one earth into six. Mind-altering events and disroganization prevent their assistance.

During the Mars Attacks Image event Liberty and Justice were stationed in Detroit when Kid Avenger blew the whole city up. Though they survived both were captured by the aliens and Liberty was experimented on, raped and impregnated by them. She is saved and all her attackers are slain. Being pro-life she refused to have an abortion and gave birth to an alien-human hybrid she called Damian. Damian would go onto become the time traveling villain Damian Darklord/Darklord. Liberty was kidnapped by the Covenant of the Sword, under the direction of her own son, and Justice was badly assaulted by them but was able to get message of Liberty's capture to their father Superpatriot. He was last seen in hospital where he told Sgt. Marvel and She-Dragon what he had told Superpatriot. Neither appeared again before Universo destroyed their Earth.

Current Earth

When The Dragon killed Liberty's son he created a parallel world without any of Darklord's meddling and became stuck there. This is the Earth were the Savage Dragon series is currently set. Not much was revealed about the twins on this Earth and they appeared infrequently as background characters until they were both killed during a huge battle between that Earth's new Vicious Circle and various heroes. The battle was as a result of the new version of the old criminal organisation kidnapping The Dragon's daughter Angel. Several other characters were killed during the issue's course, most notably the Underground Freak The Shrew.

FRATERNITY

A fraternity is a brotherhood, though the term usually connotes a distinct or formal organisation and a secret society. There are known fraternal organisations which existed as far back as ancient Greece and Rome, and analogous institutions in the late medieval period called confraternities, which were lay organisations allied to the Catholic Church. These confraternities evolved into purely secular fraternal societies such as Freemasonry, which in turn was used as a model for many modern fraternal orders and societies. The development of modern fraternal orders was especially dynamic in the United States, where the freedom to associate outside governmental regulation is expressly sanctioned in law.

There have been hundreds of fraternal organisations in the United States, and at the beginning of the 20th century the number of memberships equaled the number of adult males. In 1944 Arthur M. Schlesinger coined the phrase "a nation of joiners" to refer to the phenomenon. Alexis de Tocqueville also referred to the American reliance on private organisation in the 1830s in Democracy in America. There are many attributes that fraternities may or may not have, depending on their structure and purpose. Fraternities can have differing degrees of secrecy, some form of initiation or ceremony marking admission, formal codes of behaviour, disciplinary procedures, very differing amounts of real property and assets.

Types of Fraternities

The only true distinction between a fraternity and any other form of social organisation is the implication that the members freely associate as equals for a mutually beneficial purpose, rather than because of a religious, governmental, commercial, or familial bond, although there are fraternities dedicated to each of these topics. On most college campuses fraternities are divided into three groups such as social, professional and honourary. Fraternities can be organised for many purposes, including university education, work skills, ethics, ethnicity, religion, politics, charity, chivalry, other standards of personal conduct, asceticism, service, performing arts, family command of territory, and even crime.

There is almost always an explicit goal of mutual support, and while there have been fraternal orders for the well-off there have also been many fraternities for those in the lower ranks of society, especially for national or religious minorities. Trade unions also grew out of fraternities such as the Knights of Labour. The ability to organise freely, apart from the institutions of government and religion, was a fundamental part of the establishment of the modern world. In Living the Enlightenment, Margaret C. Jacobs showed the development of Jurgen Habermas' 'public space' in 17th century Netherlands was closely related to the establishment of lodges of Freemasons.

College and University Fraternities

- Fraternities have a long history in colleges and universities, and form a major subsection of the whole range of fraternities. In Europe, students were organised in nations and corporations since the beginnings of the modern university in the late medieval period, but the situation can differ greatly by country. In the United States, fraternities in colleges date to the 1770s, but did not fully assume an established pattern until the 1840s. They were strongly influenced by the patterns set by Freemasonry. The main difference between the older European organisations and the American organisations is that the American student societies virtually always include initiations, the formal use of symbolism, and the lodge-based organisational structure derived from usages in Freemasonry. In Germany the Corps are the oldest academic fraternities. Twenty-eight were founded in the 18th century and two of them still exist.

Trade Guilds

The development of Fraternities can be traced from trade unions or guilds that emerged in England. These guilds were set up to protect and care for their members at a time when there was no welfare state, trade unions or National Health Service. Various secret signs and handshakes were created to serve as proof of their membership allowing them to visit guilds in distant places that are associated with the guild they belong. Over the next 300 years or so, the idea of "ordinary" people joining together to improve their situation met with varying degrees of opposition from "People in Power", depending on whether they were seen as a source of revenue or a threat to their power. For example, when Henry VIII broke from the Roman Catholic Church, the Guilds were seen by him as supporters of the Pope, and in 1545 all material property of the Guilds was confiscated.

Elizabeth I took away from the Guilds the responsibility for apprenticeships, and by the end of her reign, most Guilds had been suppressed. The suppression of these Trade Guilds removed an important form of social and financial support from ordinary men and women. In major cities, some Guilds survived by adapting their roles to a social support function. Eventually, these groups evolved in the early 18th century into more philosophical organisations focused on brotherly love and ethical living. Among guilds that became prosperous are the Freemasons and the Odd Fellows. In many instances fraternities are limited to male membership such as the Dutch 'Alpinisten Vereniging Gelderland Midden' but this is not always the case, and there are mixed male and female, and even wholly female, fraternities. For example, for general fraternities: the Grande Loge Mixte de France, the Honourable Fraternity of Ancient Freemasons, the Grande Loge Féminine de France, the various Orders of Odd Fellows, Orange Order and Daughters of Rebekah and the Order of the Eastern Star.

3

Demands on Modern Social Work

It is common to find clients who expect much from you. Usually they expect immediate material assistance. For example, if they experience financial difficulties, they expect to be given money. It is important for you to explain to your clients what your roles are, instead of raising false hopes. It is important for you not to take on the personal problems of your clients as your own, as this could cause problems for you. You should present yourself as a person who can assist them to understand their concerns and manage them. While you, your clients, and the general public, may see social work as the embodiment of social services, you are dependent on public sponsorship. Social work is not about providing solutions to problems, but it provides an arena in which clients can review their concerns, and see how they can manage them best and live an effective life. Social work links clients with services, resources and opportunities, which might provide them with the help they need. This contributes to problem-solving for clients. It is important to recognize in social work the fact that it is an adaptable service, and one which is more responsive and accountable to a particular locality and its people. Social work is concerned with the provision of welfare services, when people's capacity for responding to the demands of life is strained, when capacity growth seems unattainable, and when important decisions elude resolution. Social work should assist clients to deal with life, engage in growth-producing activities, and make effective decisions. Naturally when people have a problem, they look for help. Usually, they think they have no capacity to solve their problem unless someone helps them to do so. And even when help comes, they expect the helper to produce the magic which will solve their problems. Social workers must make the role of their work clear when they are approached by a client. Their role is to assist the client to know why they need help and where they can get it.

EXPECTATIONS OF CLIENTS

Naturally, the presence of a social worker, when there is a problem, raises hopes in a client. Clients usually think that someone with a solution to their problem has come. As a result, they may present themselves as people who are completely helpless, even when they are able to do something themselves to resolve their concerns. A social worker should not take over the problem of the client. Instead, he/she must assist the client to re-examine it and consider possible solutions to it. People who experience difficulties/problems require assistance that should help them deal with them, and live more effectively. It is important that people who experience difficulties/problems are helped to overcome them. Children who experience difficulties require support.

As children cannot present their own interests, it is the responsibility of the state, through social welfare services, to take special responsibility for them. Social work plays a key role in family conflicts with children. It serves children whose parents neglect or abuse them. Social work is also important in schools, because it is in the schools where the inaccessible population is to be found. Social work in schools should be the application of social work principles and methods to the purpose of the school. Goals should centre upon helping pupils attain a sense of competence, a readiness to continue learning, and an ability to adapt to change. Increasingly, the focus of school social work should centre on cognitive areas such as learning, thinking and problem-solving, as well as traditional areas of concern, like relationships, emotions, motivation and personality. It is important for the school social worker to be concerned with the relationship of the school to other social institutions in the community.

INTERNATIONAL ORGANIZATIONS IN SOCIAL WORK

THE THREE MAJOR INTERNATIONAL ORGANIZATIONS

Organizing into associations is one of the hallmarks of the professions. Although his use of the term is outdated, Abraham Flexner pointed out in a 1915 speech to the U.S. National Conference of Charities and Correction that a profession is a "brotherhood" and tends to self organize. Within just a few decades of the first offerings of social work education in Europe and North America, social workers and others interested in social welfare came together for professional meetings and began to organize what are today the three major international organizations in the field of social work and social welfare.

This stage will describe the International Federation of Social Workers, the International Association of Schools of Social Work and the International Council on Social Welfare. Beginning with a discussion of the First International Conference on Social Welfare that gave the organizations their impetus, parts on each of the organizations will describe their history, mission, membership, and major programmes and initiatives. Areas of collaboration and conflict will be addressed and the substance will conclude with brief forward-looking recommendations. A few key leaders will be mentioned, although it is not possible to give adequate attention to their contributions to the international character of social work.

THE FIRST INTERNATIONAL CONFERENCE AND ITS ANTECEDENTS

There is no firm date to mark the beginning of social work. Better documented are the beginnings of social work education and here it is known that by the very late 19th century, social work courses had been offered in England, the United States and the Netherlands, with Germany following in the early years of the 20th century. Social workers were active in important international movements of the early 20th century, especially movements for peace, women's rights, and improved labour conditions.

As leaders in social welfare from various countries met each other, the benefits of exchanges of ideas became evident. This led to a proposal for an international conference on social work and social welfare, an idea that originated when European and Japanese social workers participated in the U.S. National Conference of Social Work in 1919. The official proposal for a conference was made in a letter from Dr. Rene Sand of Belgium to Julia Lathrop of the U.S. in 1923. Endorsement by national associations and by the League of Red Cross Societies followed. In 1926, an organizing committee met in Paris; the Committee was comprised of representatives from 17 countries in Europe, Asia and North America and from a number of important international organizations. Among these were the League of Nations, the International Labour Organization, the League of Red Cross Societies, the International Migration Service, and the Save the Children Fund.

Leading the way were Dr. Alice Masarykova of Prague as President and Dr. Rene Sand as Secretary General of the conference. Plans grew until the final event spanned two weeks and included international meetings of a number of organizations. The first International Conference of Social Work was held from July 8-13 1928 in Paris and was attended by 2,481 delegates from 42 countries. It is remarkable that so many traveled great distances almost 80 years ago. Yet, one of the conference speakers applauded the ease of travel in the day: "In the last hundred years, the technical application of human invention has wrought nothing short of a revolution in international relations. The high seas— obstacles for so long to the free interchange of goods and ideas—have become a great medium for the exchange of both...Ships, railways, aeroplanes, telephones, wireless telegraphy, broadcasting—all these have made the world smaller, have brought us into close contact with one another".

The Conference was only the first of what became the international social work and social welfare conferences. Two more were held before World War II interrupted international collaboration: 1932 in Frankfurt and 1936 in London. A planned conference for 1940 was never held; a planning meeting in Paris in 1946 and much less grandiose conference in 1948 in Atlantic City, New Jersey in the U.S. began the effort to rebuild the international social work/social welfare movement. Particularly significant is that the 1928 conference "gave birth" to the three international organizations that are the topic of this stage. Although they have been slightly renamed, both the IASSW and the ICSW have been in continuous existence since the 1928 meeting. The IFSW, originally the International Permanent Secretariat of Social Workers, disappeared for a time, but was officially reconstituted in 1956.

MISSION AND PURPOSE

The International Federation of Social Workers (IFSW) is a global organization striving for social justice, human rights and social development through the development of social work, best practices and international cooperation between social workers and their professional organizations. Association members work together through the international organization towards developing the common goals of the profession and in working on issues of concern to social workers globally.

IFSW tries to achieve this international identity by:

- Encouraging cooperation between social workers of all countries;
- Providing means for discussion and the exchange of ideas and experience through meetings, study visits, research projects, exchanges, publications and other methods of communication;
- Establishing and maintaining relationships with social work organizations and their members and representing them to international bodies relevant to social development and welfare;
- Sponsoring biennial international symposia and conferences;
- Developing and publishing policy statements to guide social work practice worldwide;
- Advocating for the protection of human rights of practicing social workers; and
- Providing consultation to the United Nations on issues of human development and human rights.

HISTORY AND ACTIVITIES

The IFSW celebrated its 50th jubilee in Munich in 2006, having grown from just 12 member organizations in 1956, to over 80 today. However, the heritage of the modern IFSW stretches back to the First International Conference on Social Work held in Paris in July 1928, where it was agreed that an international association of social workers be formed. At the 1932 Second International Conference on Social Work held in Frankfurt, provisional statutes of the International Permanent Secretariat of Social Workers (IPSSW) were agreed.

The IPSSW operated from Berlin, Geneva and Prague until 1956 when the International Federation of Social Workers was formed in Munich with 12 national member organizations and a new Secretariat was established in New York, sharing office with the National Association of Social Workers. Of major concern to the new organization was the question of ethics and in 1957 work began on the establishment of what has become today 'Ethics of Social Work – Statement of Principles'. The President and Executive promoted the voice of social work at the United Nations and its bodies so much that by 1959, just three years after re-establishment, the IFSW was approved for consultative status with the United Nations Economic and Social Council (ECOSOC), with a special relationship later extended by UNICEF and the International Labour Organization (ILO). Teams of representatives are in action at the United Nations in Geneva, Nairobi, New York and Vienna.

IFSW now also has formal partnerships with Amnesty International, CONGO (Conference of Non-Governmental Organizations in Consultative Relationship with the UN), Council of Europe; European Union, Habitat, IASSW and ICSW. Encouraging a discourse of international social work was greatly strengthened by the decision to launch the Journal of International Social Work. IFSW joined its partner organizations, ICSW and IASSW in sponsoring the journal in 1959. The Journal remains one of the most significant refereed journals on international social work available today. While early conferences were held jointly, by the mid 1960's it became apparent that for various reasons the three foundation organizations, IFSW, IASSW and ICSW, had begun to move in their own directions; since then, some of the conferences have been held separately and some together.

Regional IFSW seminars and conferences have been a strong feature, particularly of the European region, and have extended with differing levels of success across all IFSW regions. The IFSW Executive Committee decided to establish a permanent and paid secretariat in 1972 in Basel, Switzerland, appointing Catherine Chuard, followed by Andrew Mouravieff-Apostol as the Secretary General (1975-1992), assisted in his work by his wife Ellen. Both enjoyed extensive networks within the United Nations system and Ellen remains today as the IFSW Main Representative to the UN Geneva.

From 1975 to 1992 Andy was IFSW Secretary General, and was elected lifelong Honourary President when he retired in 1992. For IFSW, Andy was the cornerstone. He communicated with social workers of all countries with warmth, knowledge and diplomacy and became like a father for the international social work community.

His lifetime spanned close to a century and his history and background reflect the international character of the profession. Born in France in1913 of Russian/Ukrainian parents, his family were abroad when the 1917 revolution in Russia broke out it was impossible for the aristocratic family to return home; Andy was only able to return to Russia at the time of perestroika in the late 1980s. Working first as a journalist and then as a foreign correspondent in England before and during World War II, he also served in the Free French military forces.

After the war Andy left journalism and took up a position with the World Council of Churches and later with the United Nations High Commissioner for Refugees. He served in many countries, but mainly in South America, where he met his future wife Ellen. The couple settled in Geneva, where Andy until his death worked as a professional interpreter at the United Nations and other international bodies.

The strengthening of the secretariat also heralded an era of increased activity in membership levels and by IFSW through its representative status with various organizations. The secretariat later moved to Oslo, Norway in 1992 and then in 1999 to Berne, Switzerland, where it is located today, with Tom Johannesen as the Secretary-General.

The late 1970's saw considerable work undertaken on the definition of social work. This document was endorsed at the Brighton Conference in 1982 and remained unaltered until 1996 when a committee was established to revise and prepare a new definition of social work, ultimately adopted by both practitioners and educators in 2001. The 1980's were particularly active years for the IFSW in the area of human rights and social justice. By this time the IFSW had well established representative teams to the United Nations in New York, Geneva and Vienna.

This focus of concern led the Federation to a strong engagement in the UN International Year of Peace 1986, recognized by the UN officially declaring IFSW a 'Peace Messenger'. Eight years later the United Nations designated IFSW as 'Patron of the International Year of the Family' for exemplary support of the UN programme. Many outstanding social workers have contributed over the years to IFSW and its development. Among these are Jane Hoey whose major contribution to social work was in the establishment and enforcement of standards in public welfare administration in the United States, and in whose name a fund has been established to promote social work in developing regions of the world.

Another is Chauncey Alexander who served as the first US President of IFSW 1980-1982, developing the concept of global policy documents, the international code of ethics, and mentoring and promoting other social work associations. Social work grew out of humanitarian and democratic ideals, and its values are based on respect for the equality, worth, and dignity of all people. Human rights and social justice serve as the motivation and justification for social work action. IFSW promotes human rights by publishing statements on human rights issues and related matters and by raising awareness within the profession about the profession's commitment to its human rights heritage. IFSW has adopted an International Policy on Human Rights describing its commitment and giving guidance to social workers and social work organizations on human rights policy matters. To implement the human rights agenda of IFSW a special commission has been set up—the Human Rights Commission.

Apart from its work on behalf of imprisoned and persecuted social workers around the world, the Commission has successfully developed two landmark publications with international partners, on human rights and social work and social work and the rights of the child. IFSW and its member Associations have also produced other academic publications from time to time. Social Work and Globalization was produced as a special issue on the occasion of the IFSW and IASSW joint Conference in Montreal, 2000. Other publications include a series of edited books on social work in different countries, Social Work Around the World, which is now on its fourth issue.

Regional newsletters and journals are also published wherever possible. A series of international policy documents has been developed and are regularly revised. Current policy documents cover Displaced Persons, Globalization and the Environment, Health, HIV/AIDS, Indigenous Peoples, Women, Migration, Older Persons, Peace and Social Justice, Protection of Personal Information, Conditions in Rural Communities, Refugees and Youth. A highlight in the 1990's was IFSW's strong involvement in the World Summit for Social Development in Copenhagen in 1995. A special issue of the IFSW Newsletter was presented to a broader audience focusing on social work contributions to a new world order for social development in the areas of poverty eradication, unemployment, social integration and transition in Eastern Europe.

Also the Fourth UN World Conference on Women in Beijing the same year had a strong IFSW presence. The start of the new century brought with it a significant range of challenges for the social work professions. A worldwide shift in political orientation towards conservative and in some instances ultra-conservative governments has meant that working to develop social services has been particularly difficult in more developed countries. Issues concerning the alleviation of poverty, human rights and HIV/AIDS continue to be major concerns. IFSW has responded to some of the major international issues experiences in recent years such as the Asian tsunami, serious human rights violations in the Sudan and the challenges faced by orphans and vulnerable children in Africa, through projects initiated by its regional bodies and in cooperation with partner organizations.

MEMBERSHIP

IFSW is the international organization representing professional social workers, although membership is through national social work organizations, not individual status. Only one national professional organization in each country may become a member of the Federation. Such an organization may be a national organization or a coordinating body representing two or more national organizations. Each member association or coordinating body must observe the IFSW Constitution and should require from its members regular professional training based upon an organized sequence of social work education incorporating ethical standards of practice and a body of knowledge compatible with social work principles. At present, there are national organizations in 84 countries in membership, representing just under 500,000 social workers across the world.

Association members collaborate together through IFSW towards developing the common goals of the profession and in working on issues of concern to social workers internationally. IFSW is divided into the five geographical regions of Africa; Asia-Pacific; Europe; Latin America and the Caribbean; and North America, each of which is represented by a regional president. An international elected executive committee steers the work of the Federation with a global President and Secretary General heading the body. The general executive meets every two years at the same time as an international Conference, at times held jointly with IASSW and ICSW. IFSW also has a very successful programme called 'Friends of IFSW,' providing affiliating social workers, social work students and organizations a link to international social work.

CHALLENGES: PAST AND FUTURE

IFSW has faced significant challenges at various times in its history, often due to political and ideological differences among its many members. However the international executive committee and the General Meeting of the member associations has made every effort to work in as harmonious a way as possible and to reconcile and overcome these issues. Serious problems have ranged from conflicts in places as varied as the Middle East, Sri Lanka and Zimbabwe. However the contentious issue of South Africa was one of the most significant, when by 1963 the attention of the world began to focus on South Africa and its Apartheid policy.

The South African European Social Workers organization was a member of IFSW at that time and despite continued work on their part to establish a coordinating body of European and non-European social workers, due to government policies in that country, such an organization could not be established. The principles of non-discrimination are foundation principles for social work and after many years of agonized debate and attempts to resolve this very difficult and delicate situation South Africa was expelled from membership in 1970 and was not eligible to re-enter membership again until 1998. In fact, South Africa has yet to achieve membership of IFSW due to the persistent problem of being able to form a coordinating body between the white, coloured and black South African social work associations.

There are various future priorities and challenges that face IFSW, including:

- A core concern is to ensure that key policy statements are up-to-date and relevant. In this context both IFSW and IASSW have agreed a four-year process for the review of the international definition of social work and the international statement of ethical principles, leading to the 2010 joint conference in Hong Kong. Thereafter these core statements will be reviewed every 10 years.

- Social work practice is becoming increasingly international with the migration of social workers from many countries in the developing world to the developed. A challenge for IFSW is to link with other organizations that are trying to improve conditions in the originating countries and stem this migration as far as this is possible.
- Conflicts and consequent human rights abuses have intensified throughout many regions of the world in recent years and this challenges IFSW to take an even higher profile in defence of human rights. IFSW already issues statements of concern where violations of peoples' rights occurs, such as in Darfur, but the challenge for IFSW is to ensure that these words are translated into actions.
- A similar challenge for IFSW is to respond as effectively as it can to natural disasters such as the Asian tsunami of December 2004.
- The IFSW's engagement with debates on poverty, ways to achieve the Millennium Development Goals and tackle the consequences of HIV/AIDS remain important areas of concern for the organization.

An enormous commitment by many volunteers and a small but dedicated secretariat has over 50 years given rise to a significant organization with good reason to celebrate its achievements. Through a number of world and regional conferences, the development of core international documents to guide social work concepts and practices, and ongoing representation at the United Nations and other international bodies, IFSW is today a key global voice of international social work practice.

THE INTERNATIONAL ASSOCIATION OF SCHOOLS OF SOCIAL WORK (IASSW)

The International Association of Schools of Social Work is the main organization representing social work education and educators around the world; in 2008, it will celebrate its 80th anniversary.

MISSION

The primary mission of the IASSW is to strengthen social work education around the world. This has remained constant since the founding. The most recent formal review of the mission statement took place in 2000 and resulted in the following mission statement: The International Association of Schools of Social Work is an international association of institutions of social work education, organizations supporting social work education and social work educators.

Its mission is:

- To develop and promote excellence in social work education, research and scholarship globally in order to enhance human well-being;

- To create and maintain a dynamic community of social work educators and their programmes;
- To support and facilitate participation in mutual exchanges of information and expertise;
- To represent social work education at the international level.

The statement also commits IASSW to adhere to UN human rights declarations and conventions and to pursue social justice and social development.

HISTORY AND ACTIVITIES

A special part of the 1928 conference focused on social work education and was led by Alice Salomon of Germany. The delegates at the conference decided to "write to all the training schools of social work asking them whether they would be prepared to become members of an International Association of Schools". In addition to Alice Salomon, the founders of the International Committee of Schools of Social Work, as it was originally called, consisted of representatives from the Netherlands, Belgium, and Switzerland, soon joined by the United States, France, England, and Poland. Of the 111 schools of social work identified at the time, 46 schools from 10 countries agreed to become founding members of the new association.

By 1939, membership had grown to 75 schools from 18 countries; by then, however, all German schools had withdrawn from membership. In the early years, the International Committee sponsored seminars to exchange knowledge and strengthen social work education, including "summer schools"— seminars that intensively explored significant topics for social work. The organization continued to be led by Alice Salomon as President. She was pressured by her colleagues in Germany to resign after the Nazis came to power; Salomon was suspect for many reasons, including Jewish ancestry and her commitment to peace and internationalism.

She resigned several times as President, but each time, her IASSW colleagues renamed her President. Just before she was expelled from Germany, Salomon completed the first world survey of social work education, published by the ICSSW in 1937. She produced an in-depth sociological and comparative analysis of social work education in 32 countries. The International Committee established working relationships with the ILO and with the Commission on Social Questions of the League of Nations.

A particularly important achievement was that the ILO set up a Centre of Documentation for schools of social work in 1929. "For the next ten years the ILO attempted, with moderate success, to collect and index the statutes, programmes of study, annual reports, publications, research and seminar reports, and lists of theses or other student reports from more than 100 schools of social work." As was true for each of the 3 organizations, World War II had a devastating effect. Not only were communications disrupted for the war period, but many teachers and students died and educational facilities destroyed. The plight of the school at Warsaw is recorded in early letters of the IASSW: "I appeal most warmly in the name of the Board...to make their members send all they possibly can collect, books, documents, reports, *etc.* regarding social work to Mrs. Helena Radlinska, one of the founders of our Committee, professor of the State University of Lodz. Mrs.

Radlinska had the great misfortune to see destroyed besides her private house, the School of Social Work, founded by her at the University of Warsaw as well as the University itself, and to lose by death two-thirds of the teaching staff. In spite of this great misfortune starting anew at the age of 75 years Mrs. Radlinska does what she can to rebuild a School of Social Work at the University of Lodz." Kendall labeled the years 1945-1954 the "Restoration Years".

A small conference was held in Atlantic City in the U.S. in 1948 and Rene Sand had agreed in 1946 to take on the Presidency of the International Committee of Schools of Social Work. Ironically, although devastation was significant, Kendall reports that the war and its aftermath created a new demand for social workers and thus, "by 1948, 359 schools were counted in 41 countries" in a report issued by the new United Nations.. Social work as a profession and social work educational institutions began to disappear in the Communist countries, but grew substantially in the newly independent countries in Asia and Africa.

In the 1950's and 1960's, IASSW extended its outreach to programmes in developing countries. The Congress was held in Madras, India in 1952, marking the first time the conference was held outside of Europe or North America. By 1956, the board of directors included members from Australia, Guatemala, Japan and India. The name of the organization was officially changed to the International Association of Schools of Social Work, although many member units are not independent schools but programmes within larger institutions. A major, but sadly temporary, milestone was the establishment of a Secretariat in 1971 with a paid Secretary General. Katherine Kendall served as the first paid Secretary General from 1971-1978. Originally in New York, the Secretariat moved to Vienna in 1978.

Kendall was succeeded by Margarite Mathieu of Canada and then Vera Mehta of India. In the early 1990's, the organization experienced financial difficulties caused by the increased expenses of maintaining the Vienna office. A decision was taken by the Board to return to a volunteer-run organization and the Secretariat was closed in 1992. While finances have since permitted the hiring of an Administrative Assistant based in the office of the President, from 1993 IASSW has functioned without a professional executive officer. As is true for ICSW and IFSW, IASSW holds a biennial world conference.

These have been held regularly since 1928 except for the war years. At various times, the conferences have been held jointly with IFSW or with both

IFSW and ICSW; in 2006 and 2008, the 3 organizations held/will hold separate conferences before joining in 3-way collaboration in 2010.It might be argued that the Biennial world conference with its call for documents and the co-sponsorship of the journal, International Social Work, are particularly important to the mission of the IASSW as both address the purpose of advancing scholarship and research in social work and social work education. IASSW played a lead role in the establishment of the journal and guided it in its early years.

To further this objective of encouraging scholarship and research, IASSW has recently expanded its publication activity and has launched a book series through Venture Press. IASSW also assisted the Caribbean sub-regional group to launch The Caribbean Journal of Social Work in 2002. In the 1970's IASSW secured significant funding to pursue a 6 year multi-country project on family planning and social work education.

The project was implemented in 20 countries—as diverse as Iran, the Philippines, Kenya, and Jamaica. Curricula, field placements, project reports and a number of important publications resulted from the effort. The family planning project put IASSW on the forefront of a cutting edge issue and reflected sound working relationships with major governmental and private funding bodies.

While no initiative of this scale has been implemented since then, IASSW was active in the 1980's and 1990's to promote and assist the development of social work education in Eastern Europe, Russia and China. Consultations and seminars were sponsored to help countries establish or re-establish social work. Through recent efforts to strengthen the regional association of schools of social work in Africa and assistance in the establishment of sub-regional organizations in the Caribbean in the 1990s and in Southeast Europe in 2006, promotion of the growth and development of social work education continues to be a programme priority of the IASSW. In an effort to promote international exchange and innovation, IASSW began a programme of small projects in 2004. A consortium of at least 3 schools in two or more countries with different cultures or social work educational systems may apply for funding for a project that advances social work education internationally. The projects must enhance international and cross-cultural collaboration.

To date, among the projects that have been funded are one to develop a web site on field education for Chinese schools of social work; a collaboration of schools in Kenya, the Philippines and England to develop a module on disaster management; a project sponsored by 18 schools in 9 different countries on indigenous social work education and practice; and a 10 country project on international social work and political conflict resolution that is setting up a network to enhance social work education and research in conflict and post-conflict situations. IASSW led the effort to develop Global Standards for Social Work Education and Training, adopted by both IFSW and IASSW in 2004. This comprehensive document is the first set of standards for social work education at the global level. Although compliance with the standards is voluntary, they have been hailed by schools of social work—especially in the developing world—as helpful targets that will contribute to upgrading of social work training. IASSW also joined with IFSW in developing and endorsing the Global Definition of Social Work and the Statement of Ethical Principles.

MEMBERSHIP AND ORGANIZATIONAL STRUCTURE

There are two categories of membership in the IASSW: school members and individual members. Social Work educational programmes at the tertiary level are eligible to join as school members. Individual educators may also join, but individual member votes count as 1/10 of a school vote. Currently, there are member schools in more than 70 countries spread across Africa, Asia and the Pacific, Europe, Latin America, and North American and the Caribbean. Schools are also organized into regional associations. Although the regions differ greatly in their degree of formality and organization, each regional President serves on the IASSW Board and Executive Committee as a Vice-President.

The Board of Directors is large and includes the elected officers of President, Secretary and Treasurer; 4 elected at-large members; regional representatives, including the Vice-Presidents; and national representatives. Chairs of task forces and committees also attend board meetings where they have a voice, but not a vote. Current committees and task forces include the International Exchange Task Force, the Nominating Committee, an award committee, the World Census Committee, the Women's Caucus, Publications, Human Rights, the Projects Committee, and the UN representatives team.

CHALLENGES: PAST AND FUTURE

IASSW has faced several challenges over its almost 80 years of existence. Among them were the devastation and disruption caused by World War II and the financial difficulties of the early 1990's that led to the loss of Secretariat. In the 1980's, the organization faced a different kind of struggle over the membership of South African schools. The world's attention on the evils of the South African apartheid system intensified during the late 1970's and 1980's. A major initiative was to isolate the South African government by expelling South African organizations from participation in world bodies and events (although South Africa continued to be a member of the United Nations). The issue extended to social work education. Throughout the 1980's there was extensive work to assess the degree to which the South African schools were working to oppose apartheid and to ensure multiracial social work education. When the IASSW leadership decided to work with the reform-oriented South African schools and allow the JUC to retain membership, the schools in the Nordic region withdrew. Although reconciliation and re-entry of the Nordic schools occurred after the end of apartheid, the struggle over South Africa had a longlasting effect on the organization. Future challenges include pressures arising from changes in the educational sector, where mergers of social work programmes into larger departments with other disciplines are becoming more common.

When social work has less autonomy and less visibility, there is diminished allegiance to the profession and schools are less likely to maintain membership in social work organizations such as the IASSW. While the Global Standards are a major advance, they are voluntary and some are concerned that free trade regulations will lead to externally-imposed criteria for social work education. IASSW needs to carefully monitor such developments and be prepared to respond. The process of developing the standards also gave renewed attention to the continuing challenge to achieve some universality— definition of what is essential and core education for professional social work— while encouraging diversity and indigenization of curricula.

THE INTERNATIONAL COUNCIL ON SOCIAL WELFARE (ICSW)

The International Council on Social Welfare differs from the IFSW and IASSW because it is interdisciplinary and includes lay as well as professional members. The ICSW is "a global non-governmental organization which represents a wide range of national and international member organizations that seek to advance social welfare, social justice and social development".

MISSION

ICSW describes its mission as: "to promote forms of social and economic development which aim to reduce poverty, hardship and vulnerability throughout the world, especially amongst disadvantaged people." The statement continues: "It strives for recognition and protection of fundamental rights to food, shelter, education, health care and security. It believes that these rights are an essential foundation for freedom, justice and peace. It seeks also to advance equality of opportunity, freedom of self-expression and access to human services."

HISTORY AND ACTIVITIES/PROGRAMMES

The ICSW, under the earlier name of the International Conference on Social Work, was formed in 1928 out of the Paris conference with Rene Sand, a chief organizer of the 1928 meetings, as its founder and Alice Masarykova as first president. Sand soon succeeded Masarykova as President in 1932. Organized to promote the interests of the social welfare sector and to ensure international exchange of information and views, the ICSW held international conferences in 1932 and 1936, resuming in the post-World War II years. Records of the planning for a 1940 conference and all records of the early ICSW were destroyed in the bombing of London. Rene Sand's own story shows the disruption of organizational activities during the war years.

He was taken prisoner in 1940 when the Nazi army invaded Belgium and was held in Tyrol, Austria until he was liberated in May of 1945. He resumed his active presidency of ICSW until 1948 when he encouraged younger leaders to take over. ICSW regrouped after the war, focusing initially on relief for war-torn areas. A special meeting was held in 1947 in Holland on the theme: "Urgent Social Problems in the War Stricken Areas of Europe". The ICSW was one of the first NGOs to gain consultative status with the United Nations. Conference locations marked progress of the ICSW in the post-war years. The 1952 conference in Madras, India, was the first held outside the West.

In 1956, the conference was held in Munich with participants from 55 countries. As Katzki observed, support for the conference in Germany showed that "participants recognized in ICSW a force that could help heal wounds and contribute to a better understanding amongst peoples". Geographic reach was extended through the 1962 conference in Brazil and the 1974 conference in Nairobi, Kenya. It is worth noting that ICSW gave early recognition to human rights. The 1968 conference theme "Social Welfare and Human Rights" supported the United Nations International Year of Human Rights.

The documents delivered at the conference contain messages relevant to this day. The human rights theme was echoed in 1976 in Puerto Rico: "The Struggle for Equal Opportunity-Strategies for Social Welfare." The organization sought ways to expand its activities beyond the biennial conferences. In 1966, the name of the organization was changed to the International·Council on Social Welfare to more accurately convey that membership and scope of activity are not limited to social work.

Katzki records that by 1968, ICSW had almost 50 national committees in membership and that many of these were in developing countries. Efforts continued to strengthen national committees and build regional networks. A particularly important area of activity is consultation at the United Nations. ICSW has the highest level of NGO consultative status with the United Nations and relates to the Economic and Social Council as well as to the ILO, UNICEF, UNESCO, WHO and other bodies.

The Category I consultative status allows ICSW to attend ECOSOC meetings, circulate written statements to members, address a council committee, and submit items for ECOSOC consideration. For at least 25 years, ICSW has emphasized social development. In 1982, ICSW officially described itself as: International Council on Social Welfare: A World Organization Promoting Social Development.

The emphasis on social development intensified in preparations for and participation in the 1995 United Nations World Summit on Social Development held in Copenhagen. ICSW participated in the preparatory meetings for the

Summit and organized a global NGO preparatory meeting. More than 60 NGO leaders attended this meeting in Helsinki in 1994.

Over several years prior to and during the Summit, ICSW distributed copies of its policy documents on poverty and other Summit issues, monitored the official deliberations, and worked collaboratively with other NGOs. The Chair of the ICSW Summit Working Group, Julian Disney, reported success: "ICSW widely circulated about a dozen policy documents and proposals for inclusion in the Summit agreements and we are pleased that many of our recommendations are reflected in the final documents". After the Summit, the organization has continued to participate in the activities of the Commission on Social Development and to monitor progress on the commitments agreed at the Summit. In 1997, ICSW signed a Memorandum of Understanding with UNDP to ensure closer cooperation on matters related to civil society, poverty eradication and social development.

ICSW has continued to represent issues of social welfare and social development at numerous international meetings, including the World Economic Forum, the International Labour Conference, WHO, and the UN Commission for Social Development.

More recently, ICSW has been critical of the narrow definition of poverty expressed in the Millennium Development Goals and called for inclusion of the ideas expressed in the Summit Commitments. ICSW identifies employment as an important component of the fight against poverty, yet employment is neglected in the MDGs.

The emphasis of the 2007 Social Development Commission UN meeting is on decent work for all, a theme actively supported by the ICSW. ICSW makes its contribution through research and dissemination of information, exchange through conferences, and development of policy recommendations based on its research and linkages with local and national organizations. ICSW experienced leadership difficulties early in the 21st century, when the elected President was harassed and jailed in his home country of Bangladesh. This coincided with a time when the organization was also without a permanent Executive Director. non-etheless, programmes have continued. Global conferences were held in Malaysia in 2004 and in Brazil in 2006, with more than 1000 participants from 44 countries.

A four-year plan for ongoing programmes was adopted in 2004. Regional activities have intensified as ICSW carries out its goal of "strengthening civil society in all parts of the world". Initiatives included efforts in Central and West Africa and the Black Sea area. In Europe, work at the European Regional Conference emphasized a "European Social Model" to promote balanced social and economic progress, equal rights, and solidarity. A link with the South Asia Partnership has worked on such critical issues as trafficking, democracy and disasters.

MEMBERSHIP

There are several different membership categories. National Committees of ICSW are country level bodies that represent non-governmental organizations in the social welfare/social development field. There are currently national committees in 32 countries that are members. In addition, ICSW has International Member Organizations—global and/or regional organizations that support ICSW goals; and a number of members classified as Other Organizations who can affiliate within regions; and finally, Government Associates. There are currently member organizations in at least 50 countries.

CHALLENGES: PAST AND FUTURE

The disruption caused by the arrest of the President of the ICSW in 2000 and obviously posed a serious challenge to the organization. But, the ICSW has recovered and is actively pursuing an ambitious programme. In 2004, ICSW adopted a 4-year global programme with seven areas of work. These are: social welfare and social development; networking; communicating with stakeholders; global advocacy on "socially responsible global governance"; regional cooperation; North-South partnerships; and South-South policy dialogue. A challenge is the lack of strong national committees in some countries. The Executive Director, "the emphasis of ICSW's current global programme is to strengthen national umbrella organizations in the South. This is fundamental to achieving our goal of influencing governments to take seriously the road to reducing poverty in their countries and their regions". While establishing strong and sustainable national civil society organizations in the Global South may be particularly difficult, the problem also exists in industrialized countries. The United States, for example, no longer has a strong national committee and its participation in the ICSW has diminished.

AREAS OF CONFLICT AND COLLABORATION AMONG THE THREE ORGANIZATIONS

The three organizations have many common areas of interest and activity. All hold conferences, support the journal International Social Work, maintain consultative status at the UN and aim to represent social work and social welfare at a number of NGO committees and activities. All emphasize the value of international exchange and communication and all have continued to seek ways to strengthen their organizational activities and contributions between and beyond conferences. IFSW and IASSW have successfully collaborated in and sponsored an annual Social Work Day at the UN in New York. In 2007, a World Social Work Day has been launched by the IFSW and creates additional opportunities for collaborative efforts.

At some points in history, there have been conflicts within and between the organizations, especially over the status of apartheid South Africa. At other times, disagreements or barriers to collaboration have been more mundane—disputes over conference locations, expenditures, or hurt feelings over failure to give due credit to contributions of the collaborating partners. While mundane, these can be difficult to resolve and can pose obstacles to successfully speaking with a unified voice on the international scene. Perhaps more distressing have been the consequences caused when the organizations and their leaders have been persecuted for their advocacy work. Over the course of history, each organization has suffered. In the 1930's, the President of IASSW was pressured by her own German colleagues to resign as she was deemed unfit by the Nazis.

More recently, the elected President of the ICSW. Qazi Faruque Ahmed of Bangladesh, was unable to fulfill his duties as he and his local organization were persecuted by the government of the country. While pressure from ICSW members and others resulted in his release from jail, Dr. Ahmed was unable to serve as President due to this situation. Oppression and conflict have taken their toll many times, including the early 1990's when the head of the IFSW's Kuwait Association of Social Workers was captured and later killed by the Iraqi invaders. As a profession concerned with social justice and human rights, social work is seen as highly political and therefore as a threat to oppressive governments. This continues to put social work organizations and their leaders in danger.

The commonality of goals and programme priorities suggest that the organizations can share successful strategies and sessions learned. All three organizations are working to strengthen the regions, identify and encourage growth of membership in Africa, Asia and Latin America, and promote increased communication and networking. Now that the organizations have agreed to co-host their world conferences, more emphasis on sharing information and successes can begin.

MODERN SOCIAL WORK

Pierre Bourdieu was perhaps the greatest sociologist since the classical generation of Max Weber and E´ mile Durkheim. Yet, despite occasional ritualistic invocations of his key concepts and references to certain famous texts, social work remains largely unfamiliar with his ideas. Bourdieu contributed more than just a set of such terms as "cultural capital" and "habitus." He provided a new relational approach to the study of fields of domination and struggle, a new way of thinking about how power operates within social life. This thesis seeks to demonstrate the potential usefulness of Bourdieu's approach, which diverges significantly from much of contemporary research in the social work discipline.

After a brief survey of his core theoretical insights by way of illustration and provocation to further research, an analysis of one particular empirical field that is highly relevant to the discipline: the field of homeless services in New York City. It discusses this field in terms of its two constituent components: on the side of production, the field of shelters, and on the side of consumption, the field of homeless clients. Finally, the object steps back from this dual analysis to explore the implications of Bourdieu's ideas for social work enquiry and practical intervention.

This work does not present a detailed portrayal of shelters and their clients or a definitive blueprint for improving homeless services. Rather, it sketches in bold strokes what a Bourdieuian analysis of the field of homeless services might look like and how it might contribute to both the theory and practice of social work. Specifically, it shows how Bourdieu's theory of fields moves beyond social work's traditional systems perspectives by illuminating, as those perspectives do not, the full significance of field specific contestations: symbolic capital is accrued in widely varying forms and volumes by social service providers as well as recipients. Such capital becomes both a stake and a weapon in their respective struggles over legitimate authority within helping systems.

CONSTRUCTING THE OBJECT

The first and most important task in any Bourdieu-inspired analysis is to construct the object of study, and such a task always entails thinking systematically in terms of fields. Bourdieu conceives of fields as relatively autonomous social microcosms, exhibiting, like Weber's life- or valuespheres, their own distinctive structures and dynamics and functioning just as to their own inner logics.

He posits a multiplicity of such spaces in any complex and differentiated society. Modern society, he claims, is marked not by the ascendancy of any one singular logic like that of the social relations of production but by the existence of a number of more or less independent social universes that, although empirically interrelated and mutually determinative, nonetheless obey, again to some extent, their own inner laws and principles.

"What happens in," he writes, "cannot be understood by looking only at external factors". Bourdieu characterizes even the national society itself as a field, terming this the social space as a whole, but within this social macrocosm he also delineates a number of less expansive spaces, such as the legal field, the economic field, the field of cultural production and the field of bureaucratic powers. Also included within the social space as a whole are exceedingly circumscribed and even microcosmic social worlds, such as individual families.

In between, at a level identified as intermediate in terms of scope and complexity, are also such fields as the one discussed below: that of homeless services in one particular metropolitan setting. Bourdieu conceives of fields as "configuration[s] of objective relations between positions" such that any given field can be conceptualized as a structure of relations not between the concrete entities themselves but, rather, between the nodes that those entities happen to occupy. In other words, Bourdieu takes as his units of analysis not concrete or empirical entities but what he calls constructed or epistemic objects.

These objects are defined in terms of where they are situated within a relational system. For Bourdieu, to construct an object means to break with preconstructed, taken for- granted understandings of that object in favour of "situating [it] at a determinate place in social space". This is important because one gains a way of systematically taking into account forces that act upon and are determinative of these objects from elsewhere or from outside: "Like heavenly bodies belonging to the same gravitational field," objects within a space "produce effects upon one another from afar".

Bourdieu indicates that the nodes or positions within a field are "objectively defined, in their existence and in the determinations they impose upon their occupants, agents, or institutions, by their present and potential situation in the structure of the distribution of species of power whose possession commands access to the specific profits that are at stake in the field, as well as by their objective relation to other positions". In other words, positions within a field, including those that mark the dominant and dominated poles of that field, must be analysed in terms of the distinctive profiles of capital associated with them.

Bourdieu refers here to "species of capital" in the plural: while capital most often connotes material or economic resources, for him it also encompasses a wide range of other types of resources, any of which, when accrued by actors within the field at hand, can enable them to climb to positions of relative privilege within the field. Within any given field, different specific entities can be said to engage in the struggles ongoing within that field as bearers of different amounts and combinations of capitals, some yielding greater advantages within that particular field than others.

The concepts of field and capital are intrinsically interlinked; just as "a capital does not exist and function except in relation to a field," so too, conversely, the distribution of capital "constitutes the very structure of the field". Capitals function both as weapons and as stakes in the struggle to gain ascendancy within fields. Any field is a structure or temporary state of power relations within what is also an ongoing struggle for domination waged by the deployment or accumulation of relevant capitals, a struggle for successful monopolization "of the legitimate violence which is characteristic of the field in question".

Bourdieu's perspective brings to the foreground the structural tension between occupants of dominant and dominated positions within any social microcosm. It requires that any field be conceived of as a terrain of contestation among occupants of positions differentially endowed with the resources necessary for gaining and safeguarding an ascendant position within that terrain.

Indeed, much of the contestation among actors can be said to concern the legitimate valuation that is to be accorded the precise species of capital in which they happen to be well-endowed; that is, such conflict is about gaining the capacity to produce a recognition of the legitimacy of this capital distribution among the other contending parties.

Especially significant in all such struggles is what Bourdieu terms symbolic capital, or capital in any of its forms insofar as it is accorded positive recognition, esteem, or honour by relevant actors within the field. Contestations over symbolic authority are a crucial feature of field dynamics, and those actors who succeed in amassing it gain considerably thereby in their efforts to assume a dominant position within the field as a whole. Within the social space as a whole, the most consequential struggles over symbolic capital take place within what Bourdieu terms the field of power, a relational reframing on his part of the more conventional idea of a ruling class.

He defines this field of power as a space of contention for ascendancy among dominant actors from all the other fields that constitute the social order. Since the field concept is meant to be applicable at all scales, from the most expansive to the most circumscribed, each of the more delimited social microcosms, too, can be said to feature something like its own internal field of power. All such "gaming spaces" whether large or small, exhibit certain structural properties that can be said to be invariant and universal. One of these properties is a bipolar structure, such that these spaces all revolve around an opposition between what Bourdieu terms temporal and spiritual power.

At the level of the social space as a whole, this opposition typically translates to structural tensions between the holders of economic, political, or social privilege, on the one side, and of intellectual pr-eeminence, on the other. In more delimited spaces, this polarity takes other but still structurally homologous forms. Close homologies, Bourdieu indicates, can often be found between what are outwardly very different kinds of gaming spaces. Looking ahead to this object's analyses, for example, the authors find a bipolar structure between those homeless shelters that are relatively rich in the symbolic capital of order and those that are relatively rich in the capital of authenticity.

So too, the same structure is observed between those homeless clients who are relatively well-endowed in staff-sanctioned capital and those who are relatively well-endowed in client-sanctioned capital. Bourdieu specifies another invariant property of gaming spaces. This has to do with the mutually opposed interests and strategies of action that one typically finds within such spaces. Actors' interests are largely shaped by the location of those actors within the overall distribution of capital and, thereby, within the structure of power relations constitutive of a contested space.

Their strategies of action are also largely determined by such positioning. On the one hand, Bourdieu predicts that dominant actors or entities pursue a conservation strategy, one in which their overriding aim is to preserve the principle of hierarchization, the distribution and valuation of species of capitals, that happens to be most favourable to them and to safeguard or even enhance their position within this hierarchy. On the other hand, he predicts that dominated actors or entities adopt a subversion strategy, in which their aim is to transform the field's system of authority, including its relative valuation of different capitals and, potentially, the very rules of the game just as to which it ordinarily functions, to their own benefit.

Subversion strategies typically entail, he adds, a claim "to be returning to the sources, the origin, the spirit, the authentic essence of the game, in opposition to the banalization and degradation which it has suffered". Bourdieu claims that, in analysing any field, it is important to determine precisely how its constituent actors, differently positioned as they are within the field in respect to the distribution of capital operative therein, perceive themselves, their competitors, and the field as a whole, in all its opportunities and challenges.

Actors, he asserts, gravitate in the direction of one or another of these opposing strategies. One final invariant property of fields is that actors and entities within them not only have interests grounded in the discrete positions they happen to occupy relative to others in the field but also have shared commitments to and investments in the field overall. Bourdieu describes these ties as an *illusio*, or "objective complicity which underlies all the antagonisms". In the study of fields, it is crucial always to enquire into the tacitly shared interests, concerns, and ultimate beliefs that constitute the admission fee, as it were, into those fields; these attachments also guarantee that the dynamism and processuality constitutive of fields do not entail perpetual upheaval.

Bourdieu points out that such unspoken agreements are often lodged at the level of what he terms the habitus. By this, he means the system of dispositions that become like second nature to actors as a result either of childhood socialization within the family or, later in life, of more specific mechanisms of socialization. Such dispositions include deeply ingrained modes of perception, emotional response, and action within the world but also manners and bearing, ways of speaking, forms of dress, and personal hygiene.

Since these systems of dispositions serve as a generative principle for strategies of action, differences at the level of habitus help to explain the different conservation and subversion strategies that actors find themselves inclined to pursue; indeed, their very habitus often become forms of capital and, thus, weapons and stakes in struggles. Those actors who occupy the most dominated positions in the field tend also to be those with habitus least well-suited for the contestations specific to that field.

However, commonalities at the level of habitus also serve to bind all these actors together, even despite the structural tensions that tend to separate them. *"A fight presupposes agreement between the antagonists about what it is that is worth fighting about; those points of agreement are held at the level of what 'goes without saying'".*

THE FIELD OF HOMELESS SHELTERS

The field of homeless services in New York City provides an illustration of how a Bourdieuian field analysis might be constructed. This enquiry commences by analysing the space of production of homeless shelters: the providers of homeless services. The second half of the thesis lays out a similar framework in respect to the field of homeless clients: the consumers of those services. The intent is twofold: to highlight how one might conduct an actual field analysis and to demonstrate how such an approach might lead to alternative ways of understanding social work systems and practices.

While other examples from social work could have been selected instead, the case of homeless services in New York City is featured because of the second author's intimate and firsthand knowledge of that field, accumulated over 5 years during the late 1990s as a director of social services and as the programme director of one of the city's homeless shelter programmes. Her experiences of the day-to-day operations of that shelter, her frequent meetings with other shelter administrators and staff from both the New York City Department of Homeless Services and the Coalition for the Homeless, her supervision of casework staff and MSW field students, and her extensive contact with clients serve as the principal data upon which this illustrative analysis is based.

PRINCIPLES OF DIVISION

Even with such intimate familiarity with the field, constructing the object of study is at best a highly challenging endeavor. Speaking practically, how are the field's most pertinent indicators, properties, or principles of division to be identified? How are its parameters to be ascertained? Bourdieu suggests that enquiry should be guided at first by a basic sense of the field or space at hand. But these early intuitions about the principles of division operative within that field should be empirically tested and gradually refined until they yield an objective space, defined perhaps just as to criteria quite different from those that originally guided the study.

What follows is an attempt to convey how such a process might unfold. Ultimately, this enquiry ventures well beyond the initial categories used by the actors who work within the field of homeless shelters. It breaks with what Bourdieu calls the *doxa* of that field, the taken-for-granted, unquestioned, spontaneous, and commonsensical understandings that prevail across that space. The analysis demonstrates that even insiders to the field do not always possess an immediate or unimpeachable knowledge of the divisions operative within it.

Specifically, it rejects three alternative ways of mapping the field of homeless shelters, three different principles of division that are commonly deployed by those who staff shelter organizations: single-adult versus family shelters, general versus specialized shelters, and public versus private shelters. The first of these principles of division, that between a single adult system and a family system, derives its legitimacy and official sanction from New York City's DHS, which has organized more than 200 shelters from the perspective of this division.

Initially, it seems to be a reasonable principle of categorization, since single adults and families require very different types of social services and housing. However, while this division makes sense for the DHS, it fails to illuminate how shelters are actually organized within this space; that is, how different types of capitals that are highly salient within this field are differentially distributed among the various shelters comprising it. More specifically, a wide variety of shelters exist within each system and across the two systems, some shelters enjoy particular distinctions and others do not. In both systems, for example, there are shelters that social workers at assessment centers understand to be of fine quality. Social workers speak highly of these places to their clients and work hard to get those clients transferred to or placed on the waiting lists at these locations.

But, within both systems, there are also other shelters that assessment social workers may from time to time invoke in threatening fashion.

Since this sort of hierarchy exists within both systems, and being part of the family system affords shelters no clear advantage over affiliation with the adult system, this distinction between single-adult and family shelters must be rejected as the principle of division along which the space is organized. Nor is a second division, that between general and specialized shelters, entirely adequate for the current purposes.

General shelters are typically very large and chaotic places. Specialized shelters by contrast, are organized with a particular client population in mind. These sites are usually smaller than general shelters and have an intake or special referral process. Admissions criteria, such as gender, a minimum age, veteran's status, and a willingness to stay clean and sobre, are some of the many and varied prerequisites for referral.

At first glance, such a division of the field in terms of general and specialized shelters seems like a viable way to proceed. Specialized shelters seem to be the dominant ones in the sense of being the most privileged, while general shelters seem to belong in the dominated sector of the space.

In the second author's experience of the field, some shelters did, in fact, seem to enjoy a certain distinction among social workers as well as clients, the DHS, and homeless advocates on account of being specialized. Among these were the shelters that work with a particularly difficult client population.

For example, the Center for Urban Community Services serves homeless women with mental illness, and Valley Lodge works with homeless older adults.

But providing services for a difficult population does not always accord a shelter symbolic authority in relation to other shelters. Some mental health shelters have reputations clearly inferior to those of others that similarly specialize in mentally ill populations. And while certain employment shelters or shelters for clients trying to remain clean and sobre might well be seen as pathways to specialized housing, others of their ilk altogether lack such a distinction.

Once again, it becomes clear that a conventional and pregiven division does not fully explain how the space of shelters is organized: it lumps together entities that are highly distinct while distinguishing between entities that belong together. Finally, there is the distinction between public and private shelters.

Although New York City's DHS owns and operates many homeless shelters, in the 1990s it also began contracting with private not-for-profit organizations for services to homeless clients. Two sharply distinguished categories of shelters resulted, the distinction between them seeming at first glance to be a viable way of understanding the field.

It would not be difficult to establish that homeless clients at city-run shelters typically wait longer to see caseworkers than clients at the private shelters, that city caseworkers are often overloaded with caseloads up to three times the size of those of their private counterparts, and that city caseworkers lack the training and credentials of their private counterparts. Researchers would also readily find that caseworkers at the public shelters are less invested in helping their clients because of the conditions. This is made even worse by the poisoned-well effect of the negative climate pervasive in city- and state-run agencies.

Among shelter staff and clients, circulating impressions that certain public shelters are more dangerous than others, that they are larger, and that they have a worse staff further contribute to this effect. In the second author's practical experience of the field, it was clear that a negative attitude towards cityoperated shelters was pervasive among staff, clients, and homeless advocates alike. The movement towards privatization among specialized shelters even suggests, in fact, that the DHS concurs with this assessment.

However, there are problems with dividing the field between public and private shelters. While efforts have been made to privatize most of the shelters, the city plans to provide state-of-the-art programming in some of the remaining city-run shelters.

Conversely, some private shelters are poorly run and have acquired a negative reputation among professionals as well as clients. Thus, the distinction between private and public shelters proves insufficient for grasping the underlying logic of the field; we cannot clearly place all the privately run shelters at one end of the field and all the city-run shelters at the other.

Those unfamiliar with homeless services in New York City might propose race as yet another possible principle of division of the field, arguing that the racial composition of shelters might affect their positioning in relation to one another within that space.

In this study, the authors reject race as the primary way of understanding the underlying logic of the field, although it is certainly an important feature of the context within which homelessness is a social problem. In the New York City shelter system, clients are assigned a shelter; they do not self-select.

The second author saw no evidence that such assignments were based on race. Nor do shelters with a large proportion of white clients enjoy clear advantages relative to those with large numbers of African Americans, Puerto Ricans, Dominicans, and so forth, for white clients are not necessarily easier to work with in a shelter, nor are they necessarily easier to place in housing—two important factors, from the second author's experience, in determining whether a shelter will identify a client as desirable.

The separation between racial groups in New York City is not nearly the clear-cut principle of division that one might expect at first glance.

DOMINANTS AND DOMINATED

Thus, all of the several aforementioned ways of understanding the field's organization fall well short, requiring that the current enquiry move in a very different direction, following the same tacking motion indicated by Bourdieu: "There is thus a sort of hermeneutic circle: in order to construct the field, one must identify the forms of specific capital that operate within it, and to construct the forms of specific capital one must know the specific logic of the field".

Specifically, the thesis proposes two other alternative principles of hierarchization that are simultaneously operative and exist in some tension with one another but that serve to distinguish the dominant from the dominated shelters.

The first of these revolves around the struggle between order and chaos. Shelters that control clients' choices and behaviours accumulate a field-specific capital of order and come to occupy the dominant sector of the field.

These shelters provide a smooth and timely processing of clients from the assessment phase on through to housing placement. They excel at constraining clients' actions by imposing shelter rules and by getting clients to comply with conditions of service plans, such as engaging in money management.

They also control clients' behaviours by getting clients to agree to participate in housing interviews in boroughs that may not be their first choice, by helping clients to interview well by coaching them in interview skills and by getting clients to agree to accept suboptimal housing when offered.

Although the DHS distributes housing appointments in a presumably fair manner, these advantages in controlling clients relative to housing appointments helps to distinguish the more privileged shelters from the less privileged ones. By contrast, shelters that are less able to control clients' behaviours and choices, those with a high level of chaos, occupy the dominated regions within the field.

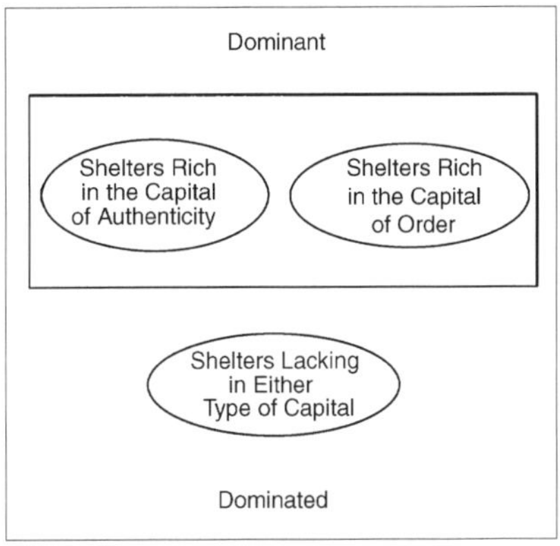

Fig. Field of Homeless Shelters

The other principle of hierarchization revolves around the struggle between authenticity and inauthenticity. There is much to be gained from "returning" to the putative "authentic essence" of the game. Certain shelters derive a special authority or legitimacy from being the real deal, from working with the most disadvantaged clients. These are the shelters that can point to being on the front lines or in the trenches, fighting the good fight against homelessness.

Although these organizations, often drop-in centers, tend to be run-down and resource-poor spaces, staff willingness to take on certain types of clients and client problems that other shelters hope to avoid establishes them at the dominant end of the field. Some mental health shelters and shelter programmes for dual- diagnosed clients and most drop-in centers, especially those with homeless outreach teams are found within this category. Of course, it should also be noted that shelters well-endowed in this capital of authenticity stand in considerable tension with those others that are rich in the capital of order.

Conceiving of that sector as itself a space analogous to, and homologous with, the field of power in the broader social space, one faces a familiar structural opposition: the pole of temporal authority opposes the pole of spiritual or cultural authority. In addition, there are still other shelters that lack altogether in both species of capital. Together, these capital-poor shelters occupy the dominated regions of the field of homeless shelters.

In what follows, we provide by way of illustration some examples of each of these various types of shelters, at both the dominant and dominated regions of this space. George Daly House a shelter for 88 homeless adults, ages 45 and older, serves as an example of a more privileged shelter in the dominant pole of the field, on the side of order. The shelter occupies a converted music school in the East Village neighborhood.

The building has been completely remodeled to create a transitional shelter with mostly single rooms. By contrast, many of the larger shelters offer only barracks-style sleeping areas. The floors at GDH are always polished to a high shine.

Its walls, which are kept freshly painted are hung with original art and photography and coordinate nicely with the large, overstuffed, dark green leather sofas in the lobby. Bookshelves, as well as end tables with lamps and silk orchid flower arrangements, create the effect of an upscale hotel lobby. Classical or jazz music can be heard throughout the building and in a well-tended garden space filled with flowering dogwood trees, manicured boxwoods, climbing vines, and flowers.

While most shelters' gardens or patios would be filled with stackable plastic furniture or rusting metal folding chairs, that of GDH offers teak benches, chairs, and matching tables with dark green wood and canvas umbrellas. While disarmingly elegant for a shelter, GDH's reputation as one of the most privileged shelters, a reputation communicated among clients via word of mouth and to staff of other shelters and homeless advocates during public forums such as shelter directors' meetings, stems primarily from its proven track record.

This record includes getting clients to comply with shelter rules governing behaviour, good results with service plans concerning money management, and high rates of success in getting clients to accept available housing. Regarding compliance with shelter rules, for example, GDH maintains a zero tolerance policy for alcohol or drug use and threatening behaviour. Clients who appear to be under the influence of alcohol are questioned by a member of the staff who may elect to administer a Breathalyzer test.

Staff also regularly conduct urinalysis screens to detect illegal drug use. Clients who are found to be drinking or using drugs must meet with their caseworker and enroll in treatment. Clients already in treatment are required to intensify their treatment programme. Clients who refuse or who continue to drink or use drugs are transferred to another shelter.

Threatening or violent behaviour results in an immediate shelter transfer. Further research might examine if this shelter's records contain comparatively few DHS incident reports concerning fights or threatening behaviour among clients. It might also be useful to compare GDH with other shelters on the frequency of complaints made against shelter staff to either the client advisory board or the Coalition for the Homeless. Finally, one might compare degrees of compliance with service plans and timeliness of placement into housing.

A subsequent part of this object explores some of the conservation strategies employed by dominant shelters of this sort that help to perpetuate their reputation for order. Peter's Place, a drop-in center, is a good example of a shelter located at the other side of the field's dominant sector, on the side of authenticity. From a cramped and often disheveled space, this programme serves homeless men and women ages 45 and older. Upon entering this crowded setting, an observer first notices the lockers that line several walls.

These tall, battleship gray, rectangular boxes are available for storing clients' belongings; clients must provide their own locks. Beyond these banks of gray are rows of tables and gray folding chairs. Clients are seated there day and night, reading, talking, eating, and sleeping. Just around the corner from this large client area are the cramped offices and desk spaces of the Peter's Place staff. The staff spend most of their time interacting with the clients.

Clients who are relatively new to Peter's Place are assessed by social workers. This process begins after a client has returned several times: Why would one begin an assessment, after all, if the client is a one-timer? Staff greet returning clients in a welcoming manner and ask how they have been faring. Peter's Place, like other drop-in shelters, is a preferred shelter service among those clients who are either unwilling to participate in more structured shelter programmes or who have effectively been kicked out of the other shelters.

This population is comprised of the stereotypical street homeless. The media often depict them as disheveled, drunk, and psychotic. They move about with all their belongings and are often seen sleeping on subway trains. Peter's Place clients come and go at will.

They are not denied access if under the influence of drugs or alcohol, provided they are not threatening. Challenging behaviours are expected, and even threatening clients are welcomed back once they have calmed down. While drop-in centers like Peter's Place exercise very little control over their clients, homeless services programmes of this sort non-etheless occupy some of the most dominant positions within the shelter field because they are seen as doing the real work required to address the needs of homeless clients.

They are therefore high in the capital of authenticity. Less privileged shelters, those with less order and also lacking in authenticity, occupy the dominated end of the field. These are the places understood as poorly run, impersonal, and potentially dangerous. Such shelters are seen as inadequate with respect to basic services, structure, and safety. Numerous ethnographic studies support these assessments with descriptive firsthand accounts and client-staff interviews.

Facilities at this end of the field include the larger general shelters. Morale is low at these facilities, and researchers would likely find a high level of staff turnover. Not only do staff at these shelters have more difficulty in controlling clients, but they also lack a feeling of pride in taking on the true mission of social work. Again, further research might consider if these shelters have more clients from the dominated end of the field of clients and if they are less successful than privileged shelters in preventing clients from engaging in incidents of violence or threatening behaviour. One might also assess whether these shelters are less successful in heading off client complaints to internal and external boards or less successful in finding housing or transitional placements for clients in a smooth and timely manner.

STRATEGIES OF CONSERVATION AND SUBVERSION

Crucial to understanding the dynamics of the field of shelters is the distinction between the conservation strategies of shelters that occupy positions of specific authority within the field and the corresponding subversion strategies of shelters seeking to challenge and discredit this authority. To maintain their ascendant positions, the most order-privileged shelters engage in image or reputation protection by taking advantage of their right to refuse certain clients.

This is a right gained by shelter administrators during contract negotiations with the DHS, a right to an interview or acceptance process wherein clients can be screened for appropriateness just as to predetermined admission criteria. The shelters that possess this right make full use of it to protect their accrued symbolic capital. That is, order-rich shelters effectively accept those homeless individuals who are most likely to help maintain their positive reputation or position relative to other, more chaotic shelters or dropin centers. The obvious effect of this right of refusal is that the less desirable homeless, those with challenging behaviours who are not compliant with their service plans, stay in the less privileged shelters.

Image or reputation protection through right of refusal is one of the numerous causal mechanisms or "recurrent causal sequences of general scope" that a field analysis can identify and underscore, casting doubt upon the conventional distinction in social science between description and causal explanation. More covert conservation strategies among shelters rich in order capital, strategies that also effectively keep out less desirable homeless people, are seen in the imposition of organizational rules and procedures: in this case, shelter rules.

A shelter that insists on zero tolerance for drugs and alcohol, that enacts a strict curfew, or that requires clients to participate in money management will attract those homeless men and women who are willing to submit to such restrictions. Such requirements will also deflect others who reject rules and structure. Since the DHS is mandated to provide shelter for anyone who requests it, regardless of circumstances, it is not difficult to identify the results of these power plays and to see the source of conflict.

Homeless clients who are identified by the DHS as chronic, long-term stayers, especially those with aggressive dispositions and less social capital, tend to remain in the less privileged shelters. By contrast, temporarily homeless people, those who typically bear larger amounts of capital of various kinds, make the move rather quickly into more privileged settings. A close examination of shelter transfer patterns, with careful attention paid to which clients move where and how quickly, might test the hypothesis that shelters with more order capital are able to attract and receive clients who themselves are endowed with more personal capital, that is, clients with habitus more conducive to following restrictions, engaging in self-regulation, and exerting self-discipline.

Bourdieu points out that the habitus of working-class people, shaped under conditions of comparative stability and orderliness, tend to be more conducive to the working out and following of a rational life plan. By contrast, the habitus of subproletarians that have been formed and perpetuated under conditions of uncertainty, incoherence, and arbitrariness— subproletarians characteristically lacking secure employment and often also homeless—tend to be particularly ill suited to a regularization of daily life conduct.

Subversion strategies tend to be employed by the dominated dominants of a field in order to legitimate a claim to ascendancy within it. In the case of the field of homeless shelter programmes, those shelters that are richest in claims to authenticity are precisely the ones most likely to engage in subversion strategies in seeking to better their position relative to those that manifest a high degree of order. Staff in the authentic shelters frequently highlight the serious obstacles that they face on a daily basis, thereby drawing an invidious distinction between themselves and their counterparts in the more orderly settings.

Such distinctions serve to undercut the latter's own claims to legitimacy. Rather than minimize the number and severity of difficulties confronting their programme, the dominated dominants identify these difficulties themselves as badges of honour. War stories abound, and the worse off or more challenging their clients, the better. For them to be at the dominant end of the field at all, however, other shelters, the DHS, homeless advocacy groups, and the consumers of shelter services must recognize and grant validity to the claims that they make.

Indeed, shelter staff at the less privileged and capital-rich shelters willingly acknowledge the especially difficult work that these authentic programmes undertake. The latter's undeniable hard work and the almost insurmountable challenges that they face earn them a sort of mystique among shelter providers. So too, word on the street among homeless clients often characterizes these shelters as compassionate, dependable, port-in-the-storm kinds of settings.

A plausible hypothesis is that shelter directors at these highly challenged shelter programmes and drop-in centers utilize their own claims to authenticity to connect positively with DHS contract managers and with Coalition for the Homeless watchdogs. Such strategies help these shelters to further their influence with both the DHS and the coalition, two entities with opinions that truly matter. Shelters that are without the symbolic capital of either order or authenticity engage in subversion strategies similar for both of the dominants.

For example, capital-poor shelters attack their better-endowed counterparts by charging that the order-rich shelters handpick their clients or by criticizing authenticity-rich shelters as horribly chaotic places. Capital-poor shelters also attempt somehow to account for both their lack of order, relative to the dominant shelters, and their lack of authenticity. It was the second author's experience that complaints are frequently heard at shelter directors' meetings regarding the unfair advantages enjoyed by better-endowed shelters, regarding staffing shortages, and regarding the inadequate resources available for dealing with challenging clients.

In respect to exit options, for example, it was often pointed out that it is far easier for the dominant shelters to transfer challenging or rule-breaking clients to the less privileged shelters than the other way around, leaving the dominated shelters with clients whom they do not want. Staff members from dominated shelters resented the ability of their more privileged counterparts to dump difficult clients into their laps. Their complaints about this asymmetry served as a way for these dominated shelters to claim symbolic authority in relation to their better-off counterparts.

The field of homeless shelters is a space riven with tensions and mutually opposing strategies of action. However, it is also worth noting that all of those involved in this field, regardless of the particular position they occupy within it, are heavily invested in the work of helping homeless people; homelessness is recognized across the board as a problem that is worth addressing. Their underlying belief in the game, or *illusio*, serves as the fundamental premise upon which the entire field is based, a shared understanding that goes without saying.

The very willingness of the various actors in this field to engage in struggle over the mechanisms of service delivery, definition of a challenging client, reasonable lengths of stay, and whether or not shelters ought to maintain their right of refusal supports this shared framework of investments and commitments. Bourdieu reminds us that small victories or "partial revolutions" that "constantly occur in fields do not call into question the very foundations of the game, its fundamental axioms, the bedrock of ultimate beliefs on which the whole game is based.... Those who take part in the struggle help to reproduce the game by helping—more or less completely, depending on the field—to produce belief in the value of the stakes".

THE FIELD OF HOMELESS CLIENTS

Having explored the field of providers of services to the homeless, this object now turns to a consideration of the consumers of those services. It illustrates how a Bourdieuian framework can be utilized to raise questions about the homeless clients within these shelters, the positions that they occupy within a field of homeless clients, and how their location within this space influences the quantity and quality of services that they receive. In-depth studies of the homeless are plentiful. This rich collection of qualitative and quantitative research, far too extensive to discuss adequately here, provides scholars interested in that vulnerable population with a range of useful approaches, both theoretical and methodological.

What follows is not an attempt to replace these studies or to discuss homelessness in general. Rather, it is an attempt to investigate in particular those homeless individuals who are located within the field of shelter clients, insofar as they are located within this field. The primary source of data is the second author's experience as a director of social services and as a shelter director. In these roles, she supervised caseworkers, met directly with clients and discussed particularly challenging cases with representatives from the Coalition for the Homeless and the DHS.

PRINCIPLES OF DIVISION

To begin once again, two familiar questions are revisited: What are the specific dimensions along which the field of homeless clients is organized? And what separates those who occupy the relatively more privileged positions within that field from those who occupy its relatively less privileged locations? As in the analysis of the field of shelters, this discussion of the field of homeless clients extends beyond pregiven and taken-for-granted categories. It requires rejection of an alternative principle of division that comes from the common sense of the social work universe, one that is commonly deployed by the DHS and by those who staff the shelters: the distinction between the chronically and the transitionally homeless.

These labels, together with a third label, the episodically homeless, pertain to a person's length and pattern of stay in the shelter system. Over time, they have come to be associated with various stereotyped characteristics or features. As before, it is necessary to begin by examining these doxic categories and by identifying the reasons why they fail to illuminate how individuals are organized within the space at hand. The transitional or temporarily homeless category consists of those men and women with infrequent or one-time shelter stays. These are the homeless clients with the lowest incidence of medical, mental health, and addiction problems; they often get back into housing once the basic reasons for their housing loss are addressed.

Typical reasons for housing loss include loss of employment, family composition changes, and safety issues that resulted either in eviction or in a voluntary decision to abandon the home. Temporarily homeless clients are identified by shelter staff as capable of living on their own and are seen as motivated to do whatever it takes to be successful in a housing interview. They are often thought by caseworkers to be comparatively easy to work with, and it is widely held that once they have housing, these clients will happily put the whole experience behind them. It seems reasonable that these clients would be the bearers of the greatest volume of personal capital in the field of homeless shelter consumers. The real story, however, is not nearly so simple. Some temporarily homeless clients lack a feel for the game, an ability to grasp the relationship between client and caseworker. Many are new consumers of social service assistance and consequently present themselves as deserving special consideration or as being somehow different from or better than the rest of the caseworker's clients.

These attitudes, ultimately rooted in the clients' habitus, may impede the delivery of services, alienate these individuals from other shelter clients, and result in their being deemed more rather than less challenging by the shelter staff. In the end, such attitudes may prevent these clients from experiencing a positive transition from shelter to housing. By contrast to the temporarily homeless, men and women who are chronically homeless would at first glance seem likely to occupy the least privileged positions within the field.

They are defined by the DHS as shelter clients who have infrequent yet lengthy shelter stays. Their longer length of stay, as compared with those of other clients, is determined by a number of different factors, such as immigration status, health problems, poor interviewing skills or a lack of familial connections. Irving Piliavin and associates also find a higher incidence of long-term homelessness among individuals with a history of out-of-home care. Moreover, they find that those with untreated alcohol problems are at great risk for longer lengths of stay and frequent returns to homeless services systems; often afflicted with mental illness and addiction, those with untreated substance problems are understood to be difficult clients.

Despite the formidable challenges faced by such clients, however, it was certainly the second author's experience that chronically homeless shelter clients did not lack in all forms of personal capital. Some are actually very well liked by both staff and clients. They may be identified, for example, as helpful around the building, pleasant to meet with, agreeable regarding their service plan, sought after by other clients, and generally well respected within both client and staff circles. The chronic, long-term homeless sometimes acquire, as a consequence of their long exposure to the shelter system, an insider's knowledge of how things work.

This experience contributes to, rather than reduces, their personal capital. The episodically homeless, defined by the DHS as those clients who return to the shelters again and again, would be expected to occupy an intermediate sector of the space of homeless clients. Some of them make relatively few requests for shelter, but others return quite frequently. This category of homeless clients, however, comprises an exceedingly heterogeneous population and, as a result, is very difficult to characterize. For example, while psychosocial and emotional forces often lead these clients to return to shelter, the nature of these forces varies widely. In some cases, their problems closely resemble the kinds of cognitive and affectual disturbances found among the chronically homeless. But in other cases, these clients return to shelter because it becomes for them a sort of microcommunity. Researchers would likely find that while many who are described as episodically homeless find group living claustrophobic, a fair number of others derive emotional benefits from the congregate setting. That is, clients who develop strong connections to their peers experience difficulties in making the transition to independent living.

A plausible hypothesis is that when these clients are placed on their own in rooms or apartments, some experience a feeling of loneliness for which they are ill prepared. This loneliness is starkly contrasted with the social environment of the shelter. Still other clients are forced to seek shelter because of social developments largely outside of their control. Such developments include neighborhood gentrification, changes in economic climate and the resulting increases in unemployment, the growing burdens of health care, and housing loss.

Some of the individuals in this category gravitate rather easily towards more privileged positions within the field of shelter clients; others quickly find themselves in the dominated regions of that space. The authors' initial impression was that length and pattern of stay enable one to understand the logic of the field of homeless clients: that temporarily homeless men and women likely occupy the most privileged positions within the field of homeless shelter clients, the episodically homeless occupy the mid-range positions, and the chronically homeless occupy the least privileged positions.

Yet, through reflection, as well as in ongoing dialogue between theory and the empirical material at hand, the authors came to see that the manner in which homeless clients interact with staff and with other clients plays the most important role in determining their position. While a shelter client may not have a lot of influence in the overall system, he or she may wield a fair amount of power, earn a fair amount of distinction, and secure privileges internal to a particular shelter.

In relation to their counterparts, clients earn capital both from the staff and from their fellow clients. These two often competing species of capital and principles of hierarchization cut across the categorical distinctions that we have been discussing. Specifically, the unequal distribution of these two species illuminates the difference between those clients who are successful within the shelter system and those who occupy less advantaged places within it.

STAFF-SANCTIONED AND CLIENT-SANCTIONED CAPITAL

The authors' hypothesis, staff-sanctioned capital, or, more broadly, the placement of a homeless client somewhere along a continuum between good and challenging, emerges from the cumulative impression that staff members develop of a client in response to the latter's attitude concerning shelter rules, policies, and expectations, reasons for housing loss, and purpose of shelter stay. Not all clients adhere to the rules and policies that shelters establish, which usually include curfews, restrictions on visitors, limited access to smoking spaces, no food during non-meal times, restrictions on the amount and type of personal possessions, and limited access to telephone communication.

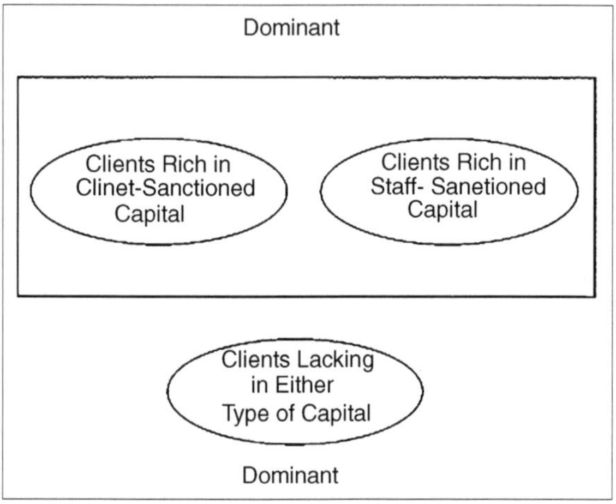

Fig. Field of Homeless Clients

But when they do, conforming to staff expectations of appropriate bearing and conduct as well as being submissive and respectful, they are accorded a certain measure of value and esteem. Along with that personal capital, they are given greater opportunities to obtain housing; shelters, much like academic organizations that hold degree-conferring power over students, are gatekeepers to housing opportunities that are generally unavailable to people outside the shelter system. Many clients naturally and easily gain such privileges, being already rule abiding, non-challenging, flexible, and polite.

Others adopt in more strategic fashion the outward appearances of a good client in order to get through the system and obtain housing. While certainly there are clients who understand active participation in case plans as an opportunity for self improvement, clients are a captive audience, and case plans are presented to them as a necessary rather than optional condition of shelter stays. How else to explain the spectacle of a 57-year-old client allowing a 24-year-old caseworker to criticize his or her money management style?

Another determinant of staff-sanctioned capital is the way in which a client understands his or her housing loss. The client who takes personal responsibility for that loss paradoxically earns more symbolic capital from the staff than the client who identifies other people as its cause. Perhaps the client who admits personal responsibility is understood to be more willing to learn from past mistakes, or perhaps shelter caseworkers espouse an ethic of personal responsibility that centers on patterns of action within their clients' own scope of influence, rather than on macroscopic forces such as declines in affordable housing stock or neighborhood gentrification.

In her study of homeless women and the shelter industry, Jean Williams affirms, "Shelters do not ignore low-income housing shortages or the value of the minimum wage as reasons for homelessness, but many of the most important facets of their programmes address the perceived *behaviours* of the homeless. Dysfunctional behaviours are believed to have been instrumental in the process of becoming homeless". Amy Dworsky and Irving Piliavin also note that this "individual deficits framework assumes that people become homeless because they possess or lack certain attributes... which can include personal disabilities or human capital deficiencies."

The homeless shelter client who accepts responsibility for his or her housing loss accrues more staff-sanctioned capital. Shelter staff identify such a client as easy to work with and as someone who will be easy to place in housing. Should this client prove difficult to place in housing, staff often argue to the DHS that he or she should be allowed to remain in the shelter beyond the time limits specified in that shelter's policy, pointing to external reasons for the delay.

Discourse analyses of clinical staff meeting minutes, along with indepth interviews of caseworkers or observation of shelter interactions, would provide researchers with illuminating insights into how certain clients acquire large amounts of staff-sanctioned capital and the implications of such capital. A client's access to staff-sanctioned capital is also determined by the ways in which that client understands his or her caseworker and the shelter. Good clients, those with a large endowment of such capital, tend to treat the shelter with a certain attitude of grateful reverence, behaving much like a guest in someone else's home.

They help to keep the shelter clean, complain only when absolutely necessary, try to frame complaints as requests or suggestions, and avoid making negative statements about the shelter facility and staff. Clients are expected to make themselves at home within a shelter and yet not to become too comfortable. In contrast to good clients, their more challenging counterparts engage in behaviours and statements suggesting permanent residency; they communicate or behave in ways that indicate that they have little intention of leaving in a timely manner.

Other clients identified by shelter staff as problematic are those who treat the facility like a prison and its staff like guards, those who are loud and disruptive, those who vandalize, those who frequently complain about the quality and quantity of services, and those who similarly complain about provisions. These challenging clients treat caseworkers not as counselors or guides but as scapegoats or servants; for example, a client might be heard saying to his or her caseworker: "You're my social worker; you're supposed to work for me."

They regard the shelter not as a temporary safe haven but as a permanent home or as a prison. Some shelter clients, those with little prior experience as recipients of social services, also see themselves as different from the rest of the shelter clients. This attitude results in requests for special privileges, such as increased access to the caseworker, leniency concerning curfews, or indulgence when they bend shelter rules. The more successful such clients were prior to their shelter experience, the less able they often are to accept their present circumstances or to receive help from someone whose experience and training they view with skepticism.

Often they act as if they know more than their caseworker and can do the worker's job, in fact, better than the caseworker can. While more challenging types of clients may not gain for themselves much staff-sanctioned capital, it is non-etheless possible for them to garner a large amount of client-sanctioned capital.

This is a second type of symbolic capital operative inside the field of homeless shelter clients. Unlike staff-sanctioned capital, however, client-sanctioned capital is generated and bestowed entirely by other shelter clients. Client-sanctioned capital flows to those who directly and routinely challenge shelter staff, rules, and structure. Clients who garner large volumes of such capital are those who are strong advocates for themselves and others within the shelter environment.

They become known inside the shelter as persons to consult when a caseworker is not being helpful, when a client has been denied a weekend pass, or when a client does not think that he or she is getting a fair shake regarding housing appointments. Sometimes these bearers of client-sanctioned capital take the lead in urging their peers to refuse currently available housing appointments, encouraging them instead to wait for subsidized or *New York New York* (NYNY) housing. In providing such advice, these influential clients forfeit their own chance to earn staff-sanctioned capital in favour of accumulating the esteem of their fellow clients. Since they often complain to shelter advocacy groups both within and without the shelter, they are seen by the shelter staff as challenging and difficult. These are the clients with connections. Some can quote the Callahan decree from memory and are on a first-name basis with staff at the Coalition for the Homeless. They may even have earned the coveted title of shelter monitor. This is a high-status volunteer position with the coalition. It allows them on-the-spot inspection access to any shelter in search of infractions of the Callahan decree.

By contrast, those clients who separate themselves from other clients or who adopt an attitude of superiority do not accrue such clientsanctioned capital. In homeless shelters, clients with large endowments of either type of capital may be on the fast track to housing. In the first instance, clients who have accrued staff-sanctioned capital may move through the shelter quickly because of preferential treatment. Such treatment may result in weekend passes, easier access to caseworkers, and recommendations for housing.

Clients with large amounts of client-sanctioned capital, conversely and paradoxically, may also move quickly through the shelter because staff are anxious to get them out of that environment, where their perspectives and conduct may have a negative influence upon other clients. Shelter staff are very cognizant of the effects that challenging clients can have upon other clients. Shelter environments are not static but always evolving and dynamic contexts, and the presence of putatively difficult clients can affect matters in sometimes significant and dramatic ways.

At bottom, what is most troubling to the shelter staff is the tendency of those clients who are well-endowed in clientsanctioned capital to seek to delegitimate the officially sanctioned rules of shelter life. In Bourdieu's terms, such clients seek to transform "the representation of this world which contributes to its reality" by denouncing the "tacit contract of adherence to the established order which defines the original *doxa*" of that space. This strategy of action among so-called difficult clients undercuts the staff-sanctioned recognition enjoyed by certain of their counterparts. It also makes it all but inevitable that the shelter staff will move these difficult individuals on or at least make a serious effort to do so.

EMPIRICAL ILLUSTRATIONS

The configuration of the field of homeless shelter clients can be effectively illustrated through a series of composite profiles. These sketches are fictional constructs that combine individual client characteristics with stylized background features and narrative trajectories drawn from multiple homeless individuals. In order to protect subjects' confidentiality, pseudonyms are used throughout.

These composite sketches are meant to illustrate the different kinds of persons who occupy key positions within the space of homeless clients. The profiles are also meant to demonstrate that length of shelter stay and pattern of shelter use are inadequate criteria for understanding the division of the homeless client field.

Ben, an Example of a Client Well-endowed with Staff-sanctioned Capital

Ben lost his housing when he lost his job; he worked for a restaurant equipment company, but the firm downsized. For 4 years, he has been in and out of most of the adult shelters available for men. Ben has two grown children with whom he is in touch only a few times a year. They resent his divorce from their mother and his subsequent remarriage; Ben characterizes his relationship with them as, "okay but not close." He has a number of extended family members in the area, but, having stayed with many of them for a few weeks to a month at a time, he has effectively worn out his welcome.

At age 47, Ben is too young for subsidized apartments for adults over the age of 50 and must settle for single-room occupancy housing. He finds its cramped quarters, shared bathroom, and shared kitchen to be very unpleasant. After 6 years in recovery for alcohol addiction, he also does not care for the drinking or evidence of drug use that he encounters in these converted welfare hotels, and although he reports that he has increased the number of Alcoholics Anonymous meetings he attends each week, he feels that these depressingly edgy, unsafe housing environments threaten his sobriety.

He frequently leaves these SRO placements, returning to his previous shelter. Ben is a people person. Shelter staff and many of his fellow clients enjoy his company when he is in the building, and he usually finds something complimentary to say to his caseworkers. He routinely praises the shelter director for imposing strict rules and for running a tight ship. These rules, he informs her, help everyone there to feel safe.

They also support his own efforts to stay sobre. Shelter staff wish that more of their clients were like Ben. Shelter clients, by contrast, like him well enough, but some see him as more than a little annoying. Ben has figured out how to play the game. He follows shelter rules, is friendly and engaging with staff, praises the director for how he or she runs the shelter, and provides compelling reasons why substandard housing is not for him.

This client is endowed with enough staff-sanctioned capital to stay on at the shelter until he becomes old enough for senior housing or to move into an apartment if shelter staff manage to locate one of the scarce studio or one-bedroom apartments sometimes made available to single adults.

Charlotte, an Example of a Client Well-endowed with Client-sanctioned Capital

Charlotte was evicted from her apartment after having one too many conflicts with her landlord. She had allowed her nephew to stay with her, which was against her lease, and had stopped paying rent in the meantime because the landlord had failed to replace a rotten bathroom floor. In fact, she had filed a civil suit against the landlord for failing to keep the premises in good repair. In court, the judge ordered the landlord to make repairs.

However, Charlotte was unable to pay the past rent she owed, so the landlord evicted her for failing to pay that rent and for having a guest in excess of the 14-day period allowed under her lease. Charlotte sent her daughter to stay with the child's grandmother and entered the shelter system. All of Charlotte's furniture went into a storage locker, and the bill for her storage exceeded her monthly Supplemental Security Income check. Charlotte resents her caseworker and does not hesitate to tell her so: "If you really wanted to help me, you'd find me an apartment I can afford and get my storage bill paid!"

Charlotte also frequently challenges the shelter director for what she views as draconian rules and policies, often breaking them defiantly. She enjoys engaging the other clients in conversation over cards and often offers them assistance with their problems. She tells them, "You ought to sue; that's what I'm going to do! Make those bastards pay!" Charlotte has connections, she tells the other clients, and she is not afraid of using them. This helps her to earn a large volume of client-sanctioned capital. Clients like her because she is funny, forthright, and on their side.

She says the things to staff that clients are thinking but are afraid to say. Staff members are eager to see Charlotte leave the shelter programme as quickly as possible. She poisons the well with her loud pronouncements during mealtimes, and she intimidates her caseworker. Indeed, this is Charlotte's third shelter in 6 months. Shelter directors have been transferring her like a hot potato to their unsuspecting colleagues at other shelters. She may even wind up with one of the scarce studio or one-bedroom apartments, just to ensure that this litigiously minded woman goes on her way.

Leo, an Example of a Client Lacking in Either type of Capital

Over the last 6 years, Leo has been in a few men's shelters but has never chosen to stay more than a few days at a time. This temporary status has prevented shelter staff from getting a full picture of his history and from providing the kind of assistance that might help him to find permanent housing. Leo's employment history is filled with short-lived, part-time, and temporary jobs, such as sweeping stores or stocking shelves. He sometimes receives a general relief income from income maintenance centers, but he hates having to comply with the work that these centers assign him; in fact, he is frequently a no-show and has to negotiate to get his general relief case reopened.

When not sleeping on trains, Leo uses drop-in centers for hot meals, showers, and a place to obtain clean clothing. There is no warm relationship between this client and the shelter system. Leo thinks that shelters are too much about rules and resents their insistence on planning for the future: "I take things as they come. What good is planning? Nothing ever turns out right anyhow." Leo's cynical outlook is reinforced daily by the difficulties he encounters living on the street: the delinquents who pick on him for sport, the police who hassle him, and the public at large who react to him, if not with avoidance, then with visible disgust.

Unsurprisingly, Leo acts the part of the kicked dog. When in a drop-in center, he becomes easily annoyed with the staff and clients alike. On good days he mumbles profanity and sarcastic comments, while on the more volatile days he calls people out. Most fellow clients do not take up Leo's invitations to fight, but his behaviour does often result in temporary suspensions from drop-in centers. His behaviour also makes him an unlikely candidate for referral to one of those relatively more privileged shelters that are steeped in the capital of order.

THE INTERNET AND SOCIAL WORK: A PERSONAL PERSPECTIVE

A vast array of social work Web sites have sprung up. The first systematic social work invasion of Web service was in educational institutions. Michael McMurray (Colorado State University) was the first, most notable effort. A long-lived and well-managed example is the University of South Carolina's SWAN (Social Work Access Network).

At the time of this writing well over 25 per cent of all accredited social work academic programmes have Web sites. Clearly, Web pages that are owned and operated by large institutions are the most reliable. Nevertheless, I believe the future power of the Web lies elsewhere. Although psychotherapy on the Internet existed prior to the popularity of the Web, employing the Web as a medium of psychotherapy has mushroomed. During a recent survey, well over 1,000 psychotherapists were capitalizing on the Web.

Each time Marson and Brackin study psychotherapy on the Web, the number of therapists increases. NASW News is chronicling efforts of private practitioners in this arena. Clearly, the Web will have a profound effect on future strategies for psychotherapy and other forms of social work practice. For example, Schein-Levi and Pollack (1997) demonstrate how social workers can employ the Web for enhancing parenting skills.

According to Anderson et al. (1995), the most widespread use of the Internet among the general public is not browsing the Web, but e-mail and listservs. Marson (1997) confirms this finding among social workers. A personal history will help explain the importance of these two uses. When I first learned of access to the Internet, I also learned about listservs and immediately searched for a listserv that addressed social work issues.

In my search, I discovered the Social Work discussion list. SOCWORK started as an idea for introducing students at the School of Social Work, University of Toronto, to computer communication technology. Bellamy (1987), and Bellamy and Mielniczuk (1988) offer historical details of how and why the list became operational on February 3, 1988. It began with 11 students and four faculty and staff. Within four months there were 20 members. By May 1989 there were approximately 75 members and a new management under the watchful eye of Harry Chaiklin at the University of Maryland. It was about this time that I discovered SOCWORK and joined the list when there were fewer than 80 subscribers. During Harry's tenure, two major developments occurred. First, after much prodding among various members of the listserv, the Council on Social Work Education subscribed to SOCWORK. Second, staff from the National Association of Social Workers WASW] subscribed. Participation by our two major professional organizations established an aura of legitimacy and personal subscriptions to SOCWORK surged.

Later, when the subscribers grew to approximately 700 in the spring of 1995, Cindy Jones from the University of Arkansas inherited SOCWORK. Soon SOCWORK had over 1,000 subscribers and many thought the listserv was out of control. As a result, in the fall of 1996, Ogden Rogers from the University of Wisconsin at River Falls became the new manager. The number of subscribers shrank to less than 300, but SOCWORK became more manageable. Listservs are now flourishing and are being systematically evaluated for their contribution to the profession.

Berman (1996) provides an excellent example of such research in his analysis of two listservs. Noticing the congressional proposals to decentralize social services, the Consortium of State SOCWORK Listservs was founded in 1993 by Steve Marson at the University of North Carolina at Pembroke. With decentralization, each state has gained greater control over social service resources.

The direction of the services may greatly depend on the ability of state social workers to spread knowledge to grassroot organizations and to lobby the state house in a favourable direction. State social work listservs should prove to be vital for the speedy dissemination of needed information. Social workers have a long history of technology avoidance. This avoidance was first noted by Richmond (1911) when she had to encourage turn-of-the-century social workers to exploit the telephone as a tool for practice. Towards the end of this century and with the inaugural issue of a newsletter entitled Computer Use in Social Services Network (CUSSN), Dick Schoech (1981) took Richmond's place as the nurturer of technology.

Schoech's newsletter evolved into a journal entitled Computers in Human Services which continues to lay the ground work for integrating and advancing computer technology in social work. For example, it served as a platform for Hanna (1995) to report on early efforts to combine and link many existing electronic networks through the Internet. Prior to this effort, electronic and political barriers prohibited members of one network from sending e-mail or conference with members from other human services networks.

INTERNET AND KEY SOCIAL WORK ORGANIZATIONAL EVENTS

Four happenings in recent history have had an influence on social work and the Internet. In the late 80s, CSWE board members and NASW staffs became active on the Internet. A CSWE staff member coordinated a meeting of two Internet enthusiasts. Although they communicated often over the

Internet, they first met face to face at the CSWE 1990 Annual Programme Meeting.

Here, they gave birth to the Baccalaureate Programme Directors Association's Committee on Information Technology and Social Work Education. In 1992, the unofficial committee offered its first workshop at the BPD annual conference. At the 1995 APM, the committee became an important part of BPD's table of organization as a standing committee. The most stirring moment in the short history of technology and social work professional organizations was at the 1992 APM. Marshall Smith requested the floor in an open meeting of CSWE's Accreditation Board.

In a very eloquent, short, but powerfully moving speech, Marshall expressed the importance of the Internet for the accreditation process. He made a plea that board members consider accepting self-studies via the Internet. Marshall was ahead of his time. Now we are wagering on which school will take the bold step to be the first the submit a self-study via electronic means. One positive intermediate step was taken to achieve this goal. Through the advocacy of BPD's Committee on Information Technology and Social Work Education, CSWE's Directory of Colleges and Universities with Accredited Social Work Degree Programmes included e-mail addresses. Soon web page locations will be published in the Directory. These actions lay the ground work for the electronic transmission of self-studies and a more efficient means of educational research.

Technical and confidentiality problems related to document transfer are on the verge of being resolved. Third, in early 1995, Rita Vandivort, of the NASW national office, established a listserv for technologically capable social workers to plan an Internet symposium at the upcoming NASW conference. As a staff member of NASW, she was able to acquire funds to put together an impressive Internet demonstration facility at the Philadelphia conference.

Members of the technology committee involved in the planning were overwhelmed and profoundly impressed with the Internet resources that Rita was able to pull together. It was a success beyond anyone's imagination. Since the Philadelphia conference, the use of an Internet lab continues to be an important feature of the NASW annual conference.

Perhaps more than any single event in the history of social work and the Internet, the lab at the NASW conference has had the greatest influence on the utilization of the Internet among seasoned social work practitioners. Fourth, in the fall of 1992, Ogden Rogers proposed that SOCWORK subscribers who were also CSWE members meet face-to-face. Ogden dubbed the group "OffLine." Subscribers/CSWE members had been communicating with each other on a wide variety of levels. Close friendships were established, accreditation consultation support was given, and in some cases enemies were made! Steve Marson organized this group's first "get-together" during the 1993

APM in New York. The second get-together in 1994 in Atlanta was also a great success. During a SOCWORK discussion, subscribers decided to formalize OffLine in order to avoid scheduling conflicts. Since the formalization of Offline, the "social" get-togethers have been well attended and led to more serious academic conferences.

RECOMMENDATIONS

The profound influence of the Internet and technologies that the Internet will spawn in the future is undisputed. Social work and the entire social welfare system will not escape utilizing the Internet anymore than social workers were able to escape the use of the telephone during Richmond's era. As a result, we have an ethical obligation to systematically encourage others to employ the Internet in their daily activities.

Competence and comfort with the Internet leads to and enhances one's creativity in using the Internet, which in turn leads to improved human services. Such statements are grandiose and easy to state. How does one operationalize this? Reading and recalling recent history is a good place to start.

Our short history and experience offers some simple guidelines:

- Like Richmond, professors and field instructors must shepherd their students (particularly non-traditional students) into feeling comfortable with the Internet.
- Leaders both in education and practice must share their ideas by writing, presenting documents at conferences, and offering workshops about technology. Tom Hannah, Dick Schoech and Rita Vandivort are good conternporary role models for the rest of us.
- Leaders of professional organizations must be nurtured into accepting that computer technology and the Internet have vast implications for their organization's benefit. This can only be accomplished by a one-by-one strategy and face-to-face interaction. In addition, technologically competent professionals must organize themselves to vote for leaders who recognize the importance of the Internet. Actions like Marshall Smith's speech is a good illustration. Members of CIFTSWE make efforts to support candidates that have a history of supporting technology.
- Leaders of professional organizations should be shown that technology committees made up of volunteers are a cost effective manner of spreading the advantages that the Internet and computers have for human services. The development and actions of CIFTSWE provide an excellent example.
- Workshops must be freely offered in a non-intimidating manner to those professionals and educators who are technophobic. CIFTSWE's annual workshops are good illustrations of an effective strategy.

- Technophobic professionals must be approached in the same manner as Richmond approached social workers at the turn of the century. They must be nurtured, reassured, and shown that such technology is not dehumanizing but improves the quality of care. Vandivort's coordination of NASW's Internet lab at annual conferences represents an excellent example.
- Technologically competent professionals should meet socially (*i.e.*, OffLine) and professionally (*i.e.*, conferences). These meetings must be used to share ideas on effective methods of spreading the good news of technology and the Internet.
- Technologically capable human service professionals need to lead the way to make Internet technology user-friendly and practical. As stated earlier, CIFTSWE is developing a structure for the confidential transmission of CSWE self studies and research via the Internet.

CONCLUSIONS

The key to advancing the Internet in social work is the theme found in the history of the development of the Internet. As a social worker, two aspects of Internet history are striking. The concept of "unintended consequcnces" is first apparent. The present use of the Internet is nothing like the original notion expected by its designers. A vast array of commercial and non-commercial applications for social work practice now exist. We are just witnessing the tip of the iceberg.

Second, and closely related to the concept of unintended consequences, is social work values. The values to which most social workers cling are contrary to the values behind the original design of the Internet. Recall that the original intent of the Internet was to deliver weapons of mass destruction. Now, we see social workers employing it as a system to deliver social services. The success of the Internet must be attributed to the cooperative nature of it's users. I find that the massive level of cooperation found in the Internet is unprecedented in the twentieth century. In the end, social work success in employing the Internet will be limited only by the cooperative nature of those using it in practice and research.

4

Social Work Profession

SOCIAL WORK AS A PROFESSION

- Professional social workers assist individuals, groups, or communities to restore or enhance their capacity for social functioning, while creating societal conditions favourable to their goals. The practice of social work requires knowledge of human development and behaviour, of social, economic and cultural institutions, and of the interaction of all these factors.
- The U.S. Department of Labour's Bureau of Labour Statistics, social work is one of the fastest growing careers in the United States. The profession is expected to grow by 30 per cent by 2010; currently, nearly 600,000 people hold social work degrees.
- Social workers are highly trained and experienced professionals. Only those who have earned social work degrees at the bachelor's, master's or doctoral levels, and completed a minimum number of hours in supervised fieldwork, are "professional social workers."
- The Council on Social Work Education, 22,163 junior and senior students were enrolled in baccalaureate social work Programmes in 2000; there were also 20,369 full-time and 13,446 part-time students enrolled in master's degree Programmes. In the same year, 15,007 individuals graduated with MSW degrees and 11,773 graduated with BSW degrees. In addition, 229 doctoral degrees in social work were awarded in 2000. Currently there are over 8,000 social work professors teaching in the United States.
- Social workers help people overcome some of life's most difficult challenges: poverty, discrimination, abuse, addiction, physical illness, divorce, loss, unemployment, educational problems, disability, and mental illness. They help prevent crises and counsel individuals, families, and communities to cope more effectively with the stresses of everyday life.
- Professional social workers are found in every facet of community life—in schools, hospitals, mental health clinics, senior centres,

elected office, private practices, prisons, military, corporations, and in numerous public and private agencies that serve individuals and families in need.

They often specialize in one or more of the following practice areas:

- Addictions Prevention/Treatment
- Adoption and Foster Care
- Advocacy, Consulting and Planning
- Child Abuse and Neglect
- Child Welfare Services
- Chronic Pain
- Community Mental Health Employee Assistance
- Community-Based Services
- Criminal Justice
- Crisis Intervention
- Depression
- Development Disabilities
- Difficulties in School
- Disaster Relief
- Domestic Violence
- Eating Disorders
- Employment Services
- Family Planning
- Family Preservation Services
- Genetics
- Gerontology Services
- HIV/AIDS
- Homeless Family Assistance
- Hospice and Palliative Care
- Hospital Social Work
- Housing Assistance
- In-Home Services
- Institutional Care
- International Social Work
- Mental Health Therapy
- Military Social Work
- Outpatient Treatment
- Parent Education
- Political Development
- Private Practice
- Public Welfare
- Rural Social Work
- School Alternative Programmes

   - School Violence
   - Senile Dementia and Alzheimer's
   - Veterans Services
- The Substance Abuse and Mental Health Services Administration, professional social workers are the nation's largest group of mental health services providers. There are more clinically trained social workers—over 190,000 in 1998—than psychiatrists, psychologists, and psychiatric nurses combined. Federal law and the National Institutes of Health recognize social work as one of five core mental health professions.
- Over 40 per cent of all disaster mental health volunteers trained by the American Red Cross are professional social workers.
- "There are over 170 social workers in national, state and local elected office, including two U.S. Senators and seven U.S. Representatives. These include: Sen. Barbara Mikulski, Sen. Debbie Stabenow, Rep. Ciro D. Rodriguez, Rep. Barbara Lee, Rep. Ed Towns, Rep. Allyson Schwartz, Rep. Carol Shea-Porter, Rep. Luis Gutierrez, and Rep. Susan Davis."
- Today, 48 special interest social work organisations contribute to the vitality and credibility of the social work profession.

BEGINNING OF SOCIAL WORK AS A PROFESSION

In its broadest significance, it is simply the opposite of the word amateur. A person is in this sense a professional if his entire time is devoted to an activity, as against one who is only transiently or provisionally so engaged. The professional nurse, baseball player, dancer, and cook thus earn a livelihood by concentrating their entire attention on their respective vocations and expect to go on doing so; whereas the amateur nurse enlists only for the duration of the war, or the amateur baseball player, during youth or college life.

Social work is from this point of view a profession for those who make a full-time job of it; it is not a profession for those who incidentally contribute part of themselves to active philanthropy. However, I have not been asked to decide whether social work is a full-time or part-time occupation, whether, in a word, it is a professional or amateur occupation.

I assume that every difficult occupation requires the entire time of those who take it seriously, though of course work can also be found for volunteers with something less than all their time or strength to offer. The question put to me is a more technical one. The term profession, strictly used, as opposed to business or handicraft, is a title of peculiar distinction, coveted by many activities. Thus far, it has been pretty indiscriminately used. Almost any occupation not obviously a business is apt to classify itself as a profession. Doctors, lawyers, preachers, musicians, engineers, journalists, trained nurses, trapeze and dance masters, equestrians, and chiropodists—all speak of their profession.

Their claims are supposed to be established beyond question if they are able to affix to their names one of those magical combinations of letters that either are or look like an academic degree. On this basis, chiropody would be a profession because the New York School of Chiropody confers the degree of M.Cp., and social work might qualify at once with the degree S.W. Some years ago, the president of a western university told me that he had compiled a list of all the degrees ever conferred by his institution.

In the list appeared a very ominous combination of letters—nothing less, in a word, than N.G. I was relieved to be informed that this was not an effort to characterize the entire academic output but signified only "graduate nurse." If the academic degree decides, nursing is a profession for that reason, even were there no other. We need waste no time in endeavoring to formulate the concept of professional, if the concept is to include the indiscriminate activities touched on above.

If there is a dancing profession, a baseball profession, an acting profession, a nursing profession, an artistic profession, a musical profession, a literary profession, a medical profession, and a legal profession—to mention no others—the term profession is too vague to be fought for. We may as well let down the bars and permit people to call themselves professional for no better reason than that they choose in this way to appropriate whatever of social distinction may cling to a term obviously abused. But to make a profession in the genuine sense, something more than a mere claim or an academic degree is needed. There are certain objective standards that can be formulated. Social work is interested in being recognized as a profession only if the term is limited to activities possessing these criteria. The social worker wants, I assume, to be a professional, if at all, only in the sense in which the physician and the engineer are professional, and he wants to make common cause with them in defending the term against deterioration.

In this narrower and eulogistic sense, what are the earmarks of a profession? One has, of course, no right to be arbitrary, notional, or unhistorical. The nature of a profession has undergone a readily traceable development, and the number of professions has not remained stationary. Occupations that were once non-professional have evolved into professional status.

These changes will continue to go on. The definition that we may formulate today will therefore need recasting from time to time, and internal modifications will occur in many of the activities that we shall mention. My present concern, however, is not to consider the evolutionary aspects of the problem, but rather to ask what are at this moment the criteria of a profession and to consider whether social work conforms to them. There are a few professions universally admitted to be such—law, medicine, and preaching.

From these, one must by analysis extract the criteria with which, at least, one must begin the characterization of professions. As we proceed, we shall consider how far the conception has been widened or modified by the addition of new professions; and finally, to what extent social work measures up to the standard thus reached. Would it not be fair to mention as the first mark of a profession that the activities involved are essentially intellectual in character? Manual work is not necessarily excluded; the use of tools is not necessarily excluded. The physician is not the less a member of a profession because his fingers feel a pulse and his hands sound a patient's chest; the engineer is not the less a member of a profession because he employs instruments and tools. But in neither of these instances does the activity derive its essential character from its instruments.

The instrument is an incident or an accident; the real character of the activity is the thinking process. A free, resourceful, and unhampered intelligence applied to problems and seeking to understand and master them—that is in the first instance characteristic of a profession. Wherever intelligence plays thus freely, the responsibility of the practitioner is at once large and personal. The problems to be dealt with are complicated; the facilities at hand, more or less abundant and various; the agent—physician, engineer, or preacher—exercises a very large discretion as to what he shall do.

He is not under orders; though he be cooperating with others, though the work be team work rather than individual work, his responsibility is not less complete and not less personal. This quality of responsibility follows from the fact that professions are intellectual in character; for in all intellectual operations, the thinker takes upon himself a risk. If then intellectuality with consequent personal responsibility be regarded as one criterion of a profession, no more merely instrumental or mechanical activity can fairly lay claim to professional rank; for the human mind does not, in instrumental or mechanical activities, enjoy the requisite freedom of scope or carry the requisite burden of personal responsibility.

The execution or application of a thought out technique—be it crude or exquisite, physical or mental—is after all routine. Someone back of the routineer has done the thinking and therefore bears the responsibility, and he alone deserves to be considered professional. We are accustomed to speak of the learned professions. What is the significance of the word learned in this connection?

Does it imply that there are unlearned as well as learned professions? I suspect not, for the intellectual character of professional activity involves the working up of ideas into practice, involves the derivation of raw material from one realm or another of the learned world. Professions would fall short of attaining intellectuality if they employed mainly or even largely knowledge and experience that is generally accessible—if they drew, that is, only on the usually available sources of information. They need to resort to the laboratory and the seminar for a constantly fresh supply of facts; and it is the steady stream of ideas, emanating from these sources, which keeps professions from degenerating into mere routine, from losing their intellectual and responsible character. The second criterion of the profession is therefore its learned character, and this characteristic is so essential that the adjective learned really adds nothing to the noun profession. Professionals are therefore intellectual and learned; they are in the next place definitely practical.

No profession can be merely academic and theoretic; the professional man must have an absolutely definite and practical object. His processes are essentially intellectual; his raw material is derived from the world of learning; therefore he must do with it a clean-cut, concrete task. All the activities about the professional quality of which we should at once agree are not only intellectual and learned but definite in purpose. The professions of law, medicine, architecture, and engineering, for example, operate within definite fields and strive towards objects capable of clear, unambiguous, and concrete formulation.

Physicians rely mainly on certain definite sciences—anatomy, physiology, pharmacology, *etc.*—and apply these to the preservation and restoration of health. Architecture relies on mathematics, physics, *etc.*, and applies these to the designing and construction of buildings. Ends may of course be concrete and practical without [being] physical or tangible.

University professors, engaged in teaching, in the training of teachers, in the increase of knowledge or the development of thought, stand the tests that we have thus far enumerated: their work is intellectual, learned in quality, and definitely practical in object. Each of the unmistakable professions already mentioned for the purpose of illustration possesses a technique capable of communication through an orderly and highly specialized educational discipline. Despite differences of opinion about details, the members of a given profession are pretty well agreed as to the specific objects the profession seeks to fulfill, and the specific objects that the practitioner of the profession must master in order to attain the object in question. On this basis, men arrive at an understanding as to the amount and quality of training, general and special, which should precede admission into the professional school; as to the content and length of the professional course.

These formulations are meant to exclude from professions those incapable of pursuing them in a large, free, and responsible way; and to make sure that those potentially capable are so instructed as to get the fullest possible benefit from the training provided. A profession is a brotherhood—almost, if the word could be purified of its invidious implications, a caste.

Professional activities are so definite, so absorbing in interest, so rich in duties and responsibilities, that they completely engage their votaries. The social and personal lives of professional men and their families thus tend to organize around a professional nucleus. A strong class consciousness soon develops. But though externally somewhat aristocratic in form, professions are, properly taken, highly democratic institutions. They do indeed tend to set up certain requirements for matriculation, so to speak; but democracy, I take it, means not the annihilation of distinctions, but rather the abrogation of gratuitous and arbitrary distinctions.

If membership in a profession were conditioned on some qualification not essentially related to the activities involved—on birth or wealth or some other accident—professions could be fairly charged with being snobbish or aristocratic; but if qualifications are determined by the nature of the responsibility alone, and if membership depends solely on satisfying terms thus arrived at, then professions must be adjudged thoroughly democratic in essence. There is, of course, always danger that the interests of an organization may conflict with those of the body politic.

Organizations of physicians, lawyers, and teachers may find the personal interests of the individuals of whom they are composed arrayed against those of society at large. On the whole, however, organized groups of this kind are, under democratic conditions, apt to be more responsive to public interest than are unorganized and isolated individuals. In any event, under the pressure of public opinion, professional groups have more and more tended to view themselves as organs contrived for the achievement of social ends rather than as bodies formed to stand together for the assertion of the rights or the protection of interests and principles. I do not wish to be understood as saying that this development is as yet by any means complete.

Such is far from being the case. Organizations of teachers, doctors, and lawyers are still apt to look out, first of all, for "number one." But as time goes on, it may very well come to be a mark of professional character that the professional organization is explicitly and admittedly meant for the advancement of the common social interest through the professional organization. Devotion to well-doing is thus more and more likely to become an accepted mark of professional activity; and as this development proceeds, the pecuniary interest of the individual practitioner of a given profession is apt to yield gradually before an increasing realization of responsibility to a larger end.

Let me now review briefly the six criteria which we have mentioned; professions involve essentially intellectual operations with large individual responsibility; they derive their raw material from science and learning; this material they work up to a practical and definite end; they possess an educationally communicable technique; they tend to self-organization; they are becoming increasingly altruistic in motivation.

It will be interesting to submit various forms of activity to the test in order to determine whether these criteria work. We begin with a crude and obvious example—plumbing. Plumbing possesses certain professional characteristics:

it is definite in purpose, possesses a technique communicable through education, and has developed a very definite organization. Nevertheless, plumbing is not a profession.

The plumber is a mechanical performer, acting on the instrumental rather than the intellectual level; the data which he uses are the property of common experience, not immediately or recently derived from the realms of science and learning; finally, there is as yet no convincing evidence that the spirit of plumbing is becoming socialized. Plumbing is still prosecuted too largely for the plumber's profit. It is therefore a handicraft, not a profession. Banking is an activity with certain professional characteristics.

Its purpose is definite; it gives a good deal of scope to intelligence; it develops a distinct class consciousness. But the disqualifications are plain: Banking is as yet far from being to a sufficient extent the application of economic science; it is largely a matter of what is vaguely called business sense or business experience, common sense or rule of thumb. The scientific possibilities unquestionably exist, and recent legislation marks a distinct advance in the direction of scientific or professional banking in the stricter use of those terms. For the present, however, banking practices are still too largely empirical to square with the modern conception of professionalism.

There are, of course, other defects. A prominent banker recently described himself as "a dealer in credits." The motive of financial profit is thus too strongly stressed. It is true that at times of crisis the banking interests of the country have mobilized for the protection of the general public. But in these instances, trade interest and general interest so largely coincide that it is a question whether the motive can be regarded as an example of professional altruism; in any case, it is exceptional, due to common danger from the outside rather than to spiritual striving from within.

For the present, therefore, banking is to be regarded as a trade with certain professional learning. Is pharmacy a profession? Is trained nursing a profession? The pharmacist compounds the physician's prescription, for which task he requires a considerable degree of expertness, a knowledge of certain sciences—especially chemistry—and a high degree of caution, since either the slightest error on his part, or inability to detect an error on the part of the physician, whether due to ignorance or carelessness, may have very serious consequences. Recurring to our criteria, I should say that pharmacy has definiteness of purpose, possesses a communicable technique, and derives at least part of its essential material from science. On the other hand, the activity is not predominantly intellectual in character and the responsibility is not original or primary.

The physician thinks, decides, and orders; the pharmacist obeys—obeys, of course, with discretion, intelligence, and skill—yet in the end obeys and does not originate. Pharmacy, therefore, is an arm added to the medical profession, a special and distinctly higher form of handicraft, not a profession.

Nor is this distinction merely a verbal quibble, for it has an important bearing on the solution of all educational questions pertaining to pharmacy. I am conscious of endeavoring to pick up a live wire when I undertake to determine the status of the trained nurse. But if consideration of various activities serially will throw any light upon the problem as related to the social worker, there are obvious advantages in discussing the twilight cases. The trained nurse is making a praiseworthy and important effort to improve the status of her vocation. She urges, and with justice, that her position is one of great responsibility; that she must possess knowledge, skill, and power of judgement; that the chances of securing these qualifications, all of them essentially intellectual, improve, as the occupation increases in dignity.

It is to be observed, however, that the responsibility of the trained nurse is neither original nor final. She, too, may be described as another arm to the physician or surgeon. Her function is instrumental, though not, indeed, just mechanically instrumental. In certain relations, she is perhaps almost a collaborator. Yet, when all is said, it is the physician who observes, reflects, and decides.

The trained nurse plays into his hands; carries out his orders; summons him like a sentinel in fresh emergencies; subordinates loyally her intelligence to his theory, to his policy, and [is] effective in precise proportion to her ability thus to second his efforts. Can an activity of this secondary nature be deemed a profession? On the answer, an entire educational policy depends. I have spoken of the trained nurse, the sick-room attendant, and I have raised, without endeavoring finally to dispose of, certain questions suggested by her relationship to the physician. Meanwhile, it is only fair to add, we are developing nursing along other lines. The public health nurse is a sanitary official, busy in the field largely on her own responsibility rather than in the sick room under orders. Whether the term nurse is properly applicable to her, whether a differentiation in training and terminology is not likely to occur as public health work comes into its own, I need not undertake to decide.

With medicine, law, engineering, literature, painting, music, we emerge from clouds of doubts into the unmistakable professions. Without exception, these callings involve personally responsible intellectual activity; they derive their material immediately from learning and science; they possess an organized and educationally communicable technique; they have evolved into definite status, social and professional; and they tend to become, more and more clearly, organs for the achievement of large social ends. I need not establish this position separately in reference to each of them. Let the case of medicine suffice.

The physician's function is overwhelmingly intellectual in quality and his responsibility absolutely personal. He utilizes various instruments, physical and human: microscope, stethoscope, sphygmograph, orderly, pharmacist, dietician, nurse. But his is the commanding intelligence that brings these resources to bear; his the responsibility of decision as to the problem and how it is to be solved.

There are, of course, physicians in abundance to whose processes the word intellectual cannot be properly applied—routineers, to whom a few obvious signs indicate this or that procedure, by a law of mechanical association; but these poorly trained and ill-equipped medical men have no place in modern medicine. They are already obsolete, mere survivals destined soon to pass away. In the next place, medicine derives its material immediately from science. Indeed, an imposing array of sciences has been developed, very largely out of problems encountered and needs felt in medical practice: anatomy, physiology, pathology, bacteriology, and pharmacology. These sciences have now achieved independence in the sense that, like chemistry and physics, they possess inherent interest and are capable of development without immediate reference to disease.

They nevertheless furnish the data with which the physician very largely operates, and his professional development may be determined by the degree to which he substitutes in his observation and thinking data thus derived for data empirical in character. Medicine qualifies on other points equally well: it has the definite, practical end already noted, viz: the preservation and restoration of health; it lends itself admirably to an effective and orderly educational discipline, calculated to attain the definite status; finally, though neither the organization as a whole nor the members as individuals can claim to be exempt from selfish and mercenary motives, it must in fairness be said that the medical profession has shown a genuine regard for the public interest as against its own, that it is increasingly responsive to large social needs, and that there are not wanting signs of a development that will minimize personal profit somewhat as it is minimized in teaching.I hope that these examples have made our criteria so clear that they can now be applied to social work. Is social work a profession in the technical and strict sense of the term?

The Bulletin of the New York School of Philanthropy under the title The Profession of Social Work makes the following explanation:

- The School of Philanthropy is primarily a professional training school, of graduate rank, for civic and social work. The word philanthropy is to be understood in the broadest and deepest sense as including every kind of social work, whether under public or private auspices. By social work is meant any form of persistent and deliberate effort to improve living or working conditions in the community, or to relieve, diminish, or prevent distress, whether due to weakness of character or to pressure of external circumstances. All such efforts may be conceived as falling under the heads of charity, education, or justice, and the same action may sometimes appear as one or another according to the point of view.

The activities described in these words are obviously intellectual, not mechanical, not routine in character. The worker must possess fine powers of analysis and discrimination, breadth and flexibility of sympathy, sound judgement, skill in utilizing whatever resources are available, facility in devising new combinations. These operations are assuredly of intellectual quality. I confess I am not clear, however, as to whether this responsibility is not rather that of a mediating than an original agency. Let me explain as concretely as I can. The engineer works out his problem and puts through its solution; so does the physician, the preacher, the teacher.

The social worker takes hold of a case, that of a disintegrating family, a wrecked individual, or an unsocialized industry. Having localized his problem, having decided on its particular nature, is he not usually driven to invoke the specialized agency, professional or other, best equipped to handle it? There is illness to be dealt with—the doctor is needed; ignorance requires the school; poverty calls for the legislature, organized charity, and so on. To the extent that the social worker mediates the intervention of the particular agent or agency best fitted to deal with the specific emergency which he has encountered, is the social worker himself a professional or is he the intelligence that brings this or that profession or other activity into action?

The responsibility for specific action thus rests upon the power he has invoked. The very variety of the situations he encounters compels him to be not a professional agent so much as the mediator invoking this or that professional agency. In speaking of social work as mediating, I do not intend to say that other professions are mutually independent and act independently. Indeed, the collaboration of different professions in the doing of specific tasks is a characteristic feature of latter-day organization. Architects, engineers, sanitarians, lawyers, and educators cooperate in the building of a school or a tenement. But it is to be noted that this is a division of labour among equals, each party bearing, subject to general consent, primarily responsibility for his particular function, the definiteness of that function and the completeness of the responsibility differing I take it, from the function and responsibility of the social worker under similar conditions. Consideration of the objects of social work leads to the same conclusion. I have made the point that all the established and recognized professions have definite and specific ends: medicine, law, architecture, engineering—one can draw a clear line of demarcation about their respective fields.

This is not true of social work. It appears not so much a definite field as an aspect of work in many fields. An aspect of medicine belongs to social work, as do certain aspects of law, education, architecture, *etc.* Recur for a moment to the scope of interest indicated in the extract above quoted from the prospectus of the New York School: the improvement of living and working conditions in the community, the relief or prevention of distress whether individual or social in origin. The prospectus of the Boston School for Social Workers enumerates the various kinds of positions occupied by its graduates as follows: care of children, church or religious work, civic agencies, industrial betterment, institutional and medical social service, neighbourhood work and recreation, organizing charity, probation and parole.

The field of employment is indeed so vast that delimitation is impossible. We observed that professions need to be limited and definite in scope, in order that practitioners may themselves act; but the high degree of specialized competency required for action and conditioned on limitation of area cannot possibly go with the width of scope characteristic of social work. A certain superficiality of attainment, a certain lack of practical ability, necessarily characterize such breadth of endeavor. If, however, we conceive the social worker, not so much as the agent grappling with this or that situation, but rather as controlling the keyboard that summons, cooperates with, and coordinates various professional specialists, this breadth of attainment is very far from being a matter for reproach.

It imposes upon the social worker the necessity of extreme caution, of considerable modesty, because in these days a considerable measure of certainty is possible to any one person only within a restricted field. Would it not be at least suggestive therefore to view social work as in touch with many professions rather than as a profession in and by itself? Perhaps the same idea can be brought out in other ways.

A good deal of what is called social work might perhaps be accounted for on the ground that the recognized professions have developed too slowly on the social side. Suppose medicine were fully socialized; would not medical men, medical institutions, and medical organizations look after certain interests that the social worker must care for just because medical practice now falls short? The shortcomings of law create a similar need in another direction.

Thus viewed, social work is, in part at least, not so much a separate profession, as an endeavor to supplement certain existing professions pending their completed development. It pieces out existing professions; breathes a new spirit into them; and binds them together in the endeavor to deal with a given situation from a new point of view. Lack of specificity in aim affects seriously the problem of training social workers. Professions that are able to define their objects precisely can work out educational procedures capable of accomplishing a desired result.

But the occupations of social workers are so numerous and diverse that no compact, purposefully organized educational discipline is feasible. Well-informed, well-balanced, tactful, judicious, sympathetic, resourceful people are needed, rather than any definite kind or kinds of technical skill. Insofar as education can produce this type, the education is not technically professional so much as broadly cultural in a variety of realms of civic and social interest. The vagueness of the enterprise in which they are engaged must have troubled the instructors themselves, if I may judge from a remark once made to me by one of them: "We don't know just what to teach them." In this connection, it is worth noting that the heads of schools for social workers are trained men with subsequent experience but not trained social workers. Dr. Graham Taylor is a theologian by training; Dr. Brackett and Dr. Devine are economists. In addition to knowing a specialty well, they are all well-informed in many other directions.

This breadth of interest and attainment reinforced by practical experience makes them competent heads of schools for social workers—this, rather than any particular training aimed at the particular job. Let me add, however, that what I have just said does not imply that schools of philanthropy are superfluous. Looking at them as educational ventures, I suspect that they are as yet feeling about for their proper place and function. There is an obvious convenience, however, in having an institution which focuses as far as possible the main lines of social activity; an obvious advantage in having an institution that emphasizes the practical side of what might otherwise be more or less academic instruction in many branches.

But instruction of this kind is not exactly professional in character; it supplements and brings to bear what good students might well acquire in the course of their previous higher education. If social work fails to conform to some professional criteria, it very readily satisfies others. No question can be raised as to the source from which the social worker derives his material—it comes obviously from science and learning, from economics, ethics, religion, and medicine; nor is there any doubt on the score of the rapid evolution of a professional self-consciousness, as these annual conferences abundantly testify.

Finally, in the one respect in which most professions still fall short, social work is fairly on the same level as education, for the rewards of the social worker are in his own conscience and in heaven. His life is marked by devotion to impersonal ends, and his own satisfaction is largely through the satisfaction procured by his efforts for others. There is, however, another side even to this aspect of professional activity. Professions may not be cultivated for mere profit. Neither, let me add, can they develop on the basis of volunteer or underpaid service. Most men and women are fortunately so placed that the careers they adopt must afford them the income necessary to their existence and development. Well-trained men and women cannot, as a rule, be attracted to a vocation that does not promise a living wage in return for competent service.

Am I mistaken in thinking that not infrequently the inner joy attached to philanthropic endeavor has seemed to those in control a more complete satisfaction of the worker's legitimate desires than it has seemed, for example, to the worker herself? Here again I am raising a question, not making a criticism. Now that we have run through the marks of the professions and have found that on the whole at this stage, social work is hardly eligible, it is fair to ask whether we have not been simply engaged in quibbling. Has an analysis of this kind any practical significance?It seems to me that it has. For example: the social worker is at times perhaps somewhat too self-confident; social work has suffered to some extent from one of the vices associated with journalism, excessive facility in speech and in action.

Let us suppose for a moment that our reflection on the differences between the accepted professions and social work reminds the social worker at crucial moments that he is, as a social worker, not so much an expert himself as the mediator whose concern it is to summon the expert: will not his observation be calmer, his utterance more restrained, be the difficulty he encounters economic, educational, or sanitary? He will, I mean, be conscious of his dependence, and this consciousness will tend to induce caution, thoroughness, and moderation.

For if social work is not definite enough to be called a profession, the social worker will at least be less cock-sure than the professional man whom he calls in. Is it not possible that part of the vast army of reaction is made up of those needlessly terrified by the occasionally reckless—and perhaps somewhat baseless—confidence of the reformer? If so, failure to realise the limitations of social work from the professional point of view is not without practical consequences.

Matthew Arnold somewhere quotes Goethe as saying: "To do is easy; to think is hard." There is a sense in which the remark is true. If we mean routine doing and fundamental thinking, then truly to do is easy, to think is hard. But there is a sense in which the remark is false. For if we mean by doing, effective doing, then to think is easy, to do is hard. The easy, impatient sweep of progressive recommendation, characteristic of even the best progressive journalism, is one thing; the working out of a practical problem is quite another. I know of nothing more difficult than to take hold of a definite situation in sanitation or education and to make it better.

Nor is it only or in some cases mainly the iniquity and perversity of men that are at fault; our impatience may occasionally be unjust, if it is due to any such view. The problems are in themselves intricate; our resources are inadequate; our powers, especially in dealing with others, are relatively slight and work slowly. In the sense in which we are now speaking, Goethe's saying may be reversed: To think is easy, to do is hard. I have no desire to discourage social workers; still less do I want to bring aid or comfort to the enemy. I do not want to diminish the vigour of any attack that can be made upon poverty, ignorance, disease, selfishness; but for the moment I am, ignoring all else, looking at the method of the social worker from the merely professional standpoint.

Now when social work becomes thoroughly professional in character and scientific in method, it will be perceived that vigour is not synonymous with intelligence. Moreover, vigour cannot succeed without intelligence. The battles that social work wages will not be won by phrases which too often serve as a substitute for experience and knowledge, but by trench warfare carried on by men and women who have learned every inch of the ground over which they must fight. I spoke a moment ago of journalism.

I would not be understood as discrediting effective and able journalistic work. Its limitations, however, are obvious, and by none are they more acutely felt than by some of those who are compelled by the necessities of the case to labour within them. What I mean to point out here is this: that a profession needs in these days a form of expression and record that is scientific rather than journalistic in character. The newspapers, the weekly and monthly periodicals, more or less serve social work as far as journalistic publicity is concerned.

Now while it is doubtless still advisable to concentrate this material in journals expressly devoted to social work for news-propaganda and agitation, it is important to remember that we do not thus rise above the journalistic to the scientific or professional level. A profession must find a dignified and critical means of expressing itself in the form of a periodical which shall describe in careful terms whatever work is in progress; and it must from time to time register its more impressive performances in a literature of growing solidity and variety.

To some extent, the evolution of social work towards the professional status can be measured by the quality of publication put forth in its name. I cannot pretend to such familiarity with the literature of social work as to warrant me in passing an opinion as to how far its periodical or its book literature is impressive, scientific, or professional in quality; but I believe the point is one which might be profitably considered by those who wish social work to be taken as seriously as medicine or engineering. At the moment, therefore, it may be—observe that I am not endeavoring to be very positive—it may be that social work will gain if it becomes uncomfortably conscious that it is not a profession in the sense in which medicine and engineering are professions; that if medicine and engineering have cause to proceed with critical care, social work has even more.

The father of the late President Gilman was once asked whether his son Daniel had "chosen his profession." "I don't know," he replied, "Daniel is always working rather than professing." But, after all, what matters most is professional spirit. All activities may be prosecuted in the genuine professional spirit.

Insofar as accepted professions are prosecuted at a mercenary or selfish level, law and medicine are ethically no better than trades. Insofar as trades are honestly carried on, they tend to rise towards the professional level. Social work appeals strongly to the humanitarian and spiritual element. It holds out no inducement to the worldly—neither comfort, glory, nor money. The unselfish devotion of those who have chosen to give themselves to making the world a fitter place to live in can fill social work with the professional spirit and thus to some extent lift it above all the distinctions which I have been at pains to make. In the long run, the first, main, and indispensable criterion of a profession will be the possession of professional spirit, and that test social work may, if it will, fully satisfy.

ROLE OF THE PROFESSIONAL SOCIAL WORKER

Professional social workers have a strong tradition of working for social justice and refusing to recreate unequal social structures. This means going beyond state sponsored practices which merely cater to individual needs. Social work maintains this radical kernel with the objective of transforming society as a whole.

Today many social workers internationally have strong connections with social and political movements for the emancipation of the oppressed. The main tasks of professional social workers are case management, medical social work, counseling, human services management, social welfare policy analysis, community organiing, advocacy, teaching, and social science research.

Professional social workers work in a variety of settings, including: non-profit or public social service agencies, grassroots advocacy organiations, hospitals, hospices, community health agencies, schools, faith-based organiations, and even the military. Other social workers work as psychotherapists, counselors, or mental health practitioners, normally working in coordination with psychiatrists, psychologists, or other medical professionals.

Additionally, some social workers have chosen to direct the focus their efforts on social policy or academic research towards the practice or ethics of social work. While the emphasis has varied among these task areas in different eras and countries, some areas have been the subject of controversy as to whether they are properly part of social work's mission.

UNITED STATES

In the United States of America, leaders and scholars in the field of social work have debated the purpose and nature of the profession since its beginning in the late 1800s. Workers, beginning with the settlement house movement, have argued for a focus on social reform, political activism, and systemic causes of poverty. Social workers of the Settlement House Movement were primarily young women from middle-income families and chose to live in lower-income neighbourhoods to engage in community organiing.

These workers sometimes received stipends from charitable organiations and sometimes worked for free. In contrast to the settlement house movement, the friendly visitors were women from middle-income families who visited families in lower-income neighbourhoods. Friendly visitors emphasied conventional morality rather than social activism. Others have advocated an emphasis on direct practice, aid to individual clients and families with targeted material assistance or interventions using the diagnostic and statistical manual of mental diseases DSM-IV.

While social work has been defined as direct, individual practice in the last quarter of the twentieth century, there is a growing resurgence of community practice in social work. Of broad and growing significance are the relationship counseling and Relationship Education movements which seek to assist in interpersonal social skill building which can be of great societal value in promoting marriage and family stability. Relationship education and counseling primarily aid the majority of individuals who are free of pathology or who have found that DSM-IV based services are ineffectual.

This majority can benefit from education and exposure to relationship skills that have not otherwise been discussed and distributed by social services in this time of weakened family, church, and societal conventions. Another new development in social work is the focus on informatics. For many social workers, the use of any online technology is problematic due to persistent concerns about privacy. However, other social workers recognie that clients are going on line for many purposes. Some schools of social work, such as University of Southern California are offering courses to build informatics skills at the graduate level.

Community practice is the new term of art for what used to be known as"macro practice" social work. Community practice includes working for change at the systems level, including human services management; community organiing; social policy and politics; and international social development. The National Association of Social Workers is the largest and most recognied membership organiation of professional social workers in the world. Representing 150,000 members from 56 stages in the United States and abroad, the association promotes, develops and protects the practice of social work and social workers. NASW also seeks to enhance the well-being of individuals, families, and communities through its work and advocacy.

Within the mental health field, social workers may work in private practice, much like clinical psychologists or members of other counselling professions often do. Social workers are often in the position of recommending the use of psychopharmaceutical agents, though not prescribing them.

The increasingly widespread usage of these agents in the U.S. has received little scrutiny by the NASW, despite that fact that these drugs are prescribed far more heavily in the U.S. than anywhere else in the world. Social workers in private practice may take direct payments from clients and may also receive third-party reimbursement from insurance companies or government programmes such as Medicaid. Insurance reimbursement for mental health services involves the designation of the recipient of services as mentally ill, or more specifically a label is assigned from the DSM-IV, the diagnostic and statistical manual of mental illness. This assignment, when recorded to an individual's medical history can prove to be a significant impediment to future pursuits. It can raise the cost to the individual for health or nursing home insurance; it can be the basis of denial for life insurance; and it can limit an individual's professional choices, such as in health care, motor vehicle operation, or airplane piloting.

Private practice was not part of the social work profession when it began in the late 1800s. It has been controversial among social workers, some of whom feel that the more lucrative opportunities of private practice have led many social workers to abandon the field's historic mission of assisting disadvantaged populations. The private practice model can be at odds with the community development and political activism strains of social work. Social workers in mental health may also work for an agency, whether publicly funded, supported by private charity, or some combination of the two.

These agencies provide a range of mental health services to disadvantaged populations in the US. Some social workers are child welfare workers, a role that looms large in the public's perception of social work. This role contributes to a negative view of social work in the U.S.. since child welfare authorities can remove abused or neglected children from the custody of their parents, a practice that is fraught with controversy and sometimes with scandalous incompetence. Many child welfare workers in the US do not in fact have social work degrees. Some states restrict the use of the title social worker to licensed practitioners, who must hold a degree in the field. Such restrictions are a high legislative priority of NASW.

UNITED KINGDOM

In the United Kingdom and elsewhere, a social worker is a trained professional with a recognised social work qualification, employed most commonly in the public sector by local authorities. Spending on social services departments is a major component of British local government expenditure. In Social care UK, the title "social worker" is protected by law and can be used only by people who have a recognised qualification and are registered with the General Social Care Council, the Scottish Social Services Council, the Care Council for Wales or the Northern Ireland Social Care Council. The strategic direction of statutory social work in Britain is broadly divided into children's and adults' services.

Social work activity within England and Wales for children and young people is under the remit of the Department for Children, Schools and Families while the same for adults remains the responsibility for the Department of Health. Within local authorities, this division is usually reflected in the organisation of social services departments.

The structure of service delivery in Scotland is different. Within children services some social workers are child protection workers, a role that looms large in the public's perception of social work. This role contributes to a negative view of social work in the UK since child protection workers for local authorities can remove suspected abused or neglected children from the custody of their parents, a practice that is fraught with controversy and media criticism. In mental health care, social workers can train to become an Approved Mental Health Professional, involved in the application of the Mental Health Act 1983 in England and Wales. Though now open to other professions, this involves a contributing a social care perspective to Mental Health Act assessments and is predominantly a social worker role. In 2007, the General Social Care Council launched a wide-ranging consultation, in concert with a number of other social care organisations, to agree a clear professional understanding of social work in the UK

SOCIAL WORK KNOWLEDGE BUILDING

The International Federation of Social Workers states, of social work today, "social work bases its methodology on a systematic body of evidence-based knowledge derived from research and practice evaluation, including local and indigenous knowledge specific to its context. It recognies the complexity of interactions between human beings and their environment, and the capacity of people both to be affected by and to alter the multiple influences upon them including bio-psychosocial factors.

The social work profession draws on theories of human development and behaviour and social systems to analyse complex situations and to facilitate individual, organiational, social and cultural changes." The impetus for both movements was the glaring reality of social problems and the question over how to best attack them. This debate is arguably the earliest example of a larger debate within social work–how is knowledge acquired? This debate pits positivism against post-positivism in the pursuit of achieving respect as a profession. The positivistic argument asserts knowledge has to be observable and testable, free from bias, and ultimately replicable if it is to have any merit.

Post-positivists argue there is no way to completely eliminate bias, and knowledge can be obtained via qualitative research methods. The debate reached its greatest intensity in the 1980s, reflecting the debate within the larger world of the social sciences. Subsequently, most of those interested in social work knowledge building have joined in a consensus that both perspectives are necessary to fully understand the complex realities encountered by social work practitioners. Today, most text books intended for social work research courses, while they may devote more pages to quantitative approaches, also include one or more stages on qualitative approaches, and make an effort not to favour one over the other. Meanwhile, practitioners, and often educators in social work practice, have felt left out of the debate. A frequent complaint was that social work programmes were favouring research over practice skills in faculty hiring, thus weakening their ability to teach practice skills to new practitioners. The reliance among practitioners on shared practice wisdom, and the development of skills and techniques through clinical supervision and mentorship was not considered as valid as knowledge building by either camp.

There have been attempts to bridge the gap between practice-based knowledge and knowledge obtained through more formal research approaches. One such strategy is single-subject research—also known as Single Subject Design, in which the clinician, working together with the client, carefully specifies a target of intervention, then measures its frequency, duration, intensity, or any relevant characteristics during a baseline period when no intervention is tried. Following this, an intervention is introduced, and measurement of the target problem is continued. Two claims made for SSD were that it would improve clinical work, since effectiveness of interventions could be determined, and that single cases could be aggregated into research reports, which, published, would constitute an empirically verified set of interventions for clinical use.

Although SSD has been championed by social work graduate programmes for more than two decades, there is little evidence that it has been widely adopted by social work practitioners. The current state of social work professional development is characteried by two realities. There is a great deal of traditional social and psychological research being carried out primarily by university-based researchers and by researchers based in institutes, foundations, or social service agencies. Meanwhile, the many social work practitioners continue to look to their own experience for knowledge. This is a continuation of the debate that has persisted since the outset of the profession in the first decade of the twentieth century. One reason for the practice-research gap is that practitioners deal with situations that are unique and idiosyncratic, while research deals with regularities and aggregates. The translation between the two is often imperfect. A hopeful development for bridging this gap is the compilation in many practice fields of collections of "best practices, " largely taken from research findings, but also distilled from the experience of respected practitioners.

THE ROLES OF A SOCIAL WORKER

ENABLER

In the enabler role, a social worker helps a client become capable of coping with situations or transitional stress. A social worker conveys hope, reducing resistance and ambivalence, recognizing and managing feelings, identifying and supporting personal strengths and social assets, breaking down problems into parts that can be solved more readily, and maintaining a focus on goals and the means of achieving them.

MEDIATOR

The mediator role involves resolving arguments or conflicts micro, mezzo, or macro systems. At the macro level, the mediator helps various subsystems within a community, or a community and some other system, work out their differences. At the micro and mezzo levels, mediation is helps in such areas as resolving divorce and child custody cases. A mediator remains neutral and does not side with either party in the dispute.

INTEGRATOR/COORDINATOR

Integration is the process of bringing together various parts to form a unified whole. Coordination involves bringing components together in some kind of organised manner. A generalist social worker can function as an integrator/coordinator "in may ways, ranging from... advocacy and identification of coordination opportunities, to provision of technical assistance, to direct involvement in the development and implementations of service linkages".

MANAGER

Management in social work involves having some level of administrative responsibility for a social agency or other unit "to determine organisational goals'... acquire resources and allocate them to carry out Programmes; coordinate activities towards the achievement of selected goals; and monitor, assess, and make necessary changes in processes and structure to improve effectiveness and efficiency".

EDUCATOR

The educator role involves giving information and teaching skills to clients and other systems. To be an effective educator, the worker must first be knowledgeable. Additionally, the worker must be a good communicator so that information is conveyed clearly and is understood by the client or macro system.

ANALYST/EVALUATOR

Social workers with a broad knowledge base of how various systems function can analyse or evaluate how well Programmes and systems work. They can also evaluate the effectiveness of their own interventions.

BROKER

A broker helps link clients with community resources and services. A broker also helps put "various segments of the community in touch with one another" to enhance their mutual interests. In micro and mezzo systems, this requires that the worker be familiar with community services, have general knowledge about eligibility requirements, and be sensitive to client needs. A broker may help a client obtain emergency food or housing, legal aid, or other needed resources.

FACILITATOR

A facilitator is "one who serves as a leader for some group experience". The group may be a family therapy group, a task group, a sensitivity group, an educational group, a self-help group, or a group with some other focus. The facilitator role may also apply to macro practice. In this context, a facilitator assumes "the responsibility to expedite the change effort by bringing together people and lines of communication, channeling their activities and resources, and providing them with access to expertise".

NEGOTIATOR

A negotiator represents an organisation, a group, or an individual that is trying to gain something from another group or system. Somewhat like mediation, negotiation involves finding a middle ground that all sides can lived with and achieving consensus whenever possible. However, unlike mediators, who play a neutral role, negotiators clearly ally themselves with one of the sides involved.

ADVOCATE

Advocacy involves "the act of directly representing a course of action on behalf on one or more individuals, groups, or communities, with the goal of securing or retaining social justice".

The advocate role involves stepping forward and speaking on behalf of the client system. The advocate role is one of the most important roles a generalist social worker can assume, despite its potential difficulties.

LEADERSHIP DEVELOPMENT

Leadership development refers to any activity that enhances the quality of leadership within an individual or organisation. These activities have ranged from MBA style Programmes offered at university business schools to action learning, high-ropes courses and executive retreats.

DEVELOPING INDIVIDUAL LEADERS

Traditionally, leadership development has focused on developing the leadership abilities and attitudes of individuals. Just like people aren't all born with the ability to, say, play football like Zinedine Zidane or sing like Luciano Pavarotti, people aren't all born with the ability to lead. Different personal characteristics can help or hinder a person's leadership effectiveness and require formalized Programmes for developing leadership competencies. Yet, everyone can develop their leadership effectiveness.

Classroom-style training and associated reading is effective in helping leaders to know more about what is involved in leading well. However, knowing what to do and doing what you know are two very different outcomes; management expert Henry Mintzberg is one person to highlight this dilemma. It is estimated that as little as 15 per cent of learning from traditional classroom style training results in sustained behavioural change within the workplace.

The success of leadership development efforts has been linked to three variables:

1. Individual learner characteristics
2. The quality and nature of the leadership development Programme
3. Genuine support for behavioural change from the leader's supervisor

Military officer training academies, such as the Royal Military Academy Sandhurst, go to great lengths to only accept candidates who show the highest potential to lead well. Personal characteristics that associated with successful leadership development include leader motivation to learn, a high achievement drive and personality traits such as openness to experience, an internal focus of control, and self-monitoring.

Development is also more likely to occur when the design of the development Programme:

- Integrates a range of developmental experiences over a set period of time. These experiences may include 360 degree feedback, experiential classroom style Programmes, business school style coursework, executive coaching, reflective journaling, mentoring and more.
- Involve goal setting, following an assessment of key developmental needs and then evaluate the achievement of goals after a given time period.

Among key concepts in leadership development one may find:

- *Experiential learning*: positioning the individual in the focus of the learning process, going through the four stages of experiential learning as formulated by David A. Kolb:
  - Concrete experience
  - Observation and reflection
  - Forming abstract concept
  - Testing in new situations.
- *Self-efficacy*: The right training and coaching should bring about 'Self-efficacy' in the trainee, as Albert Bandura formulated: A person's belief about his capabilities to produce effects
- *Visioning*: Developing the ability to formulate a clear image of the aspired future of an organisation unit.

DEVELOPING LEADERSHIP AT A COLLECTIVE LEVEL

More recently, organisations have come to understand that leadership can also be developed by strengthening the connection between, and alignment of, the efforts of individual leaders and the systems through which they influence organisational operations. This has led to a differentiation between leader development and leadership development. Leader development focuses on the development of the leader, such as the personal attributes desired in a leader, desired ways of behaving, ways of thinking or feeling. In contrast, leadership development focuses on the development of leadership as a process.

This will include the interpersonal relationships, social influence process, and the team dynamics between the leader and his/her team at the dyad level, the contextual factors surrounding the team such as the perception of the organisational climate and the social network linkages between the team and other groups in the organisation.

One practical example of developing leadership specifically so as to influence an organisation's safety culture is described by Burman and Evans. Both forms of development may mutually influence each other, as exemplified in the concept of "Deep Change" in Robert E. Quinn's 1996. Leadership development can build on the development of individuals to become leaders. In addition, it also needs to focus on the interpersonal linkages between the individuals in the team.

In the belief that the most important resource that an organisation possesses is the people that comprise the organisation, some organisations address the development of these resources.

In contrast, the concept of "Employeeship" recognizes that what it takes to be a good leader is not too dissimilar to what it takes to be a good employee. Therefore, bringing the notional leader together with the team to explore these similarities brings positive results. This approach has been particularly successful in Sweden where the power distance between manager and team is small.

SUCCESSION PLANNING

The development of "high potentials" to effectively take over the current leadership when their time comes to exit their positions is known. This type of leadership development usually requires the extensive transfer of an individual between departments. In many multinationals, it usually requires international transfer and experience to build a future leader. Succession planning requires a sharp focus on organisation's future and vision, in order to align leadership development with the future the firm aspires to create.

Thus successive leadership development is based not only on knowledge and history but also on a dream. For such a plan to be successful, a screening of future leadership should be based not only on "what we know and have" but also on "what we aspire to become". Persons involved in succession planning should be current leadership representing the vision and HR executives having to translate it all into a Programme.

Meir Jacob and Amit Cohen three critical dimensions should be considered:

- Skills and knowledge
- Role perception and degree of acceptance of leading role
- Self-efficacy.

These three dimensions should be a basis of any leadership succession programme.

CONTEMPORARY PROFESSIONAL DEVELOPMENT

The International Federation of Social Workers states of social work today, that:

"Social work bases its methodology on a systematic body of evidence-based knowledge derived from research and practice evaluation, including local and indigenous knowledge specific to its context. It recognizes the complexity of interactions between human beings and their environment, and the capacity of people both to be affected by and to alter the multiple influences upon them including bio-psychosocial factors. The social work profession draws on theories of human development, social theory and social systems to analyse complex situations and to facilitate individual, organizational, social and cultural changes."

A hopeful development for bridging this gap is the compilation of collections of "best practices" which attempt to distill research findings and the experience of respected social work practitioners, educators and researchers into effective interventions. Another important contemporary development in the profession is overcoming suspicion of technology and taking advantage of the potential of information technology.

QUALIFICATIONS

Professional social workers are generally considered those who hold a degree in social work. Often these practitioners must also obtain a license or be professionally registered. The education of social workers begins with a Bachelor's degree (BA, BSc, BSSW, BSW, *etc.*) or diploma in Social Work. Some countries offer Postgraduate degrees in Social Work like Master's (such as MSW, MA, MSc, MRes, MPhil *etc.*) or PhD (doctoral studies). More and more graduates of social work continue to post-doctoral studies.

It has been argued that social work education is supposed to be a lifelong process. In a number of countries and jurisdictions, registration or licensure of people working as social workers is required and there are mandated qualifications.

In other places, a professional association sets academic and experiential requirements for admission to membership. The success of these professional bodies' efforts is demonstrated in the fact that these same requirements are recognized by employers as necessary for employment.

PROFESSIONAL ASSOCIATIONS

There are a number of associations for social workers, which exist to provide ethical guidance and other forms of support for their members and social work in general. These associations/organizations are distinguished in international, continental or semi-continental, national and regional. The National Association of Social Workers (NASW) is the largest national association for social workers and provides the common code of ethics that liscensed social workers adhere to in the U.S.

They are also a key body in the academic advancement of the profession encouraging professionals to keep up with new evidence based practices and research. The main international ones are the International Federation of Social Workers (IFSW) and International Association of Schools of Social Work (IASSW).

ROLE OF THE PROFESSIONAL

The main tasks of professional social workers can include a variety of services such as case management (linking users/clients with agencies and programmes that will meet their psychosocial needs—mainly common in US and UK), counseling (psychotherapy), human services management, social welfare policy analysis, policy and practice development, community organizing, international, social and community development, advocacy, teaching (in schools of social work), and social and political research.

TRAINING, OTHER QUALIFICATIONS, AND ADVANCEMENT

A bachelor's degree is the minimum requirement for entry into the occupation, but some positions require an advanced degree. All States and the District of Columbia have some licensure, certification, or registration requirement; but these regulations vary.

EDUCATION AND TRAINING

A bachelor's degree in social work (BSW) is the most common minimum requirement to qualify for a job as a social worker; however, majors in psychology, sociology, and related fields may qualify for some entry-level jobs, especially in small community agencies. Although a bachelor's degree is sufficient for entry into the field, an advanced degree is required for some positions.

A master's degree in social work (MSW) is typically required for positions in health and school settings and is required for clinical work, as well. Some jobs in public and private agencies may require an advanced degree, such as an MSW with a concentration in social services policy or administration. Supervisory, administrative, and staff training positions usually require an advanced degree. College and university teaching positions and most research appointments normally require a doctorate in social work (DSW or Ph.D.). As of June 2009, the Council on Social Work Education accredited 468 bachelor's programmes and 196 master's programmes. The Group for the Advancement of Doctoral Education listed 74 doctoral programmes in social work (DSW or Ph.D.) in the United States. Bachelor degree programmes prepare graduates for direct service positions, such as caseworker, mental health assistant, group home worker and residential counselor.

These programmes include courses in social work values and ethics, dealing with a culturally diverse clientele and at-risk populations, promotion of social and economic justice, human behaviour and the social environment, social welfare policy and services, social work practice, social research methods, and field education. Accredited programmes require a minimum of 400 hours of supervised field experience.

Master's degree programmes prepare graduates for work in their chosen field of concentration and continue to develop the skills required to perform clinical assessments, manage large caseloads, take on supervisory roles, and explore new ways of drawing upon social services to meet the needs of clients. Master's programmes usually last 2 years and include a minimum of 900 hours of supervised field instruction or internship. A part-time programme may take 4 years. Entry into a master's program does not require a bachelor's degree in social work, but courses in psychology, biology, sociology, economics, political science, and social work are recommended. In addition, a second language can be very helpful. Most master's programmes offer advanced standing for those with a bachelor's degree from an accredited social work programme.

LICENSURE

All States and the District of Columbia have licensing, certification, or registration requirements regarding social work practice and the use of professional titles. Most States require 2 years or 3,000 hours of supervised clinical experience for licensure of clinical social workers. Due to some limitations on what settings unlicensed social workers may work and some variation in the requirements to obtain a license, those interested in becoming a social worker should research requirements in their State.

OTHER QUALIFICATIONS

Social workers should be emotionally mature, objective, and sensitive to people and their problems. They must be able to handle responsibility, work independently, and maintain good working relationships with clients and co-workers. Volunteer or paid jobs as a social work aide can help people test their interest in this field.

CERTIFICATION AND ADVANCEMENT

Advancement to supervisor, programme manager, assistant director, or executive director of a social service agency or department usually requires an advanced degree and related work experience. Other career options for social workers include teaching, research, and consulting. Some of these workers help formulate government policies, by analysing and advocating policy positions in government agencies, in research institutions, and on legislators' staffs.

Some social workers go into private practice. Most private practitioners are clinical social workers who provide psychotherapy, usually paid for through health insurance or by the client themselves. Private practitioners must have at least a master's degree and a period of supervised work experience. A network of contacts for referrals also is essential.

EMPLOYMENT

Social workers held about 642,000 jobs, in 2008. About 54 per cent jobs were in health care and social assistance industries, and 31 per cent were employed by government agencies. Although most social workers are employed in cities or suburbs, some work in rural areas.

Employment by type of social worker, in 2008, follows:

- Child, family and school social workers.............292,600
- Medical and public health social workers...........138,700
- Mental health and substance abuse social workers.......137,300
- Social workers, all other.................................73,400

JOB OUTLOOK

Employment for social workers is expected to grow faster than the average for all occupations through 2018. Job prospects are expected to be favourable, particularly for social workers who specialize in the aging population or work in rural areas.

EMPLOYMENT CHANGE

Employment of social workers is expected to increase by 16 per cent during the 2008–18 decade, which is faster than the average for all occupations. The growing elderly population and the aging baby boom generation will create greater demand for health and social services, resulting in rapid job growth among gerontological social workers. Employment of social workers in private social service agencies also will increase. Employment of child, family, and school social workers is expected to grow by about 12 per cent, which is as fast as the average for all occupations.

Demand for child and family social workers should continue, as these workers are needed to investigate child abuse cases, place children in foster care and with adoptive families. However, growth for these workers may be hampered by the budget constraints of state and local governments, who are amongst the largest employers of these workers.

Furthermore, demand for school social workers will continue and lead to more jobs as efforts are expanded to respond to rising student enrollments, as well as the continued emphasis on integrating children with disabilities into the general school population. There could be competition for school social work jobs in some areas because of the limited number of openings.

The availability of Federal, State, and local funding will be a major factor in determining the actual job growth in schools. Mental health and substance abuse social workers will grow by almost 20 per cent over the 2008–18 decade, which is much faster than the average. In particular, social workers specializing in substance abuse will experience strong demand. Substance abusers are increasingly being placed into treatment programmes instead of being sentenced to prison. Also, growing numbers of the substance abusers sentenced to prison or probation are, increasingly being required by correctional systems to have substance abuse treatment added as a condition to their sentence or probation.

As this trend grows, demand will strengthen for treatment programmes and social workers to assist abusers on the road to recovery. Opportunities for social workers in private practice will expand, as they are preferred over more costly psychologists.

Furthermore, the passage of legislation that requires insurance plans offered by employers to cover mental health treatment in a manner that is equal to treatment of physical health may increase the demand for mental health treatment. Growth of medical and public health social workers is excepted to be about 22 per cent, which is much faster than the average for all occupations.

One of the major contributing factors is the rise in the elderly population. These social workers will be needed to assist in finding the best care and assistance for the aging, as well as to support their families. Employment opportunities for social workers with backgrounds in gerontology should be excellent, particularly in the growing numbers of assisted-living and senior-living communities.

The expanding senior population also will spur demand for social workers in nursing homes, long-term care facilities, home care agencies, and hospices.

JOB PROSPECTS

Job prospects are expected to be favourable. Many job openings will stem from growth and the need to replace social workers who leave the occupation. However, competition for social worker jobs is expected in cities where training programmes for social workers are prevalent.

Opportunities should be good in rural areas, which often find it difficult to attract and retain qualified staff. By specialty, job prospects may be best for those social workers with a background in gerontology and substance abuse treatment.

EARNINGS

Median annual wages of child, family, and school social workers were $39,530 in May 2008. The middle 50 per cent earned between $31,040 and

$52,080. The lowest 10 per cent earned less than $25,870, and the top 10 per cent earned more than $66,430. Median annual wages in the industries employing the largest numbers of child, family, and school social workers in May 2008 were:

- Elementary and secondary schools....................$53,860
- Local government...6,650
- State government...39,600
- Individual and family services............................34,450
- Other residential care facilities...........................34,270

Median annual wages of medical and public health social workers were $46,650 in May 2008. The middle 50 per cent earned between $35,550 and $57,690. The lowest 10 per cent earned less than $28,100, and the top 10 per cent earned more than $69,090. Median annual wages in the industries employing the largest numbers of medical and public health social workers in May 2008 were:

- General medical and surgical hospitals................$51,470
- Home health care services...................................46,930
- Local government..44,140
- Nursing care facilities..41,080
- Individual and family services............................38,370

Median annual wages of mental health and substance abuse social workers were $37,210 in May 2008. The middle 50 per cent earned between $28,910 and $48,560. The lowest 10 per cent earned less than $21,770, and the top 10 per cent earned more than $61,430. Median annual wages in the industries employing the largest numbers of mental health and substance abuse social workers in May 2008 were:

- Outpatient care centres...$36,660
- Individual and family services............................35,900
- Residential mental retardation, mental health and substance abuse facilities....................................33,950

Median annual wages of social workers, all other were $46,220 in May 2008. The middle 50 per cent earned between $34,420 and $60,850. The lowest 10 per cent earned less than $27,400, and the top 10 per cent earned more than $74,040. Median annual wages in the industries employing the largest numbers of social workers, all other in May 2008 were:

- General medical and surgical hospitals................$55,940
- Local government..51,700
- Individual and family services.............................36,660
- Residential mental retardation, mental health and substance abuse facilities......................................36,460
- Community food and housing, and emergency and other relief services...31,890

About 24 per cent of social workers are members of a union or covered by a union contract.

RELATED OCCUPATIONS

Through direct counseling or referral to other services, social workers help people solve a range of personal problems. Workers in occupations with similar duties include:

- Clergy
- Counselors
- Health educators
- Probation officers and correctional treatment specialists
- Psychologists
- Social and human service assistants

QUALIFICATIONS FOR PROFESSIONAL SOCIAL WORK

Professional social workers are generally considered those who hold a professional degree in social work. In a number of countries and jurisdictions, registration or licensure of people working as social workers is required and there are mandated qualifications. In other places, the professional association sets academic and experiential requirements for admission to membership.

UNITED STATES

A social worker, practicing in the United States, usually requires a doctoral degree, master's degree or a bachelor's degree in social work from a Council on Social Work Education accredited programme to receive a license in most states. In some areas, however, a social worker may be able to receive a license with a bachelor's or even associate's degree in any discipline. The National Association of Social Workers is the largest organiation of professional social workers in the United States.

Depending on the university, the four year degree may be structured in different ways and draws upon many fields, including social work theory, psychology, human development, sociology, social policy, research methods, social planning and social administration. A person with a BSW is considered a "generalist" and the MSW is considered "a specialist or advanced generalist"; a Ph. D. or D.S.W. generally conducts research, teaches, or analyes policy, often in higher education settings. Various states in the United States "protect" the use of the title social worker by statute. Use of the title requires licensure or certification in most states.

The licensure or certification also requires a prelicensure examination through the ASWB with the exception of the State of California, who creates and administers their own licensing exam. Over half of all states offer licensure at various levels of social work practice, and clinical social work is regulated by licensure in all states. The pass rate for the Master's level licensing exam is around 74 per cent. A range of products and services exist to assist students in preparing for the exam including practice tests, study guides, private tutoring and prep classes.

CANADA

A four-year Bachelor of Social Work is required for entry into the field. A Masters Degree in Social Work is usually required to provide psychotherapy treatment. In Canada social workers may provide treatment but cannot diagnose. Some provinces require registration in order to legally use the title "social worker". Some provinces also require an exam prerequisite for certification through the ASWB.

UNITED KINGDOM

The main qualification for social work is the undergraduate Bachelor's degree in social work, offered at British universities from September 2003 onwards. There is also available a master's degree. These have replaced the previous qualifying award, the postgraduate Diploma in Social Work, which was first awarded in 1991 and will be phased out across the UK by 2009. Prior to this, the recognised qualification was the Certificate of Qualification in Social Work awarded between 1975 and 1991.

Purporting to be either a social worker or a student social worker without registering with the Social Work Register and holding or undergoing training for the recognised qualifications is now a criminal offence. Social workers must renew their registration every three years. These regulations offer protection to vulnerable people by guaranteeing the professional regulation of people working as social workers. They also promote workforce development, as all social workers must participate in at least fifteen days of professional training over a three year period in order to be eligible for renewal of their registration.

Lay practitioners in the United Kingdom, often referred to as Social Services Assistants or Care Workers, are unregistered social workers that often do not hold any formal social work qualification.

This is not the case in Scotland where the scope of registration for social service workers is more advanced. Within the mental health sector in the United Kingdom, social workers can train as an Approved Mental Health Professional.

With the implementation of the Mental Health Act 2007, this had replaced the previous Approved Social Worker role and is open to other professionals such as community psychiatric nurses, psychologists and occupational therapists, whilst maintaining a social work ethos. AMHPs are responsible for organising and contributing to assessments under the Mental Health Act 1983, as amended by the Mental Health Act 2007. After qualifying, social workers can undertake further training under the social work 'Post-Qualifying Framework'.

Before 2007, there were four awards available under this framework:

- *Post-Qualifying Award*: For advanced social work practice and management
- Mental Health Social Workers in England and Wales can now train to become an Approved Mental Health Professional or AMHP.
- *Child Care Award*: Qualification to work with children and young people.
- *Practice Teaching Award*: Qualification to work as a tutor, supervisor and assessor for social work students on their work placement

In 2007, the General Social Care Council and UK partners implemented a new framework which unified these awards in a simpler structure allowing broader study to count towards three levels of social work award: specialist, higher specialist, and advanced.

AUSTRALIA

A four-year Bachelor of Social Work is required for entry into the occupation of Social Worker in Australia, although some universities also offer a two-year, accelerated, graduate-entry BSW. Whilst there are no legal registration requirements, most employers stipulate that applicants must be eligible for membership of the Australian Association of Social Workers. Only graduates of courses recognised by the AASW are eligible for membership.

Continuing Professional Education is an ongoing requirement of accredited membership of the AASW and must incorporate accountability, gaining new knowledge and information and skill development.

A person with overseas qualifications can apply for consideration of recognition of their qualifications via a formal application for assessment by the AASW.

SCANDINAVIA

Socionom is the Swedish and Danish term for a person with a degree in social work and related subjects. In Sweden the "socionom"/Bachelor of Social Work education is 3.5 years.

COUNCIL ON SOCIAL WORK EDUCATION

The Council on Social Work Education is the national association for social work education in the United States of America. The CSWE sets and maintains standards of courses and accreditation of bachelor's degree's and Master's degree programmes in social work.

The CSWE specifies foundation social work programme components, but social work specialties areas are defined by the individual accredited MSW programmes. "Social work education is grounded in the liberal arts and contains a coherent, integrated professional foundation in social work practice from which an advanced practice curriculum is built at the graduate level. "

MASTER OF SOCIAL WORK

The US Master of Social Work is a master's degree in social work. In the United States, MSW degrees must be received from a graduate school that has been approved by the Council on Social Work Education.

The US MSW requires two years of graduate study, in combination with two years of internship, also called field experience. While some students obtain a Bachelor of Social Work before pursuing a Master's, most US MSW programmes accept applicants with undergraduate degrees in a broad range of liberal arts degrees. Most US MSW programmes allow students to choose a clinical or direct practice track, which focuses on direct practice with clients, or a macro practice track, with a focus on political advocacy, community organiing, policy analysis and/or human services management.

While the clinical track tends to be more popular, there has been a resurgence in community practice concentrations recently. There are also opportunities at many universities to obtain joint degrees, such as an US MSW and a Public Administration degree, US MSW and Public Health, or US MSW and Law. The US MSW practice scope has broadened in recent years to include the specialty practice areas of geriatrics and veterinary social work. In some schools the curriculum is based on a generalist model which integrates the practice of social work. The US MSW is considered a terminal practice degree in the field of social work.

The DSW or Ph. D in social work are the final degrees offered in the field of social work. The DSW is considered the professional doctoral degree, while the Ph. D in social work is viewed as the research or academic doctoral degree. There are few DSW programmes in the United States. Though US Master of Social Work is by far the most common degree title used by graduate social work schools in the United States, it is not universal. For example, Columbia University School of Social Work offers an M.S. degree in social work, the School of Social Service Administration of the University of Chicago confers an A.M. degree, and both the University of Texas and the University of Wisconsin-Madison confer the MSSW degree. The Mandel School of Applied Social Sciences at Case Western Reserve University confers the MSSA degree.

Clark Atlanta University's Whitney M. Young School of Social work is also credited with creating the administration of social work from the"Afro-centric" prospective. Clark Atlanta's school of social work has also had various stalwarts in the profession affiliated with it such as W.E.B. DuBois, Dorcas Bowles, Whitney Young, Hattie Mitchell, Naomi Ward and Rufus Lynch.

PROFESSIONAL ENTRY QUALIFICATION

Professional entry should follow completing a 3-year degree programme or its equivalent plus an assessed consolidation year in employment. To accommodate graduate level education and training will take longer than the current minimum of 2 years. What is now needed is a new degree level programme spread over 3 years, based in college, but including practice based learning.

It should be designed to ensure a proper balance of input from higher education and employment so that those completing the programme are fit to begin employment in the social work field. This should be followed by a consolidation period of one year in employment, which should include inputs from higher education before assessment by the regulatory body for registration as a qualified social worker. The objective is that at the end of the whole period of education and training, students gain a degree from the appropriate university and qualified social worker status from the regulator. The latter could in due time take the form of registration with the proposed Northern Ireland Social Care Council (NISCC). The Government's policy generally is to widen the access gates to higher education in order to create a more diverse workforce.

Social work has a good record in achieving just that. In moving to a new degree programme for social work it is inevitable that some people will be lost for whom training to a degree would be difficult. However, in keeping with the Government's general approach, it is important for social work to continue to have in it people with varied backgrounds and experience. Ideally social work should closely reflect and draw on local communities. Steps, therefore, need to be taken to keep the access gates to professional training as wide as possible.

This can be achieved through:

- Credit-rating previous appropriate professional education and experience including NVQs and relevant employment;
- Extended use of open and distance learning; and
- Full use of HE Access Programmes, Modern Apprenticeships and National Trainee schemes.

It is important to note, in this context, that here social services employers in both statutory and independent sectors have a good record of achievement in providing access to vocational qualifications. There are already examples of staff having progressed from vocational, through professional to advanced qualifications. At the other end of the scale it is important to attract postgraduate entry to social work training for those who have already obtained a degree.

Their previous experience in another graduate discipline will enrich the profession and assist in meeting the objective of a diverse workforce. However, the award at basic qualifying level should remain primary degree with higher-level academic awards being reserved to post professional development.

STANDARDS SPECIFICATION

The development of a national social work training framework underpinned by occupational standards is required. Merely lengthening the period of training will not be enough to guarantee a consistent supply of social workers fit for purpose. This can only be achieved by the statutory regulator prescribing a training framework, which clearly specifies the defined core knowledge, and competence required of the newly qualified practitioner.

The framework could also cover other matters such as, for example, student selection criteria and which parts of the training must be undertaken within a multi-disciplinary student group to be deemed effective. Rigorous specifications for student assessment would be essential.

The regulatory body in association with the Quality Assurance Agency for higher education would test for compliance with all its requirements at regular intervals.

STRATEGIC DELIVERY

Social work training has been delivered since 1989 by partnership of employers and educators approved by CCETSW. The report from the management consultants, JM Consulting, acknowledges that local current partnership arrangements are efficient in comparison with those in England. Respondents to the consultation here, non-etheless, identified areas for improvement such as the elimination of any duplication of effort in addressing common problems. It was also suggested that regional strategic planning could be improved.

It is, therefore, recommended that one strategic partnership be established to replace the current 3 partnerships to provide a strong lead for professional social work training here. This would allow employers to supply effective senior level representation more efficiently.

DIRECT COMMISSIONING OF TRAINING

It is proposed to seek a transfer from Department of Further and Higher Education Training (DFHET) of the HE funding for social work education and directly commission the training. As things stand the social work HE supply side is characteristically small-scale and inherently vulnerable within the university system.

If DFHET decides, as in recent years, to implement a policy controlling student numbers (Maximum Aggregate Student Numbers), this can adversely impact on DHSSPS workforce objectives, *e.g.* the increased numbers of qualified social workers needed to implement the Children Order.

If a university chooses to leave the social work field for any reason, the HE resource money is simply lost to social work. In order to re-engineer reliably a quality supply side, able to respond to the social policy needs of Government and social care employers, it is proposed to seek to gain control of the HE funds by an expenditure programme transfer from DFHET to DHSSPS. This would allow DHSSPS to commission directly from the HE system the training needed.

The experience of the Department which directly commissions nurse education is that clear purchasing power enables a better balance between employers and academic freedom, hence the plans to introduce a similar system for other health professional education here. Implementing this recommendation would place professional social work training on the same footing as other HPSS disciplines.

FUNDING SOCIAL WORK STUDENTS

Recent years have seen the number of applications for social work training decline, as have secondments from employment. Changes in the financial support for students have led employers and university tutors to demand Government action to halt the current rate of decline.

Employers have been concerned about the difficulties experienced in recruiting sufficient qualified social workers to allow full implementation of the Children Order and to secure sufficient levels of qualified staff for other programmes of care and service settings including residential child care. Financial pressures on students are also causing concern. Recent research by CCETSW here shows 83 per cent of students (a majority of whom are over 30 years of age) having to supplement their bursary with paid employment while undertaking their professional training.

Clearly this reduces the time and energy available for study (including practice learning) and if not addressed will reduce the benefit to be gained from the proposals in this paper.

As it stands, tutors and practice teachers have voiced concerns about the impact of relative poverty on these students and their families as well as its impact on the quality of the learning experience. Further, as word spreads about these pressures, it may be contributing to the decline in applications and consequent workforce deficiencies.

It is obviously essential to attract and retain students of the right quality and number to meet workforce needs. The numbers applying for training have declined by 22 per cent since 1995 and there is no evidence that left alone the situation will improve.

There will almost certainly be a number of successful applicants who do not take up a place. Secondment schemes currently in place were originally developed in the 1980s to train staff for the job they already held. There has been a steep decline in the numbers of secondments particularly from the statutory sector (from 66 in 1992 to 32 planned for 1999).

The position now is that some training places remain unfilled each year. Therefore, part of the answer to maintain the supply of newly qualified social workers is a new financial support regime for students and perhaps opening up the potential for employers to seek new recruits for secondment rather than depending on the existing workforce. The Department and Boards have recently introduced a Pilot Trainee Scheme with an anticipated 30 trainee posts. The total number of students to be secured through a trainee scheme is a matter for judgement. Final targets for social workers will be a matter for further discussion with employers. The best judgement at present is that given the state of the workforce we will continue to need at least 200 new social workers each year.

The Employment Survey, 1997/1998, of newly qualified social workers commissioned by SSI from CCETSW, confirms that 93 per cent quickly secured employment here on completion of training. The consultation process during the CCETSW review revealed that employers valued highly the more mature newly qualified recruits available from the postgraduate and employment based programmes.

The more mature outputs from the 2-year route non-graduate were also more highly valued than the younger, less experienced outputs from the 4-year degree programme. At present, only 25 of those qualifying each year are undergraduates. There would be implications for the employers if the supply of 200 per annum were through mainly undergraduate recruits. The implementation of any new arrangements should be reviewed at the end of the first student cohort. It will be particularly important to monitor both applications from and recruitment of undergraduate students subject to matters arising from the Dearing Report.

POST QUALIFYING EDUCATION AND TRAINING

Post Qualifying (PQ) education and training for social workers has not been addressed elsewhere. Here we have been successful in implementing the CCETSW framework for PQ education and training through the PQ Partnership. This partnership consists of the 3 Universities (including the Open University), the Further Education (FE) sector, all statutory agencies and effective voluntary sector representation. Its record speaks for itself. At October 2000, 198 of 445 Post Qualifying Awards were achieved by candidates here, and at Advanced Level 41 out of 162 Awards.

It is, therefore, intended to maintain the current Education and Training Partnership arrangements. It is recognised that the system needs additional investment to develop training, which will ensure that all client groups, service settings, and practice innovations are well covered. Despite the successful record, employer commitment could be improved. The current position reflects the enthusiasm and energy of candidates and a relatively few committed people from HE and employment.

It is intended to involve employers in discussions about both the allocation of resources to secure additional development of training opportunities and about the implementation of systems to ensure all newly qualified social workers embark immediately on a programme of continuous development in keeping with the TOPSS Training Strategy 2000-2003. Such a system will be essential when the Government's proposals for regulating the PSS workforce come into force.

Finally, PQ provides an opportunity for other disciplines to co-operate with the social work partnership to ensure that, where appropriate, the benefits of shared training are fully used. At present, as most funding for postgraduate training in other professions is outside the employment arena, it is rare for bodies such as the Postgraduate Medical Council to contribute and such examples as exist have either been funded by social services or by higher education investment.

5

Social Work Theory

INTRODUCTION

The word theory means a way of looking at a field of evidence, with a view to extracting principles from it. In trying to understand man's thinking, his development and his behaviour, it is important to have some theoretical knowledge to provide a basis for this understanding.

IMPORTANCE OF THEORY

The formulation of valid theory possesses enormous power to elevate and accelerate the expansion and development of human capabilities in any field, leading to fresh discoveries, improvement of existing activities and capacity for greater results. Science is replete with examples of theoretical formulations that have led to important breakthroughs, such as the discoveries of Neptune and Pluto, electromagnetic waves, subatomic particles, and new elements on the periodic table.

Today scientists are discovering new substances on computer by applying the laws of quantum mechanics to predict the properties of materials before they synthesize them. In fact, a broad range of technological achievements in this century has been made possible by the emergence of sound theoretical knowledge in fields such as physics, chemistry and biology.

As management expert Peter Drucker put it, "There is nothing more practical than a good theory." Valid theory can tell us not only what should be done, but also what can be done and the process by which it can be achieved. Social development can be summarily described as the process of organizing human energies and activities at higher levels to achieve greater results. Development increases the utilization of human potential. In the absence of valid theory, social development remains largely a process of trial and error experimentation, with a high failure rate and very uneven progress.

The dismal consequences of transition strategies in most Eastern Europe countries, the very halting progress of many African and Asian countries, the increasing income gap between the most and least developed societies, and the distressing linkage between rising incomes, environmental depletion, crime and violence reflect the fact that humanity is vigorously pursuing a process without the full knowledge needed to guide and govern it effectively.

Advances in development theory can enhance our social success rate by the same order of magnitude that advances in theoretical physics have multiplied technological achievements in this century. The emergence of a sound theoretical framework for social development would provide the knowledge needed to address these inadequacies. It would also eventually lead us to the most profound and practical discovery of all—the infinite creative potentials of the human being.

HIERARCHY OF LEARNING

Social development consists of two interrelated aspects—learning and application. Society discovers better ways to fulfill its aspirations and it develops organizational mechanisms to express that knowledge to achieve its social and economic goals. The process of discovery expands human consciousness. The process of application enhances social organization.

Society develops in response to the contact and interaction between human beings and their material, social and intellectual environment. The incursion of external threats, the pressure of physical and social conditions, the mysteries of physical nature and complexities of human behaviour prompt humanity to experiment, create and innovate.

The experience resulting from these contacts leads to learning on three different levels of our existence. At the physical level, it enhances our control over material processes. At the social level, it enhances our capacity for effective interaction between people at greater and greater speeds and distances. At the mental level, it enhances our knowledge.

While the learning process takes place simultaneously on all these planes, there is a natural progression from physical experience to mental understanding. Historically, society has developed by a trial and error process of physical experimentation, not unlike the way children learn through a constant process of physical exploration, testing and even tasting. Physically, this process leads to the acquisition of new physical skills that enable individuals to utilize their energies more efficiently and effectively. Socially, it leads to the learning and mastery of organizational skills, vital attitudes, systems and institutions that enable people to manage their interactions with other people and other societies more effectively. Mentally, it leads to organization of facts as information and interpretation of information as thought.

The outcome of this learning process is the organization of physical skills, social systems, and information, which are then utilized to improve the efficiency and effectiveness of human activities. It is a cyclical process in which people are continuously learning from past experiences and then applying that learning in new activities. This learning process culminates in a higher level of mental effort to extract the essence and common principles or ideas from society's organized physical experiences, social interactions and accumulated information and to synthesize them as conceptual knowledge. This abstract conceptual knowledge has the greatest capacity for generalization and application in other fields, times and places. The conceptual mind is the highest, most conscious human faculty. Conceptual knowledge is the organization of ideas by the power of mind. That conceptual knowledge becomes most powerful when it is organized into a system. Theory is a systematic organization of knowledge.

A comprehensive theory of social development would provide a conceptual framework for discovering the underlying principles common to the development process in different fields of activity, countries and periods. It would also provide a framework for understanding the relationships between the accumulated knowledge generated by many different disciplines. If pursued to its logical conclusions, it would lead to not just a theory of social development, but a unifying theory of knowledge—which does not yet exist in any field of science or art.

SEARCH FOR A SOCIAL OPERATING SYSTEM

Rapid advancement in computer technology and application has primarily been the result of dramatic progress in two parallel but interrelated fields–development of the processing capacity of the silicon chip and development of more advanced operating systems that enable users to utilize the chip's greater computing power. Chip development increases the potential power of the computer. Development of more powerful, intuitive and easier to use operating systems increases the practical power of the technology.

As a parallel, advances in scientific and technical knowledge have vastly increased the potential productivity and developmental achievements of society. But full utilization of this potential requires the capacity to consciously direct and accelerate social development processes. The discovery of methods to genetically engineer improved varieties of food crops or to control population growth through improved medical devices would have little practical value unless we also possessed the know-how to promote dissemination and adoption of these advanced technologies.

Historically, advances in our understanding of material and biological process have far outstripped advances in our understanding of social processes. As a result, vast social potential has been created, but society has not yet acquired the capacity to fully utilize it for its own development. A theory of development should aim at a knowledge that will enable society more consciously and effectively to utilize its development potentials.

WHY A FRAMEWORK HAS NOT YET EMERGED

A question naturally arises. If such a framework is possible, why with all the attention focused on development for so many decades has it not yet emerged? Social development theory has been elusive for several reasons. First, because of the very practical importance of this issue, attention in this field has very largely focused on the material results of development and on those strategies that have proven most effective for achieving those results, rather than on abstract principles or theoretical concepts.

Rapid economic progress in North America and Europe after the Second World War, which was followed by even more stunning achievements in Japan and other East Asian nations, imbued governments and the international community with the confidence that development was primarily a question of money, technology, industrialization and political will. Confident that the lessons of early achievers provided all the knowledge necessary for those that were to follow, there was an urge for concerted action and an expectation of results, rather than a quest for theoretical knowledge.

In most discussions, development was conceived in terms of a set of desirable results—higher incomes, longer life expectancy, lower infant mortality, more education. Recently emphasis has shifted from the results to the enabling conditions, strategies and public policies for achieving those results—peace, democracy, social freedoms, equal access, laws, institutions, markets, infrastructure, education and technology. But still little attention has been placed on the underlying social process of development that determines how society formulates, adopts, initiates, and organizes, and few attempts have been made to formulate such a framework.

Second, a very large number of factors and conditions influence the process. In addition to all the variables that influence material and biological processes, social processes involve the interaction of political, social, economic cultural, technological and environmental factors as well. Development theorists have not only to cope with atoms, molecules, material energy and various life forms. They must also cope with the near infinite variety and complexity of human beliefs, opinions, attitudes, values, behaviours, customs, prejudices, laws, social institutions, *etc.*

Third, the timeframe for social development theory cannot be confined to the modern day or even the past few centuries. Human development has been occurring for millennia. The basic principles of development theory must be as applicable to the development of early tribal societies as they are to the emergence of the post-modern global village. Development theory must be a theory of how human society advances through space and time.

LOOKING BEYOND THE INSTRUMENTS

Fourth, the instruments of development—science and technology, capital and infrastructure, social policies and institutions—are so compellingly powerful in their action, that they are often mistaken for its cause and source. Most efforts to understand the development process have focused on the central importance of one or a few of these instruments—primarily on money, markets, the organization of production and technological innovation. Some efforts have also been made to describe what has been learned about the contribution of education, skills, laws, public policies, strategies, social systems and institutions. While it is evident that all of these instruments can and do play an important role in social development, it has not been adequately explained what determines the development of these instruments themselves or the extent to which they are utilized by society or the process by which they can be made to generate maximum results.

Obviously, the ultimate determinants of development cannot be the instruments themselves, for none of them exists independently from society. To understand the central principles of development, we must look beyond these instruments to the creator of the instruments. Human beings fashion technology, invent money, erect infrastructures, establish policies, build institutions and adopt values to serve their needs and aspirations. Although humanity exhibits a strong tendency to mistake these instruments for primary determinants rather than created products of its own initiative, the ultimate power of determination must lie with the human beings who create and use these instruments, rather than with the instruments themselves.

Money and technology do have useful power, including a power of organization and efficiency, a power to increase the velocity of production and transactions. But they do not possess an intrinsic living power for growth or development, a source of aspiration or energy that compels their own advancement. Moore's Law describing advances in the speed of microprocessors is not driven by material forces—the microprocessor does not increase its own speed—it is driven by humanity's quest for greater productive power. The surge in value of financial markets is not driven by impersonal physical or mathematical laws governing the growth of money, but by the quest of human beings for greater material prosperity. This self-existent power for growth is an endowment of human beings, living organisms compelled to develop by a pressure within themselves, which in turn gives life and energy to the growth of the instruments and systems they create.

What has been lacking is an organized theoretical framework that describes the role of each of these instruments as aspects of a greater whole and shows each in its proper relation to the others or the greater whole of which they are all parts.

To arrive at such a framework, we have to shift our focus from the instruments of development to their creator; from the role of money and technology to the role of human beings that invent new forms of money and technology and harness them for productive purposes. The theory has to place human beings at the center and view all other aspects of development from the perspective of and in relation to human motivation and action. This conceptual knowledge of the development process should enable every society to better utilize the available instruments better, in order more fully to tap its developmental potential.

DEVELOPMENT AS A SPHERICAL WHOLE

A theory of social development should generate a framework around which all knowledge of the factors, instruments, conditions, agencies and processes of development can be integrated. Rather than singling out a specific set of determinants or giving primacy to a limited set of instruments, it would reveal the nature of the relationships and processes that govern the interaction of all these elements to generate developmental results.

Rather than generate a linear formula or 'right' perspective, it would make it possible to view the whole field and phenomenon of development from multiple perspectives that are integrated and unified ways of knowing the whole, rather than divided and separate ways of viewing the parts. The modern tendency to divide scientific enquiry into an increasing number of specialized fields of study has made the emergence of an integrated perspective very difficult. Philosopher Stephen Toulmin mourns the absence of broader conceptual thinking in physics over the past few centuries and argues the need for grand cosmological visions of the universe to unify and integrate the discoveries of many different disciplines.

Comparatively, the need for synthesis is even greater for the study of human social development than for understanding the physical and chemical evolution of the universe. For in human development, we must not only grapple with four material dimensions in space and time that preoccupy the physicist and chemist, but also integrate the dimensions of life and mind—including physical, genetic and biological determinants; social behaviours, skills, attitudes, customs, traditions, systems, formal organizations, non-formal institutions, and cultural values; and linguistic determinants, data, facts, information, beliefs, opinions, systems of thought, ideas, theories, and spiritual values—all of which interact and influence each other to impact the course of human development.

The quest for theory in social development cannot lead to any linear or logarithmic equation that adequately explains and predicts human progress. The reality we seek to understand is not of that type. It is not linear or uni-dimensional or even a combination of several dimensions. It is a complex, many-dimensional whole that evolves in many interrelated directions simultaneously. The development of society is best represented to our minds as an expansion from a point to a sphere, rather than as movement along a single line or along multiple lines of progress. Social development is the gradual discovery and unfolding of the potential of a complex, integrated whole, a living organization, a living social organism.

FROM UNCONSCIOUS EXPERIENCE TO CONSCIOUS KNOWLEDGE

Finally, social development theory remains elusive because the very nature of social learning is a subconscious seeking by the collective that leads ultimately to conscious knowledge. We experience first and understand later. Our mental comprehension perpetually lags behind physical experience and struggles to catch up with it.

Our view is that the very intensive, concentrated global experience of the past five decades provides fertile soil for the formulation of a more synthetic conceptual framework for social development. Such a framework can vastly accelerate the transfer and replication of developmental achievements around the world and make possible more conscious and rapid progress even for the most advanced societies in the world.

BASIC PREMISES

These observations suggest a starting point for formulation of a comprehensive conceptual framework:

- Social development theory should focus on underlying processes rather than on surface activities and results, since development activities, policies, strategies, programmes and results will always be limited to a specific context and circumstance, whereas social development itself encompasses a potentially infinite field in space and time.
- The theory should recognize the inherent creativity of individuals and of societies by which they fashion instruments and direct their energies to achieve greater results. It should view development as a human creative process, rather than as the product of any combination of external factors or objective instruments that are created and utilized as the process unfolds and whose results are limited to the capacity of the instruments. Society will discover its own creative potentials only when it seeks to know the human being as the real source of those potentials.
- The implication of this view is that even though it may be influenced, aided or opposed by external factors, society develops by its own motive power and in pursuit of its own goals. No external force and agency can develop a society. Paul Hoffman, the Administrator of the Marshall Plan for European Recovery who later became the first head of the United Nations Development Programme, said it succinctly: "Technical assistance cannot be exported. It can only be imported." The aspiration of the collective expressed through the initiative of pioneering individuals is the determinant and driving force for a society's own development.

DEVELOPMENT AS SELF–CONCEPTION

Material and biological sciences focus on the interaction of physical conditions, materials and forces to generate results. The tendency to view social development in the same way has led to a host of mathematical equations seeking to define and predict the consequences of combining different external variables in different proportions and under different conditions. The underlying assumption of this approach is that social development is determined by external conditions.

The hypothesis on which our attempt at theory is based is that social development is determined by human beings, not external conditions. External conditions certainly can and do influence the process. People may even act and react in predictable ways to a given set of external conditions. But the results of any development equation cannot be reliably predicted on the basis of external factors.

Human development is determined by human responses based on choices made by people. To our knowledge, external forces alone have never unleashed a process of social development, but there are countless instances in which external agents have failed to do so.

Human development is a function of human awareness, aspirations, attitudes and values. Like all human creative processes, it is a process of self-conception. As the writer, artist, composer, political visionary and businessman conceive of unrealised possibilities and pour forth their creative energies to give expression to them, the social collective evolves a conception of what it wants to become and by expressing its creative energies through myriad forms of activity seeks to transform its conception into social reality. The only major difference is that while the individual sometimes (but not always) is conscious of the conception he or she is trying to express, the society is usually (not always) unconscious of the idea and the urge that move it to create something more out of its own latent potential.

Society is a subconscious living organism which strives to survive, grow and develop. Individual members of society express conscious intention in their words and acts, but these are only surface expressions of deeper subconscious drives that move the society-at-large. The consciousness of a true collective organism is not merely the sum of its individual parts, but acquires its own identifiable character and personality.

This is why the USA has been able to assimilate such large numbers of immigrants, yet retain its distinctive (but constantly changing) national character. Immigrants are moved by the values of the collective to share in the national aspiration for greater individual freedom, practical organization and material progress. In a similar vein, the feverish collective behaviour of the stock market, fashions and pop culture are subconscious social collectives that acquire their own distinct personalities.

ROLE OF THE INDIVIDUAL

Society has no direct means to give conscious expression to its subconscious collective aspirations and urges. That essential role is played by pioneering conscious individuals–visionary intellectuals, political leaders, entrepreneurs, artists and spiritual seekers who are inspired to express and achieve what the collective subconsciously aspires and is prepared for. Where the aspiration and action of the leader do not reflect the will of the collective, it is ignored or rejected. Where it gives expression to a deeply felt collective urge, it is endorsed, imitated, supported, and systematically propagated. This is most evident at times of war, social revolution or communal conflict.

India's early freedom fighters consciously advocated the goal of freedom from British rule long before that goal had become a felt aspiration of the masses. The leaders spent decades urging a reluctant population to conceive of itself as a free nation and to aspire to achieve that dream. When finally the collective endorsed this conception, no foreign nation had the power to impose its will on the Indian people.

PROCESS OF VALUE CREATION

During the World Academy of Art and Science's meeting on development theory in Washington DC in May 1999, there was a broad consensus of participants that the formation of values was a critical aspect of the development process. We propose to re-examine the process of development as a process of value formation.

If gross physical actions are the most visible and tangible form of human initiative, the creation of values is the most subtle and intangible. Yet human existence is powerfully determined by the nature of its values. Physical skills, vital attitudes, mental opinions and values represent a gradation of internal organizing principles that direct human energies and determine the course of individual and social development.

All human creative processes release and harness human energy and convert it into results. The process of skill formation involves acquiring mastery over our physical-nervous energies so that we can direct our physical movements in a precisely controlled manner. In the absence of skill, physical movements are clumsy, inefficient and unproductive, like the stumbling efforts of a child learning to walk.

Human beings acquire social behaviours in a similar manner. Here, apart from the physical skills required for communication and interaction with other people, vital attitudes are centrally important. Each social behaviour expresses not just a movement, but an attitude and intention of the person. Acquiring social behaviours requires gaining control over our psychological energies and channeling them into acceptable forms of behaviour. Change the attitude and the behaviour changes. The developmental achievements of modern society are founded upon such intangible social attitudes as confidence in the government, trust in other people, tolerance and cooperation. Without such attitudes, our money would become valueless paper and our institutions would cease to function.

The same process takes place at the mental level. The mind's energy naturally flows as thought in many different directions without any structure to contain or organize it. The acquisition of knowledge involves construction of a mental structure of understanding that is analogous to the structure of skills and attitudes that govern expression of our physical and vital energy. It forms an organizational framework for learning and application of what is learned. Human values are formed by a similar process and act in a similar manner. Although the word is commonly used with reference to ethical and cultural principles, values are of many types. They may be physical (cleanliness, punctuality), organizational (communication, coordination), psychological (courage, generosity), mental (objectivity, sincerity), or spiritual (harmony, love, self-giving). Values are central organizing principles or ideas that govern and determine human behaviour.

Unlike the skill or attitude that may be specific to a particular physical activity or social context, values tend to be more universal in their application. They express in everything we do. Values can be described as the essence of the knowledge gained by humanity from past experiences distilled from its local circumstances and specific context to extract the fundamental wisdom of life derived from these experiences. Values give direction to our thought processes, sentiments, emotional energies, preferences and actions.

Centuries of experience have been distilled by society into essential principles. Values such as hard work, sense of responsibility, integrity in human relations, tolerance and respect for others are not just noble ideas or ideals. They are pragmatic principles for accomplishment which society has learned and transmitted to successive generations as a psychological foundation for its further advancement. The values of a society are a crucial aspect of its people's self-conception of what they want to become.

Because values are intangible to our senses and their formation is the result of a very long process, we tend to overlook their central role in development. Social values constitute the cultural infrastructure on which all further social development is based. In this sense, values are the ultimate product of past development and the ultimate determinant of its future course.

DEVELOPMENT AND VALUE CREATION IN INDEPENDENT INDIA

In Human Choice: the Genetic Code for Social Development1, we described the development process as one that releases, organizes and converts human energy into social capacity and material results. In summary, the process consists of pioneering individuals who consciously conceive and initiate new forms of activity which give expression to the subconscious aspirations and preparedness of the society. These pioneers are imitated by others so that the new activity gets replicated and diffused. Gradually, the general population comes to recognize, accept and support the new activity by formally organizing it through laws, policies, programmes, systems, organizations and education. Eventually, the activity may become so fully integrated with the society that the need for formal structures gives way to non-formal social institutions and still later becomes assimilated as cultural values of the society.

Although we describe the process as a clean linear progression, its actual occurrence is more complex. Each stage of the process interacts with those that come earlier and later to effect a general movement in a certain direction. And while the underlying process remains the same, the external results and strategies employed to achieve those results may vary significantly from one place and time to another, even within the same society.

Both the stages and the complexity of the process can be observed by examining two remarkable development accomplishments of Independent India—the Green Revolution in Indian agriculture and the high tech revolution that is making India an international software powerhouse.

The starting point for free India was a value base molded by centuries of social stagnation and foreign rule. During the British Raj, the predominant values espoused by the subject Indian population were respect for age and tradition, submission to authority, and acceptance of one's assigned place and role in society. Fear and insecurity were powerful social motives. Ambition was frowned upon. Security was cherished. Industrial and commercial activities were severely restricted by the foreign rulers. Few had the means or opportunity to acquire education. Those that did invariably sought employment in the British administration or British firms, the twin seats of power and prestige in Indian society. After Indian Independence in 1947, the values of submissiveness and obedience persisted for several decades, even though they became increasingly inadequate concepts to meet the nation's needs or respond to its opportunities. In the 1950s and 1960s, educated Indian youth sought the security and prestige of government employment, when what was really needed was entrepreneurial initiative to build the national economy.

Having achieved Independence, the leaders of India's freedom fight turned to the challenge of developing the country, but found the same lack of awareness and responsiveness from the population that the earlier freedom fighters had encountered at the turn of the century. Waging a war on poverty without the active support and participation of the people proved even more challenging than waging a war on foreign rule without an army.

Until the mid 1960s, India's economic progress was almost completely overshadowed by the explosive growth of its population, the combined effect of a release of national energies from the suppressed condition of foreign domination and the introduction of modern medical technology which drastically reduced mortality rates. Beneath the surface, the spread of democratic voting rights, implementation of legislation to eradicate caste privileges, and rising levels of education were breaking down traditional barriers, generating national pride and releasing fresh social energy, creating awareness of possibilities and preparing the society for the next stages of its collective effort. These new attitudes could be observed primarily among the youth born after Independence, often taking on the appearance of assertiveness and crude self-seeking, rather than of noble values.

This preparedness was called into action by the sudden impact of two successive years of severe drought in the mid 1960s, which threatened the country with famine on an unprecedented scale. The challenge of widespread famine—estimated by the UN to be threatening the lives of 10 million people—led to the launching of India's Green Revolution. With the support of large food imports, the country averted the immediate threat of famine. Then in response to a concerted government action to implement a comprehensive, integrated development strategy, within a very short period of five years, millions of India's farmers adopted new cultivation practices, the nation increased its food grain production by 50 per cent and achieved food self-sufficiency. Within ten years grain production had doubled. Within a quarter century it had quadrupled.

The pride and confidence generated by this remarkable achievement helped spur a dramatic change in India's social values that was reflected in many walks of life. Areas in which agriculture had become prosperous began to industrialize. There was a marked increase in demand for education and for consumer products. Indian society became more active and dynamic.

In the 1970s the preference of educated youth shifted to employment in private companies. Then in the 1980s a generation born after Independence established itself in the nation's workforce, people who had never known a foreign master or experienced subjection or feared famine. New values began to emerge among the younger generation. Talented youth began starting businesses in increasing numbers. Many sought education and work experience overseas, then returned to India to establish companies of their own. The value of security gave way to an aspiration for accomplishment. The sense of knowing one's proper place gave way to an urge for higher levels of achievement, status and enjoyment. A fundamental change in social values underpinned a fundamental shift in the direction and expression of India's national energies from minimum survival to maximum development. This shift has been by no means uniform, universal or entire. It has occurred at different rates and to different extents in different communities, classes and parts of the country, but the change in general direction became increasingly evident.

The development process that led to India's Green Revolution differed in its external expression from that which has more recently led to India's extraordinary achievements in the global software industry. The very notion that India could achieve international fame in a high technology industry was inconceivable to the national consciousness 20 years ago.

As recently as 1983, India was employing fewer than 10,000 software engineers generating about $10 million a year in software exports. Sixteen years later, India's software export revenues are approaching $4 billion. Most major US and many other large foreign computer firms have established companies or joint ventures in India to develop software for export. The country's two largest software training companies educate more than a quarter million programmers annually, roughly five times the total number of computer graduates produced by all US colleges and universities. New software companies and training institutions are sprouting up in every urban area. State governments are competing with each other for dominance in high technology. And Microsoft's Bill Gates recently christened India as "the Silicon Valley of Asia".

This phenomenal accomplishment was made possible by and has further contributed to a general shift in social values that is evidenced in the behaviour of people at all levels and in all parts of the society, including youth, students, women, farmers, lower castes, minorities and entrepreneurs. Viewed from the perspective of the traditional values that had characterized India during centuries of foreign occupation, this shift appears to some as a degradation of social values (a decline in respect for age, tradition and authority; a loss of deference, humility, and the spirit of idealistic self-sacrifice) in much the same way that the advent of democratic values in Europe seemed abhorrent to those who embraced the values of the feudal, aristocratic society that was disappearing.

Attention has focused on the vulgar self-seeking, greed, crass materialism and corruption associated with India's economic and social awakening—so much so, that the positive values that have been responsible for the country's recent accomplishments and form the infrastructure for its future progress are often overlooked. The essential knowledge India has derived from five decades of development experience has been distilled into a new set of social values based on national self-confidence, self-reliance, boldness, insistence on one's rights, greater social tolerance and social equality, and aspiration for higher accomplishment.

SAME PROCESS, DIFFERENT STRATEGIES

The challenge for development theorists is to discover in India's recent experiences fundamental principles and processes that are common to these two distinctly different instances of rapid social advancement, as well as to other instances of development in other countries, periods, and fields of activity. At first glance, the differences are far more apparent than the similarities.

Green Revolution was the result of a conscious, planned initiative by government which passed legislation, established new organizations, widely disseminated information and skills, introduced programmes and offered financial incentives to spur India's agricultural community to action. In contrast, the software revolution was the result of initiatives by individual entrepreneurial pioneers which were not planned by government and were not part of a conscious national strategy. T

he role of government was largely confined to removing administrative and tax barriers that discouraged import of computer equipment and to investment in the essential telecommunications infrastructure required to support this industry. Yet on closer inspection, India's progress in agriculture and software conform to a common process.

Both achievements were made possible by a general social readiness and awakening of the population resulting from rising levels of education, public awareness, social freedom and national confidence. Achievement of Independence and self-government prepared the ground for the Green Revolution. The breakthrough in agriculture prepared the ground for industrialization. Advances in engineering and science education, drawing on an historical Indian endowment in mathematics, the exposure of large numbers of Indians seeking higher education in the USA to the latest information technology, and the emergence of a thriving entrepreneurial business culture in India, prepared the ground for the country's active participation in the Information Revolution.

India's agricultural achievements were very largely the result of conscious initiatives taken by visionary political leaders with the support of the scientific community. The early pioneers of India's Green Revolution were public leaders, not private individuals as in the case of software. But in both cases the acceptance and spread of the new activity crucially depended on the willingness of the population to respond to the opportunity.

In the case of Green Revolution, India's planners faced the seemingly impossible task of persuading millions of illiterate, traditional farmers to adopt new agricultural technology based on new varieties of wheat and rice, which required heavy investments in hybrid seeds, fertilizers and pesticides. The organization of more than 100,000 demonstration plots of the new varieties on farmers' fields, which proved that the hybrids would not only grow but would also generate many times higher yields and profits, spurred extremely rapid diffusion of the new cultivation methods in progressive agricultural regions of the country.

In the case of software, the demonstration effect was informal and private, but equally dramatic. The spread of information about young Indian engineers who had found high paying jobs as programmers in the USA, and about Indian software export companies that were growing rapidly, generated widespread interest and spurred others to imitate these successful practices. Examples spread by word of mouth from family to family about a son or daughter who had been recruited on campus for a job overseas at ten or twenty times the equivalent Indian salaries. The business press reported the export achievements of every new software startup. State governments announced ambitious plans to promote high tech industry. Politicians vied with each other to appear most in tune with the high tech culture.

In both cases the initiatives of pioneers released an explosion of energy and initiative from the general population. Within less than half a decade in the late 1960s, millions of uneducated traditional farmers rushed to embrace the new production technology for food grains. Within a similar period in the mid-1990s, hundreds of thousands of educated youth throughout the country have been inspired to enlist in computer programming courses and seek employment in the burgeoning software industry.

For the initiative of pioneers to diffuse through society requires the active support of formal organizational mechanisms. Government had a role to play in organizing both India's agricultural and its software activities, but its role in the two instances differed markedly. In the mid 1960s, India lacked dynamic private initiative capable of responding rapidly to challenges and opportunities. An adult population born under foreign rule and slow to believe in its own greater potentials, moved hesitantly to embrace change. India also lacked the social organization needed to support rapid change. Markets were undeveloped and inefficient, so that surplus food production in one region of the country was not efficiently channeled to meet the needs of markets in food deficit regions. Information flowed slowly.

Agricultural education and scientific research, almost exclusively government activities at the time, had to be restructured and upgraded to support the new production technologies. Financial institutions were undeveloped and most wealth was in the form of tangible assets such as land that could not be readily converted into new forms of investment. As a result, the government had to play a very major role in supporting and promoting the Green Revolution through public agencies. Food Corporation of India, Warehousing Corporation, National Seeds Corporation, Fertilizer Corporation, Agricultural Price Commission and countless other agencies were established to provide the social infrastructure for modernization of agriculture.

So prominent was the role of government, that it led many to the conclusion that the government's administrative efforts were responsible for the Green Revolution and that similar results could be achieved in other fields through administrative mandate. The fallacy in this thinking was a major reason for India's slow progress in other fields following the success of Green Revolution. The country had achieved, but it had not yet drawn the essential lesson from its achievement.

The real key to the success of Green Revolution was the response of the rural population to the opportunity. India's leaders astutely recognized that unless the farmer was confident of not only growing more but also selling more grain at a profitable price, there would be no motivation to adopt the new technology. In the absence of established national markets for food grain, bumper harvests in the past resulted in falling prices and little financial benefit to the farmer. To overcome this problem, the Government instituted a guaranteed floor price for food grains and established Food Corporation to market surpluses in food deficit regions.

The importance of these formal institutions has diminished significantly over the past few decades as the new methods have become standard practice among farmers and as private firms, markets, and research organizations have grown in capacity to carry out with greater efficiency the work initially undertaken by government. Development through formal organization has gradually matured into an informal social institution in this field.

In contrast, the principal agencies of the software revolution have been private companies. The role of government in India's software revolution focused primarily on providing a conducive policy framework to encourage the spread of technology and on investment in upgrading the telecommunications infrastructure to support a global information industry. While government did broaden the availability of computer education in government colleges, the dramatic increase in availability of programmers was primarily the result of private initiative.

Software export companies recruited and trained their own staff. Software education and training centers proliferated. Investment in the software industry also came almost exclusively from private sources—banks, public stock offerings, venture capital and some foreign investment—with little government support.

Despite these differences, development in both fields has followed a similar course. The initiative of pioneers led to widespread imitation and adoption. Society accepted the new activity and established formal organizations (in one case public, in the other private) to support the new activity on a wide scale. The knowledge and skills needed for modern agriculture and computer programming have been incorporated in the educational curriculum at higher and lower levels. The social attitudes and expectations of the population have been powerfully influenced by the country's success. Progressive rural farming families teach their youth the values of modern agricultural production. Educated middle class urban families encourage their offspring to pursue careers in high technology.

DETERMINANTS OF DEVELOPMENT

We have described social development as the release and channeling of social energies through more complex social organization to enhance productive capacity and achieve greater results. This process depends upon mechanisms to direct and channel the collective energies of the society into new and more productive forms of activity. We can identify four distinctly different levels or types of mechanism that serve this function—social aspirations, government authority, social-cultural structure, and social know-how in the form of science, technology and productive skills.

SOCIAL ASPIRATIONS

Economically, development occurs when productivity rises, enabling people to produce more, earn more and consume more. To do so, they have to be motivated to learn new skills, adapt to new work processes, and adopt new technology, changes which in past ages have met with considerable resistance.

The driving force behind the whole movement is psychological. At the deepest level the energies of society are directed by the collective's subconscious aspirations. Society's self-conception of what it wants to become releases an aspiration of the collective for accomplishment. That aspiration exerts a powerful influence on the activities of the society. India's twin revolutions were spurred by a growing aspiration of Indian society for security, prosperity and enjoyment. A similar aspiration spurs middle class Americans today to invest their savings in the stock market.

We have traced the evolution of social aspirations in India from pre-Independence to the present day. The earliest expression was an aspiration for political freedom and self-determination. After Independence this aspiration evolved into an urge for self-sufficiency, a willingness to try new things and take risks. More recently it has matured into a movement of rising expectations permeating all levels of Indian society.

At the turn of the 20th Century, many Americans of humble birth saw or read about neighbours, friends or others of their class who rose rapidly out of poverty into prosperity. Their example raised the aspirations and expectations of a whole generation of Americans and the generations that followed it. So powerful was this budding movement that it prompted Henry Ford to conceive of the then outlandish notion of building a car affordable by the ordinary man. In 1900 only 8000 cars were produced in the entire USA to meet the needs of a small wealthy class. By 1929, Ford Motors alone had built 15 million Model Ts to meet the aspirations of the masses.

The revolution of rising expectations, a term first used to describe Asia's awakening in the early 1950s, is the single most powerful force yet unleashed for social development. It marks a stage in which individual members of society not only venture to dream or hope or work for higher levels of accomplishment, but in which those aspirations have coalesced into a conviction and expectation that they will achieve, possess and enjoy more than their parents or they themselves have in the past.

Expectations rise when physical security and essential material needs have been met, when fear of punishment or social ostracism is withdrawn, when rights are safeguarded democratically, when information and urbanization expose people mentally and physically to possibilities and achievements they did not previously know even existed, when technology facilitates higher productivity, and when education enlightens attitudes and elevates social awareness.

Without rising aspirations and expectations, society would not make the effort and take the risks to acquire new forms of behaviour to achieve greater results. The psychological motive is primary, the mechanical, technological and organizational processes are secondary. Some forms of economic analysis tend to view these secondary levers as the driving force and thereby miss the essential determinant of the process.

In the course of social development, society is moved by a range of different psychological motives--the quest for survival and self-preservation, the urge to possess land, the seeking for social status and power, and the pursuit of wealth. The revolution of rising expectations represents a new and more powerful motive force for development, for by its nature it is not limited, as all the others have been, to a specific class or section of society.

GOVERNMENT AUTHORITY

Like social aspirations, the authority of government has the capacity to direct the flow of social energies through the instrumentation of law, public policies, administrative procedures, controls, incentives and fear of punishment. Here too there is a graded hierarchy of stages through which government influences the development process. Monarchy is a highly centralized form of government organization with significant capacity to restrict freedom and prevent unwanted activities, but with very limited power to promote social development, because of its limited power to positively motivate and direct human initiative. Modern authoritarian states have augmented the power of government to compel and control by evolving complex organizational mechanisms to reach out into every field of social activity. Its members submit by necessity to the power of the state, but continuously seek for ways around the strictures and demands it places upon them.

As the 20th century experiments in Eastern Europe amply demonstrate, its power as an instrument for development is severely limited. Countries with authoritarian governments that have succeeded in releasing social initiative for economic development, such as China, Taiwan and South Korea, have done so by loosening social control over economic activities, while retaining it over political activities.

Modern forms of democracy greatly enhance the development capabilities of society. They are not only capable of enforcing a rule of law which to a large extent the population willingly accepts as in its own interest. They also promote far greater development of individual aspirations, thought, capacity, skill and initiative.

The accountability of a democratically elected government necessitates that it continuously institute measures perceived as beneficial to the electorate. Working through decentralized self-governing structures, it empowers more and more centers of activity in the society, leading to greater creativity and innovation. The basic human rights it endorses elevate aspirations and release human energies for higher accomplishment.

The impact of democracy on development was illustrated by Nobel laureate economist Amartya Sen when he observed that no democratic country with a free press and independent judiciary has suffered a famine in this century. India's Green Revolution is a powerful testament to the power of governmental authority, though in this and every other instance, government's role cannot substitute for social readiness and social initiative, it can only aid in preparing that readiness, releasing that initiative and organizing the new activities.

SOCIAL-CULTURAL AUTHORITY

Government exercises authority over its citizens through law, administration and enforcement. Society exercises a far more persuasive authority over its members through its ideas, attitudes, customs and values. Different societies may develop at very different rates and in different directions under very similar forms of government, due to differences in social and cultural authority.

Modern societies are far more free and tolerant than those of previous centuries, yet they continue to exert a very powerful force on their members; only, the character of that force has changed. From being predominantly negative in the form of prohibitions and strictures, now the force of social authority acts far more as a spur to initiative, than a bar. The pressure felt by middle and working class families to 'keep up with the Joneses' has become pervasive throughout the world. The bold initiative of a poor farmer in rural India to dig a bore well and become prosperous could act as stimulus for the rapid development of ten surrounding villages because the competitive pressure of social authority compelled his neighbours to keep up with his level of accomplishment.

The spread of education tends to enhance this tendency. Apart from the practical knowledge and skills it imparts, modern education also instills a greater sense of individual self-respect and social rights that impels the individual to seek and maintain status in society.

KNOW-HOW

Here we include the complete range of capacities that determine the ability of the people to physically direct their energies to achieve productive results. The most important of these are scientific knowledge, technology and productive skills. These may appear very different in nature and action from social aspirations, government and social authority, but the character of their influence on development is quite similar. They provide the direction for the efficient organization of mental, social and material energies. Each of them carries with it an inherent authority and imposes a certain discipline on the expression of social energies. This authority usually takes the form of an impersonal authority of standards, rules and systems, such as the rules for maintaining an orderly flow of air traffic.

Adopting a higher level of technology, whether that involved in the cultivation of hybrid wheat, space travel or electronic commerce requires adherence to more stringent procedures and greater organization, without which it does not work. The Internet is a recent example of a technology that promotes freer and easier commercial and personal transactions, but accomplishes it by imposing rigorous standards of discipline on users in the form of a common computer language for communication.

MOTIVES FOR DEVELOPMENT

Societies throughout the world are presently preoccupied with achieving the material results of social development. But it is interesting to note that the process itself does not appear to be driven exclusively or perhaps even primarily by material motives, although these are uppermost in the social consciousness at the present time. Even in instances where material needs and wants have approached saturation, the process shows no signs of abating in speed or intensity. On the contrary, the momentum that has led to such incredible achievements over the past century continues to accelerate. In our search for the fundamental motive that drives the process, we have to look beyond the material preoccupations by which it is currently characterized.

While it is difficult to document at the social level, at the individual level it is readily apparent that physical security and comfort are important but by no means the only or even the most powerful motives for human action. Once these needs are met, there is still the seeking for social prestige and influence, the impulse of curiosity, the thirst for understanding, the drive for accomplishment, the urge for invention and creativity, the attraction of complexity and rich variety of experience-and the irrepressible and inexhaustible quest for enjoyment that all of these activities engender.

The process of development, even the limited sphere of social development, is not driven exclusively by material motives or confined to material achievements. The goals societies and individuals seek are determined by their needs and their values. In the hierarchy of needs, physical survival, security, and comfort are primary. Vital, social and mental needs gain prominence when the basic physical needs are met. As society prospers, the vital urge for intensity, excitement, enjoyment, adventure, changing experience and self-expression become more important determinants. Beyond these lie the mental urge for curiosity, knowledge, creativity and imagination, and the aspiration for spiritual realization.

This concept of development holds very important implications for the future of humanity and the prospects for progress in the next century. Its suggests that there are no inherent limits either to the speed or to the extent of the development process, other than those imposed by the limitations of our thought, knowledge and aspirations. If we change our view, the character of this process can be transformed from the slow, trial and error subconscious process we have known in the past to a swift, sure leaping progress from height to greater height.

PHASES OF HUMAN CHOICE

Social development has always involved a tension between two poles of its existence, collective and individual. The collective strives to ensure its preservation, perpetuation and development, preparing and compelling its individual members to abide by its traditions, laws and values, and contribute their energy and effort to defend and support the community.

At the same time, individual members strive to ensure their survival, to preserve and, whenever possible, to elevate their material and social positions, personal comfort and enjoyment. For a very long period of recorded history, the collective compelled the submission and obedience of its members to support the development and free exercise of choice by a very limited number of individuals constituting its ruling elite. This tendency reached its acme in the divine right of kings, a doctrine that effectively made the whole society subservient to the whims and fancies of a single individual as an embodiment of the collective will and collective good. All served so that one person could live fully. Human progress over the past five centuries has moved very far away from this extreme pole of collective domination. The collective has discovered a new formula for its progress-all individuals should be encouraged to develop so that the collective may develop to the maximum.

The translation of this new principle into practice has taken several centuries and is still only partially realised. But the direction is clearly reflected in the continuous move towards democracy, universal education, human rights, and access to social opportunities. Society is discovering that providing the maximum human choice to its individual members is the most effective means of releasing human energy, creativity and initiative for the maximum development of the collective.

The Protestant Reformation was a landmark for Western society in the emergence of individual choice in the field of religion. A parallel shift has been identified by historians as one of the root causes for the decline of feudalism in Western Europe. The aristocracy discovered that a free farmer working for himself generated higher production and more tax revenue than an indentured serf working for mere subsistence. Since then society has experimented boldly with new ways to increase the range and quality of individual choice within a collective social framework. In subsequent centuries the rise of democracy extended human choice to the political field and the market system has institutionalized economic choice for workers and consumers.

But the collective's decision to empower individual choice can best be viewed as the first rather than the last step in human development. For the decision of the collective to encourage individual human choice is no guarantee that individuals will accept and exercise that choice or, if they do so, that they will do so wisely.

The phase of human choice that has characterized this century as the "century of the common man" can also been characterized as one in which most individual members continue to define their opinions, attitudes, values, preferences and aspirations very largely in terms that the collective sanctions and approves. Society may have consented to creative individuals exercising free choice, but for most individuals there remains a strong motivation to conform to the views and expectations of the collective and to depend on the collective as the primary determinant. So strong is this urge for conformity that even in science, a person's social position and prestige are often more powerful determinants of how the scientific community responds than the objectivity or rationality of the views expressed.

We can conceive of a time in the future when society has evolved to what we may term a second phase of human choice. In this society, not only the collective, but most of its individual members as well would have the realization that the individual human being is the determinant of its own future. This would constitute a true society of individuals, arriving at their own ideals, beliefs and values, discovering and expressing more fully their own innate potentials, rather than continuously looking to the collective as a role model for direction and support. We can imagine that this phase would be marked by an enormously enhanced level of energy, fresh initiative, innovation, invention, creativity and free expression and a far more rapid general advancement of the society as a whole in whatever fields of activity it chooses to develop. It might be a society of pioneers.

Yet such a phase, if achieved, would not in any way lessen the tension between the individual and the collective. Rather it might intensify the conflict to the point of threatening social cohesion and stability, in much the same way as the social and economic liberation of women in Western society may have affected the social institution of marriage. It might even become a society of rebels or revolutionaries with little tolerance for the status quo or the views of the collective. For an ultimate reconciliation of individuality with collective existence, we must envision a further phase of development in which social stability is achieved through the conscious understanding and consent of its individual members rather than by the force of collective authority or external limits imposed on the power of individual self-assertion. In this phase, the individual would advance beyond the discovery of his own uniqueness and inner capacity to discover the complementary truth that the individual is a portion and expression of the collective society and can achieve maximum fulfillment only by discovering and relating positively with the other aspects and expressions of self which also form part of the larger social organism.

If this comes to pass, we would then have witnessed the transition of society through three phases of emergence from undifferentiated collective existence.

- The undifferentiated phase is one in which the individuality is undeveloped and individual choice is suppressed or restricted to a very small ruling elite. The collective imposes its values on the individual.
- Gradually the collective comes to recognize the necessity and value of actively promoting the development and expression of individual human choice in its members as a means for its own greater development. The collective discovers the value of the individual human being and the power of free human choice. This is the phase which most societies are in different stages of transiting: individuality is nominally encouraged, yet the vast majority of people depend psychologically on the collective as the primary determinant and power for their development and subconsciously act in conformity with its expectations.
- In this phase, individual members of society discover the source of creative energy and unlimited human potential within themselves and draw on that source to achieve far higher levels of development in any fields they pursue. The individual discovers the value and power of individual human choice. Conflict between the collective and its members would still be possible and could even increase.
- A phase could come in which individual members discover that they are only individual expressions of the collective and that their existence is fulfilled in consciously lending their energies for the pursuit and fulfillment of the aspirations of the collective. The developed individual consciously affirms the values of the collective as his or her own. This achievement would mark a further phase in the social development of the collective. It might also prepare the possibility of a truly spiritual development for the human community founded on the twin truths of spiritual freedom and spiritual oneness.

PARALLELS BETWEEN SOCIAL AND BUSINESS DEVELOPMENT

During a workshop presentation at the November 1998 World Academy Conference on the Global Century held in Vancouver, Canada, businessman

Walt Stinson drew some interesting parallels between the principles of development theory outlined in the Human Choice paper and principles of business development set forth in several books by Fred Harmon, Garry Jacobs and Robert Macfarlane. We believe that the parallels he observed arise from the fact that both societies and businesses develop just as to the same process, one macro, the other micro.

We wish to identify some points of correspondence here as a basis for further exploration during the Madras meeting.

- In the case of both business and society, development can be defined as an upward directional movement from lesser to greater levels of energy, efficiency, quality, productivity, complexity, comprehension, creativity, mastery, enjoyment and accomplishment.
- Businesses, like societies, develop as a result of a self-conception that is sometimes conscious, often subconscious. Both the democratic union of the 13 original American colonies and India's Green Revolution were the result of the conscious self-conception of a few perceptive leaders, while the population-at-large remained only vaguely aware of the process it was participating in. In the case of business, the original self-conception is usually the creation of a founding entrepreneur, but over time many other people contribute to its formulation. A noted instance of conscious self-conception was Fred Smith's idea for establishing an overnight delivery business to compete with United Parcel Service and the US Postal Service, at a time when both were already multi-billion dollar operations. The company he founded in the early 1970s, Federal Express, became for a time the fastest growing company of all time and now has annual revenues exceeding $12 billion. Smith's conscious conception may have been partially shared by many of the company's managers and employees, but many others may have participated in the process as part of their routine employment with only a vague notion of the larger vision that inspired its leaders.
- The development of a business, like the development of a society, is fueled by the aspiration of its people. In the case of business, the aspiration of the owners and leaders is a critical determinant of how far and how fast the business grows. In the case of the society, the role of leadership is played by entrepreneurial pioneers that initiate new activities and the psychological intensity of their pursuit is a critical determinant of success. But in either case, the greater the aspiration of all the people involved, the more powerful the impetus for accomplishment.
- We stated in Human Choice that surplus energy is an essential condition for social development. Only in the presence of surplus

capacity can new activities be supported. The same is true in business. Companies struggling for survival or to meet the minimum requirements of their customers lack the excess capacity needed to plan and initiate new activities or elevate their functioning to a higher level of organization.

- New modes of activity are introduced in society by pioneering individual initiatives that are imitated and disseminated by others, diffuse through the society and are eventually accepted and integrated with the normal functioning of the society. New modes of activity are introduced in a company by pioneering individual initiatives that are imitated and disseminated by others, diffuse through the company, and are eventually accepted and integrated with the normal functioning of the company.
- Authority is a fundamental principle of organization that is essential to the survival and development of both societies and companies. Government, social and cultural authority as expressed through social norms, systems, institutions, laws, customs, and values determine the effectiveness with which surplus energy is converted by society into productive power. Corporate authority is expressed more and more through the discipline of impersonal rules, systems, coordination of activities, policies, corporate culture and values that determine the effectiveness with which surplus energy is converted by a business into productive power, rather than by top down personal exercise of authority by a management hierarchy. But regardless of whether the form is personal or impersonal, this discipline is fundamental to the successful functioning of an organization.
- Social know-how in the form of technology, practical knowledge and skills determines the conversion of productive power into material results in both society and business.
- The productivity of social resources is not subject to any inherent limits. It depends on the attitudes, information, knowledge, organization and skills creatively applied–*i.e.* on powers of mind. The productivity of a company's resources is not subject to any inherent limits. It depends on the attitudes, information, knowledge, organization and skills creatively applied–*i.e.* on powers of mind.
- In research for his upcoming book on business in 2010, Fred Harmon is exploring the relationship between the five essential components of a business—market, technology, people, capital and organization—and the five parallel components of social development—social needs, technology, people, resources and organization. As a microcosm and child of the society, companies develop by attuning themselves to the direction, trends and changing needs of the wider society of which

they are a part in each of these five major areas. This relationship is especially apparent in larger national and multinational corporations whose development is often closely tied to parallel developments in the societies in which they function.

- On the company's level of awareness, aspiration, organization, values, knowledge and skills.
- Both companies and societies depend for their development on three levels of organized infrastructure—a physical organization of production, transportation, communication, *etc.*; a social organization of legal, financial, commercial, and educational systems and institutions; and a mental organization of information, technology and knowledge. All three are needed for the achievement of progressively more complex forms of economic activity.
- For both businesses and societies, values represent that highest form of organization for directing human energies in constructive and productive activities. The quality and height of the values set the limits on the magnitude of developmental achievements.

MODERNITY AND SOCIAL THEORY

Postmodernists have launched a radical assault on modern social theory. As part of their broadside against the totalizing features of Enlightenment rationalism, Jean Baudrillard, Jean-François Lyotard, Jacques Derrida, and others reject claims about social theory's capacity to articulate modernity's complex contours and to contribute to progressive social change. Extreme postmodernists like Baudrillard make claims concerning "the end of the social" and "the end of history, " which suggest that any form social theory is obsolete.

Others, such as Lyotard, contend that "the postmodern condition" calls for a new type of theory that demolishes the bases of modern social theory's assumptions and systematic project. More specifically, postmodernists contend that modern theory's core meta-assumptions concerning "representation, " "social coherence, " and the "rational subject" result in foundationalist, essentialist, reductionist, overly totalized, and homogenized thought. We argue that the postmodernist's assault on modern social theory and historical modes of social criticism undermines their own sweeping claims about epochal change, and culminates in a one-sided emphasis on cultural and social fragmentation that ignores societal interdependencies and devalues social solidarities.

Moreover, we contend that the postmodernists have treated the modern tradition too one-sidely and monovocally, focusing almost entirely on its excesses and errors. For while positivist and hyperrationalist elements abound in their works, modern social theorists also developed themes pointing to the limits of their assumptions that anticipated the postmodern critique. They also had a much more balanced approach to the play of integrating and disintegrating forces than does postmodern theory today. Consequently, while postmodernists address some problematic features of modern theory, their caricature of the tradition and radical break with the approach ignores the extent to which it continues to provide resources for the projects of understanding social reality and promoting social reconstruction.

THE POSTMODERN CRITIQUE OF SOCIAL THEORY

Postmodernists attack classical theory's claims about mapping the social totality, detecting social progress, and facilitating beneficial social change. Since many postmodern critics are former Marxists who now reject socialism and even welfare state reformism, they advance especially scathing criticism of Marxism's global claims concerning history and universal emancipation.

The postmodern critique holds that virtually all modern social theory springs from an uncritical Enlightenment faith in science and reason and leads to "grand narratives" that legitimate political repression and distinctively modern forms of social and cultural oppression.

Postmodernists argue that social theory contributes to legitimating centralized systems of power and planning that destroy individuality and block the creative forces of language and desire. In order to avert these problems, postmodernists maintain that social and cultural critics must make a clean break with Enlightenment rationalism by rejecting classical theory's meta-assumptions about representation, social coherence, and the subject. Postmodern theorists adopt the poststructuralist strategy of severing the connection between signs and their referents, thus abandoning modern theorists' efforts to represent the "real.

"For example, Derrida treats language as a form of "free play, "independent of a "transcendental signified," and rejects claims about its capacity to objectively represent extralinguistic realities. He also believes that the modern propensity to center on "the" meaning or central proposition of a text blurs differences and diminishes the richness of linguistic creativity. His deconstructive attack on modern epistemology aims to free heterogeneous desires and signifiers from linguistic constraints.

Baudrillard goes much further, evaporating social reality into a contingent play of "simulacra. " While modern epistemology focuses on the correspondence of representations to external objects, Baudrillard claims that signs and images have replaced "the real" in the contemporary era. Speaking explicitly of a new postmodern age, he states: "We are in a logic of simulation which has nothing to do with a logic of facts and an order of reasons".

The proliferation of contradictory images and messages "implodes" the boundaries between signs and referents, and between reality and fiction, ultimately, dissolving the concepts of truth and meaning. The experience of the postmodern homo significans is constituted by language, texts, codes, and images without connection to an external world. Postmodernists treat different social theories merely as conflicting narratives, or incommensurable perspectives, rather than as portrayals of factual realities that can be judged in accordance with intersubjective standards and procedures for determining valid knowledge.

Although postmodernists do not attempt to justify their views methodologically, they privilege their own positions or narratives over competing accounts of the historical conjuncture and are especially dismissive of modernist perspectives. Secondly, postmodernists emphasize pervasive cultural fragmentation and social disintegration, rejecting the very concept of a coherent social order. They conceive of postmodernity as an exceedingly complex matrix of discontinuous processes; of ubiquitous, instantaneous, and non-linear changes; of fractured and overwhelming space; of cacophonous voices; and of divergent images and messages, all of which produce a schizophrenic fragmentation of experience.

Baudrillard speaks of "the end" of the social, of meaning, and of history, claiming that events lack consequences beyond the moment because they shift so rapidly and so radically that their impact is lost and because the saturation of "messages" reduces them to mere "noise. " Due to mass indifference following from the continuous novelty, routinization of spectacle, and excess of information, all interest in the past and concern about the future is lost. The obliteration of standards for interpreting the meaning of events and for discerning between different pieces of information produces a nihilistic relativization of experience; postmodern life is reduced to one-dimensional presence and indeterminacy that can only be felt and experienced, but not coherently interpreted. Comprehension of the social is demolished by the "eclipse of distance" by implosive dedifferentiation of boundaries, and by the consequent incorporation of spectators into a world of media and consumerist fantasy.

Social classes and other structured social relations are decomposed into a multiplicity of indeterminate and disconnected experiences and events. The extreme cultural fragmentation and incoherence of postmodern experience supposedly puts an end to modern theory's global discourses about obdurate social structures and patterned social processes. Thirdly, postmodernists herald the demise of the philosophic subject that formerly undergirded the conceptions of representation and social coherence in modern philosophy and social theory. Following Descartes and modern epistemology, classical theorists treated humanity as rational subjects who are capable of achieving an unambiguous understanding of the external world and of applying this knowledge to improve the human condition.

By contrast, Friedrich Nietzsche, the most important forerunner of postmodernist thought, characterized the modern philosophic subject as a "little changeling" who should be disposed of; he argued that "there is no `being' behind doing, effecting, becoming; the 'doer' is merely a fiction added to the deed.... ". In Nietzsche's view, the fictive subject is a byproduct of cultural homogenization and conflicting desires and strivings. However, by turning them inward to internalized norms, self control, and guilt, the myth of subjectivity transforms modern subjects into a tame and conformist shadow of what an individual could be. Like Nietzsche, postmodernists reject the concept of a rational and autonomous subject because it allegedly represses human spontaneity, difference, desire, and power.

Foucault contends that the modern subject is a product of Enlightenment efforts to make "man" an object of scientific knowledge and of social manipulation by new disciplinary and therapeutic institutions. According to his genealogical studies of the interplay of knowledge and power, the subject's highly refined capacities for self-observation and self-regulation harden modernity's "panoptical" regime of discipline and domination by elevating social control and cultural homogenization to unimagined heights.

But Foucault implies that the modern "episteme" of thought is crumbling as others have done in the past and that the subject will disappear "like a face drawn in sand at the edge of the sea". Baudrillard claims that the advent of postmodernity has already completely erased the subject and that the "drama of the subject at odds with his objects and with his image" is over. He declares that "we" are now "terminals of multiple networks" not creators of the script.

Baudrillard states:

- "You are news, you are the social, the event is you, you are involved, you use your voice, *etc.* " A turnabout of affairs by which it becomes impossible to locate an instance of the model, of power, of the gaze, of the medium itself, since you are always already on the other side. No more subject, focal point, center or periphery: but pure flexion or circular inflection.

Given the fractal and multiple nature of the postmodern self, Baudrillard declares that the reign of the "rational" subject is over. By rejecting its core meta-assumptions about representation, social coherence, and subjectivity, postmodernists undermine the very possibility of modern social theory. Yet, contrary to the postmodern caricature, most classical theorists recognized the limits of their own theoretical practices.

Because they envision the classical tradition in a monovocal fashion as if it were nothing more than a replication of the worst aspects of Enlightenment thought, postmodernists ignore the fact that the classical theorists developed epistemologically critical as well as dogmatic themes. Overreacting to its positivist features and blind to the fact that modern theorists began a critique of Enlightenment thought, postmodernists abandon altogether the vocation of classical social theory to depict and to change social reality.

CRITICAL VS. DOGMATIC THEMES IN CLASSICAL THEORY

Classical social theory addressed several types of "global" questions: "What is the structure of this particular society as a whole?"; "Where does this society stand in human history?"; and "What varieties of men and women now prevail in this society and in this period?".

By putting modern societies in broad historical perspective, by emphasizing the linkages between their differentiated social institutions, and by expressing the potentialities for normatively guided social change, classical theorists developed discourses that facilitated comprehension and discussion of, and posed responses to, the rise of modernity and its ambiguous constellation of progressive and oppressive features. Classical theorists initiated the tradition of modern social theory by conceptually delineating the historical transition from traditional society to modern society.

They created polar ideal types to systematically articulate the dominant social structures of the old and new societies and to specify the primary developmental processes that were radically transforming social life from the local to the international level. Classical theorists provided comprehensive perspectives to make sense out of the processes that were generating new modes of individuality, economy, polity, society, and culture constituting the new social order of modernity.

Classical theorists presumed that they could represent these macroscopic social realities, coherently portray their complex modes of interdependence and fragmentation, and help historical subjects transform their social worlds and actively control their fates. These meta-assumptions were sometimes employed narrowly and dogmatically and, at other times, reflexively and selfcritically. Although they initiated a revision of the tradition, classical social theorists reproduced the contradictory themes of Enlightenment thought, sometimes mechanistically replicating its excessive faith in science and reason and, at others, employing its critical rationality and epistemological selfreflexivity to their own theories and to the social world.

The positivistic side of classical theory treated science as if it was a new religion with the power to detect a lawful order behind the chaos and to provide guaranteed solutions to the new social problems. Positivists combined this excessive faith in science with a belief that reason could precisely represent the broadest features and trends of social development. They implied that social theory could unproblematically grasp reality, provide an exact system of knowledge, and serve as an instrument of enlightenment and social change.

Such dogmatic arguments grossly exaggerated theory's powers of representation, overstated the integration of society, and attributed far too much rationality to the subject. In addition, they sometimes spoke deterministically about homogeneous paths of development that operated mechanistically, ignoring regional and national differences and lacking sensitivity to particularity and differences. Theories of broad scope always depend on a precarious balancing of the general and particular, and always risk overgeneralization. However, classical theorists framed their arguments too broadly without sufficient historical specificity; nearly all of them spoke about traditional and modern societies too uniformly.

By contrast, classical theorists sometimes articulated a critical reflexivity that acknowledged the limits of representation, that treated social coherence as a precarious and unstable outcome of integrating and fragmenting forces, and that envisaged socially differentiated subjects as having limited rationality and partial integration depending on always problematic adjustments to changing historical conditions.

Yet contrary to the postmodernists, classical theorists attempted to develop intersubjective standards to rationally justify their practices on empirical-historical and theoretical grounds from which they could criticize their own and other theories. Thus, they concurred that careful conceptualization based on empirical enquiry could represent with reasonable accuracy the salient attributes of extralinguistic features of social life as well as their discursive aspects. But especially in regard to macroscopic issues most classical theorists understood that their theories could not possibly capture social reality in all its richness, particularity, and complexity.

In their critical moments, classical theorists treated their approaches as tentative arguments subject to revision or disconfirmation. Indeed, even their conception of science emphasized the need for continual revision of theory on the basis of new empirical information and arguments. Yet classical social theorists seldom addressed the hermeneutic complexities of representational thinking, nor did they closely probe the inherent uncertainties that characterize all judgements about the relationship of theory to social reality. But especially while defending the validity of their substantive positions, they often spoke with too much certainty.

In their dogmatic positivist moments, classical theorists implied a great divide between subject and object, treating the investigator as a mere spectator and "facts" as if they were unaffected by the interpretive process. Their Cartesian emphasis on the power and clarity of the impartial scientific observer resulted in extremely one-sided interpretations of social reality being granted an irrefutable objectivity and universality that blocked genuine empirical enquiry, discussion, and criticism.

Marx's critique of Hegel's theory of the state and of the German "ideologists" raised the problem of this dogmatic type of theorizing early in the classical tradition. But Marx himself made essentialist errors that derived partly from his overweening confidence in the representational powers of historical materialism. Other thinkers, such as Max Weber and John Dewey, were more sensitive to the inherently perspectival, interpretive, and uncertain nature of all theoretical practices. Still, classical theorists usually recognized that all representations of society are imperfect and must be subjected to potentially disconfirming enquiries.

This maxim of Newtonian experimentalism was earlier a centerpiece of Enlightenment thinking that had already smashed the fixed ideals of foundationalism. The critical side of classical social theory thus encouraged openended discourse because it viewed social theories as incomplete expressions of changing social conditions. And since it treated complex social phenomena as being always mediated by linguistic frameworks and inextricably entwined with social interests and ideological presuppositions, the critical approach contradicted positivist claims about exact representation of an "objective" social world. Moreover, none of the classical social theorists rejected representation entirely because they believed that, if portrayals of social reality were treated merely as narratives, the non-arbitrary, intersubjective bases for discussing, evaluating, comparing, and disconfirming social theories would be eliminated.

Classical theorists viewed society as a differentiated structural whole. Despite strong disagreement about the level of interdependence and types of connectedness, they still attempted to address the organizational properties and developmental processes that linked smaller groupings into larger interdependent societal or trans-societal units. In contrast to postmodernists, classical theorists believed that the social world has a complex coherence that could be expressed theoretically. But they were not always mindful of the fact that social organizations and groups are not clearly bounded, unproblematic totalities.

For example, the organic metaphor, employed by many theorists, reified social structure and processes, exaggerating their stability and coherence and understating their discontinuities and particularities. Yet some classical theorists anticipated the postmodern themes of social discontinuity, fragmented meaning, and the eclipse of totality. Addressing the consequences of disenchantment, Weber asserted that: "culture's every step forward seems condemned to lead to an ever more devastating senselessness. The advancement of cultural values, however, seems to become a senseless hustle in the service of worthless, moreover self-contradictory, and mutually antagonistic ends".

Weber's commentaries on increasing cultural fragmentation, his methodological broadsides against foundationalism and essentialism, his scathing attacks on secular theodicies of historical progress, his penetrating analyses of the connections between rationalization and domination, and his ardent defence of pluralism against the forces of cultural homogenization all anticipated key postmodern positions. But despite his somber vision of "unbrotherly" modernity and the "iron cage, " Weber still upheld the rational bases of modern social theory, arguing that the empirical uncertainties and ethical ambiguities arising from the conflicting values, multivocal discourses, and clashing interests of modernity must be faced with "intellectual integrity".

A complete rejection of rationalism, in his view, would simply give license to the unreflective, uncritical, and cynical pursuit of vulgar material and ideal interests that already dominated the politics and culture of his day. Therefore, while attempting to theorize the extraordinarily complex, differentiated, and pluralistic features of modernity, Weber defended a critical rationalism based on as clear as possible awareness of the limits and the uncertainty of knowledge.

Classical theory's views of representation and coherence go hand in hand with their assumptions about the individual subject's capacities for instrumentally and normatively comprehending and transforming his or her world. But they often dwelled on the homogenizing features of socialization, equating subjectivity with the passive reception of social norms and values. This conformist conception of subjectivity anchored broader theories that exaggerated societal integration and consensus and that understated the differences between individuals and subgroups. Such essentialist conceptions have frequently appeared and remain central to much social theory. For example, structural-functional theory, which dominated American sociology in the 1950s and 1960s, emphasized the unproblematic internalization of norms and implied a highly integrated vision of postwar society based on alleged "value consensus" and sweeping institutional legitimacy.

Debates over the social subject have been a particularly controversial issue among neo-Marxists, post-structuralists, and feminists because of the assumption that emancipatory change requires rational human agency. Orthodox Marxists spoke confidently about overcoming "false consciousness" and about the fragmented working class inevitably awakening as a unified revolutionary proletariat. Class fragmentation and political, ethnic, religious, and gender segmentation were at first dismissed as epiphenomena that merely postponed the revolutionary proletariat's arrival.

But when it became obvious that capital's homogenizing power was not sufficient to eradicate these social distinctions, some Western Marxists searched for a substitute emancipatory subject or a plurality of subjects, and, more recently, debated whether the conception ought to be dispensed with entirely. But other classical theorists had already developed a more critical conception of the "social-self" contradicting conformist and homogeneous portrayals of subjectivity. Mead argued that determinate individuality arises from a person's responses to his or her unique pattern of associations. In his view, socialization is a differentiating rather than a homogenizing force. Even simple societies are sufficiently complex to insure human diversity, but the individuating conditions are multiplied by modernity's diverse, increasingly voluntaristic, and rapidly changing associations.

In this setting, all persons tend to develop their own unique social network within the larger society. In responding to this complexly differentiated environment, every individual develops a multiplicity of selves, each fitted to the specialized niches of her or his contrasting social contexts. Moreover, Mead did not privilege rational or cognitive capacities of the self at the expense of sense, emotion, and other feelings. And from his pragmatist position, thought often followed practices rather than autocratically leading them. However, Mead's decentered conception of subjectivity still presumes a "complete self" that provides sufficient self-integration to maintain continuity and identity between different social settings, to facilitate new associations, and to make possible critical or rebellious selves.

Mead contended that, by having to respond to highly diverse types of persons in complex social structures, individuals expand their capacities for interpretation, sympathetic identification, and, in particular, "communication. These capacities facilitate integration of the self and society under conditions of social differentiation, and, at the same time, make possible new forms of ethical criticism, social conflict, and rebellious solidarity that increase individual and societal differentiation. According to Mead's theory of the self, voluntaristic social arrangements never emerge smoothly from collective subjectivity and normative consensus.

Instead, uncoerced social relationships must be achieved on the basis of sometimes conflictual communicative processes between differentiated individuals with divergent interests and perspectives. Moreover, these relationships are continuously negotiated in response to changing historical conditions. Mead argued that increased social differentiation produces more diversity, openness, and flexibility and not merely fragmentation and disintegration of the self as postmodernists claim. Yet his view of the subject stands out from the often simplistic, hyperrationalist, and conformist version implied by many other classical theorists. Here the postmodern critique points to serious deficiencies.

However, postmodernists still seem to be amnesic about the Counter-Enlightenment reactionaries who used the alleged irrationality of the subject to justify the need for authoritarian modes of thought and institutions to maintain social order. Mead's thought exemplifies that a more balanced view of the self is possible which abandons the imperious vision of the rational subject, yet without undermining the idea of selfhood and autonomy. Approaches that speak of the disappearance or radical fragmentation of the subject cannot account for uncoerced social action. Such views are not only empirically misguided, but can easily be turned around to support the types of repression that the postmodernists themselves oppose. Classical theorists saw modernity's new types of mass social organization and consequent interdependencies to be dialectically related to opposing forces producing social and cultural fragmentation. They generated standpoints for criticizing society and proposals for social change from the interplay of these integrating and fragmenting conditions. In particular, their "immanent" criticism emphasized the tensions and contradictions between emergent democratic ideals and possibilities of modernity with the new types of domination, oppression, inequality, and polarization.

As with their central metatheoretical assumptions, the classical theorists' historical method of social criticism sometimes resulted in dogmatic, pseudosociological pronouncements and, at others, expressed a critical sensitivity to concrete resources and possibilities for new forms of social solidarity and struggle. At their best, classical theorists expressed the growing aspirations for a freer and more democratic social life in light of the actual historical constraints and opportunities for their realization. Durkheim relentlessly attacked the reckless pursuit of private interest in modernity, but still insisted that the new division of labour produces a state of mutual "dependence" and patterns of "co-operation" that generate their own "intrinsic morality" stressing equality and freedom. Despite the prevailing state of inequality and unfreedom, he argued that traditional forms of ascription were being eroded and that growing social conflicts would eventually result in more highly developed democratic ideals favouring a more just and egalitarian social order.

In a similar fashion, Marx addressed the contradictions between capitalism's democratic ideology and its increasing poverty and class divisions. He hoped to translate this historical contradiction into an instrument of working class struggle to foster revolutionary social change. In his view, expansionary capitalism produces increased repression as well as new forms of resistance that radicalize the bourgeois conceptions of freedom, equality, and affluence and that forge new social bonds of revolutionary solidarity. Thus, Durkheim and Marx's arguments exhibit a historical sensitivity to democratic possibilities arising from the social structure and emergent social movements of modernity.

However, they sometimes spoke dogmatically about the path of societal development and possibilities for realizing freedom and justice. Although they claimed to abandon philosophical "grounds, " classical theorists often treated the progressive features of modernity too optimistically, transforming them into transcendent warranties about a more democratic future.

But, as as suggested, explain below, postmodernists, overreacting to this tendency of classical theory, speak of overwhelming social and cultural fragmentation destroying the historical bases of immanent critique and completely eliminating the possibility of progressive change. By dismissing the metatheoretical underpinnings of classical theory's empirical methodology and historical method of social criticism, postmodernists rule out the strong sociology needed to support their assertions about the rise of a postmodern era and give up the analytic means for clarifying and elaborating the historical bases of their critique of modernity. In the end, the postmodernists' totalizing claims continue in the tracks of classical social theory, but without the conceptual tools and analytic methods to provide a satisfactory account of the alleged postmodern condition.

CULTURAL FRAGMENTATION AND AESTHETIC INDIVIDUALISM

We enter a different theoretical universe when we encounter postmodern theory. Lyotard's battle cry to "wage a war on totality" and his claims about the affinity of "grand narratives" for totalitarianism are aimed generally at Enlightenment social thought, but Marxist theory is an especially important target.

Postmodernists argue that past efforts to transform bourgeois values into a revolutionary ideology, or even into welfare state reformism, have had culturally repressive consequences and that, today, cultural fragmentation nullifies all "moralizing" criticism. Since they believe that critical social theory no longer has any historical bases or any interested publics, postmodernists execute their deconstructive critique of modern theory with the intent of establishing an entirely new basis for cultural criticism.

Because of their strong normative inclination towards aesthetic individualism, postmodernists equate collectivism, consensual social values, and practically all social solidarities with repression. Following Nietzsche, they want to free modernity's new forms of desire, experience, expression, and creativity from what they believe to be repressive social regulation. Therefore, postmodern theorists have little to say about societal interdependence and social cooperation, and tend to be dismissive of theories, organizations, and movements seeking collective action or mobilization to institute progressive social change. Concurring with the Nietzschean scenario concerning the decline of individuality, Foucault's genealogy of "disciplinary" society describes the ordering and reduction of "human multiplicities" by a new secular morality that utilizes the therapeutic ideology of helping others to justify overarching social control based on moral surveillance and accounting.

While "panoptical" regimes emerged in the form of prisons, mental hospitals, and other asylums of the late 18th and early 19th centuries, the modern method of discipline and surveillance institutions spread rapidly to new sites. Consequently, the emergent professions of "medicine, psychology, education, public assistance, {and} `social work'" produced a "universal reign of the normative" based on omnipresent self-surveillance and self-discipline. The modern system of control everywhere "differentiates, hierarchizes, homogenizes, excludes.... {and} normalizes. " "Normalization, " here, refers to the processes by which individuals are produced as subjects to become useful and docile, adjusting comfortably to social domination. But Baudrillard declares that the modern disciplinary order described by Foucault, has been superseded by postmodern "simulation, " "deterrence, " "fascination, " and "discontinuous indeterminism.

"Instead of social control based on a mixture of direct coercion and self-regulation, the semiotic control system operates by "programming" and "indefinite reproduction" of disjunctive models. Change occurs randomly through mutations in sign production rather than being the creation of rational subjects.

Moralizing events, like the Watergate hearings, are merely simulations of scandal that deter people from recognizing the fundamental corruption of the bourgeois system as a whole. Since Baudrillard's postmodern "hyperreality" lacks animate critical values and social movements, the normative and societal bases for immanent criticism are demolished. Although Baudrillard's position is admittedly extreme, other postmodernists agree that the traditional Left's historical method of critique is moribund. Even Jameson who remains in the Marxist camp, speaks of "a linguistic fragmentation of social life" that impoverishes normative languages and paralyzes immanent critique. A "stupendous proliferation of social codes" and the transformation of language into a melange of contentious "jargons" and "badges" puts an end to public discourse. Thus, the discursive field lacks any trace of a "great collective project" or, even, of living national ideals. These postmodern cultural conditions end the Enlightenment dialectic of mass emancipatory movements arising from the immanent contradictions between democratic ideology and capitalism. Frankfurt School critical theorists, during their "dialectic of Enlightenment" phase, came to similar pessimistic conclusions about immanent critique.

Since the progressive side of bourgeois values seemed to be exhausted, they contended that a fundamental critique of rationalism is required to recover oppositional thought. Their search for an alternative metatheoretic basis for their cultural criticism led these theorists to Nietzsche's argument that art, in direct contrast to science and morality, is "fundamentally opposed" to the ascetic ideal. Although postmodernists forego critical theory's strong emphasis on "redemption" through artistic transcendence, their employment of the values of pluralism, difference, and the proliferation of meaning presumes an individualistic aesthetic standpoint. Their implicit normative position upholds the quest for experience and for individual development in opposition to the forces of cultural homogenization.

Since they reject foundationalism and essentialism as well as historicism, postmodernists avoid evoking any specific historical developmental scenario or universal morality in order to affirm the spontaneously arising freeplay of diverse desires and tastes. Although most postmodernists do not directly articulate a broader political vision, their aesthetic individualism requires an institutional network that favours pluralism and provides social space for the development of heterogeneous individuality.

Moreover, aesthetic individualism combined with a cynical attitude about emancipatory values and movements provides a very thin basis for social criticism or political action. While Foucault's analyses of the dialectic of domination and resistance establish the matrix for a critical micropolitics, his arguments suggest that domination, flowing from the imposition of power/knowledge, seeps from virtually all features of modern society. The system of control is so monolithic and overpowering that it is hard to envisage how any meaningful social change might take place from within.

Moreover, his rejection of macropolitics undermines efforts to develop theoretical languages to address regional, national, or international publics about global social issues and to facilitate large-scale collective actions or interventions. Lyotard argues that critical social theories which emphasize revolution or totalizing structural transformation contribute directly to totalitarian political domination. He rejects consensus as intrinsically repressive and all schemes of macro-theory and politics as "terroristic. " Instead, he wants to replace their global discourses with pluralistic theoretical practices that stress playful participation in a wide variety of language games and the creation of diverse microscopic approaches and critiques. But it is hard to imagine how these heterogeneous microtheories will escape hermetic particularism and irrelevancy. In this regard, mainstream sociology is already a "postmodern" discipline; its extreme subdisciplinary differentiation, intellectual fragmentation, and multiplicity of specialized voices have put an end to grand narratives. But the absence of broader languages to foster communication between the hyperspecialized subareas and to draw out the public significance of sociological knowledge has simply generated cynicism about professional practices within the discipline and indifference to them on the outside.

Extreme pluralism and the eclipse of broader and critical theorizing has also blocked the translation of social theory into publicly understandable discourses that could promote social change. Furthermore, if one accepts Baudrillard's claims about confused and apathetic masses capable of nothing more than mindless consumption of mass produced images and spectacles, then the formation of publics is impossible and critical theorizing is a wasted effort. No oppositional politics are possible in Baudrillard's postmodern nightmare.

Even aesthetic revolt is futile, because, when "art is everywhere, " the avant-garde becomes another variant of conformist simulation. Under these conditions theorists themselves must play the simulation game, combating indifference with greater indifference and, hopefully, contributing to the simulation machine's inevitable "implosion" from overproduction and ennui. In attempting to save cultural criticism from Marxism, postmodernists generally abandon the language of large publics and transformational politics. Those who retain a micropolitical discourse do not explain how their own criticism will somehow break through the political fragmentation and media white-out of surplus information and mass cynicism. And even if the micropolitical messages somehow get through, it is entirely unclear whether they would have much effect on the centralized organizational sites of social control, planning, and distribution that have formative impact on the macroscopic patterns of well-being and suffering. In this regard, Fraser and Nicholson argue that the postmodernist war against totality forbids the global perspectives necessary for critical social theory:

- One familiar, and arguably essential, genre of normative political theory: identification and critique of macrostructures of inequality and injustice which cut across the boundaries separating relatively discrete practices and institutions. There is no place in Lyotard's universe for critique of pervasive axes of stratification, for critique of broad based relations of dominance and subordination along lines like gender, race, and class.

Postmodernists have not demonstrated why their postpolitical aesthetic of individual development opposes rather than affirms technocracy and consumer capitalism. Because they treat social theories aimed at larger publics and at big social problems as part of the process of repressive cultural homogenization, postmodernists, in the end, break with the politically engaged theorizing of the critical tradition of social theory. Despite their attacks on totalizing theory, postmodernists themselves speak of an epochal break with modernity and claim to map the new postmodern terrain in a culturally critical fashion. But their fetishism of particularity and difference releases them from the responsibility to theorize these global structures and processes systematically, to defend the implicit normative standpoints that guide their cultural criticism, and to reflect critically on its possible political consequences of their approaches. Consequently, postmodern theories do not elaborate new possibilities for overcoming repression or point to concrete directions for democratic societal reconstruction. And when these conditions become too obvious to be ignored, they can still be trivialized as mere "simulacra, " as "deterrents, " or as indirect expressions of "cooptive" power.

CRITICAL SOCIAL THEORY

Post-WW II critical theorists feared that their war-time pessimism about "total administration, " "the culture industry, " and "instrumental rationality" had come true in the affluent "one-dimensional society" of the 1950s. In their view, the consequences of postwar affluence and the capital-labour compromise--suburbs, shopping centers, and TV–translated bourgeois values into the culture of mass consumption and integrated the working class into the system.

At the same time, liberals heralded trends towards educational expansion, increased meritocracy, new informational technologies, service sector growth, social and political pluralism, consumerism, state welfare provisioning,

Keynesian economic policy, and reduced class conflict as the "end of ideology" and the coming of "postindustrial society. " Regardless of their political differences, radicals and liberals alike agreed that the United States seemingly had unlocked the secrets of permanent economic growth and of effective technocratic management of social problems. Since these changes supposedly constituted a qualitative rupture from modern industrial capitalism, postwar society required a new theory that broke sharply with previous models of capitalism and socialism.

But postwar thinkers overestimated the degree and duration of the socio-economic reorganization and middle-class expansion. In the early 1970s, the highly competitive international economic climate eroded the capital-labour accord, while racial violence, urban decline, Vietnam protests, Watergate, resource dependency, deindustrialization, increasing class inequality and poverty, and other severe social dislocations and political conflicts ended the dream of postindustrial consensus. And by the late 1970s, free-market thinking returned with a vengeance in the ruins of welfare state politics. Aggressive claims were made about the virtues of a new service economy driven by informational technologies and by debureaucratized business organizations free of government and union interference.

Responding to these developments, to the perceived bankruptcy of the Left, and to resurgent Right-wing hegemony, postmodernists spoke again of a hypertechnocratic society lacking potential for emancipatory change and demanding new theories and politics. However, the question should be posed whether they, like their postwar counterparts, have been too general and premature in their claims about a fundamental social transition. Is postmodern theory merely a reaction to the ending of the postwar conjuncture or is it even a fleeting response to the conservative regimes that dominated Western superpowers in the 1980s?

Will a sharp change in the political economy and consequent new socio-political dynamics suddenly make the approach obsolete? As the recent events in Eastern Europe, the Soviet Union, and the Middle East make evident, sharp turnabouts are certainly possible even under the most controlled conditions.

Postmodernists cannot provide a strong retort to the above questions because they are uncritical about the historical context of their own ideas. Although they postulate major historical ruptures, the postmodernists overly general vision of history can easily inflate the significance of short-term, conjunctural changes, or passing events.

They also lack the theoretical resources to theorize the very notion of a postmodern rupture because they renounce all global theories along with the objectionable types of grand narratives. Moreover, "modern" and "postmodern" are not empirically self-evident concepts; generally, the terms are sorely undertheorized in the vast literature on the topics. Because postmodernists have jettisoned classical theory's meta-assumptions and historical mode of social criticism, they are not bound by methodological strictures stressing the need to consider countertendencies and socio-historical data that could falsify their claims about culture and politics. Analogous to their own critique of classical Marxism's homogeneous proletarian subject, postmodernists can be accused of an essentialist reduction of discontinuous and discrete cultural phenomena into a single "dedifferentiated" whole.

Given the extreme social and cultural segmentation of contemporary society, even Jameson's characterization of postmodernism as a "cultural dominant" is merely a hypothesis that demands systematic historical enquiry and support. The point is that the lack of a strong sociology makes the postmodernists vulnerable to the same type of errors made earlier by postindustrial theorists. Postmodern theory may express a new historical conjuncture or it may be nothing more than a reaction, by playful cultural critics, to a narrow range of transitory conditions.

But such judgements require a mode of discourse where arguments are open to evidential enquiry and disconfirmation. Theorizing the postmodern demands a periodization and geographical localization of an extremely broad and complex set of phenomena constituting postmodernity. The project calls for: elaboration of the societal network of interdependent institutions; analysis of the key developmental processes and features that produce institutional and socio-political changes, or "postmodernization"; description of the ensemble of artistic, musical, architectural, and other postmodern cultural forms; and enquiry into the complex of socio-cultural conditions producing the postmodern structure of experience.

Also by definition, postmodern implies an understanding of the modern that is of similar scope and complexity to the above claims about a postmodern epochal, which presumes the capacity to systematically delineate the differences between the new and the old epochs. A comprehensive postmodern social theory therefore would synchronically map society's core social structures and diachronically elaborate its central developmental patterns and processes. Properly executed, this type of global theoretic project would provide a language and concepts that raise culturally significant questions to guide enquiries about specific features of particular nations, regions, and communities; that provide models for comparative analyses of individual cases; and that offers conceptual languages inviting translation of disciplinary matters into broader public discourses.

rends towards increased internationalization of the economy, despoliation of the world's natural environment, and radical restructuring of the international political order all call for broad theorizing in the tradition of classical social theory. Even in Marx's time, capitalism's complexity, rapid change, and differentiated structure were difficult to map with precision. However, the task is even harder today with corporate capitalism's exceedingly complex connections and multiplex macroscopic structures and processes, its mix of bureaucratic and "post-Fordist" organizational forms and its vast diversity of information production and management all of which contribute to obscuring capitalism's huge networks of interdependence.

Because cultural fragmentation and pluralism cannot be understood separately from the highly internationalized flows of capital and information or from the machinations of hyper-rationalized private and public sector organizations, "the postmodern condition" increases rather than decreases the need for critical global analyses of big structures. National and transnational interdependencies have never been broader than they are today, and the discordant mix of decentralizing and centralizing tendencies require new systematic theorization and mapping. Most postmodernists want to preserve cultural criticism in the face of homogenizing forces and imposing threats to the individual.

In this regard, they have not broken completely with the critical variants of classical social theory nor with more recent theorists who have continually attempted to renew the project. However, postmodernists excuse themselves from clarifying their own implicit normative claims and political intentions. The totalizing negativity of the postmodernist stance is a product of their weak sociology and one-sided theoretical emphasis on fragmentation. Giving up the historical basis for cultural criticism without a careful reckoning of the prospects for social change merely opens the door to resignation, irrationalism, and even to revival of essentialism.

Against postmodern nihilism, the method of seeking critical standpoints historically rooted in existing or, at least, emergent social structures and movements is still a valuable legacy of modern theory. Even the postmodernists' own attacks on the excesses of Enlightenment rationalism point towards freeing this radical historicist method from the fundamentalist and essentialist elements that have hitherto limited its effectiveness. Shorn of its dogmatic features, social theory of broad scope in the classical style still provides the best resources for carrying out the postmodernists' implicit holistic problematic.

Renewed efforts to globally theorize contemporary society and to anchor normative criticism in its structural attributes and emergent political movements could benefit from the recent postmodern critiques as well as from the findings of the specialized sciences. Properly constructed, new global social theories would augment rather than undermine theories and politics of the local and particular.

Social and cultural fragmentation is a reality even if has not been adequately theorized by the postmodernists. Simple affirmation of the emancipatory tradition does not rebut the postmodernists' contentions about the contemporary era or about the exhaustion of critical theory.

Instead, their claims and challenges have to be taken seriously as objects of theoretical discourse and historical enquiry. But much postmodern thought, itself, is characterized by nihilistic pessimism deriving from its ahistorical methodology and its treatment of humanity as automata rather than as critical subjects participating in "communities of memory" and struggle. In addition, critical social theories of the contemporary era must be anchored normatively in the historical process of differentiated subjects forming themselves into publics rather than in the homogenous will of emancipatory subjectivity. To maintain political relevance, these theories should retain the themes of plurality, difference, and heterogeneity in the context of a reconstructed conception of collective emancipation.

To avoid the errors of postwar and postmodernist thinkers, critical theorists must read the current historical conjuncture in the context of the "long-duration" of social and cultural development. This does not mean that conceptions of preceding social formations and long-term developmental processes should be attributed with determining force as in much classical theory. Instead, they ought to be treated as analytic devices to prevent amnesia about tendencies of past societies that may recur again, to create distance from the immediacy of the present, and to assist in the always uncertain process of sorting narrow and transitory historical events from those that arise out of enduring conditions or structures with widespread, intergenerational impact.

Recent upheavals in Eastern Europe and the Soviet Union prove that even four decades of authoritarian control did not destroy oppositional thought or the historical bonds of national, ethnic, and religious community. It should remain an open question, subject to critical enquiry, whether cultural and human resources exist within capitalist societies, especially the United States, for a reawakening, renewal, and extension of democracy. However superficial and contradictory the state of contemporary culture, it is doubtful that historical experience has been so obliterated that all traces of community have been eliminated.

Normative ideals have a genealogy in the history of specific cultural communities. If critical theorists are serious about attaining a public, they must carry out "constructive" genealogies to uncover and reformulate the critical normative languages of their potential publics. However, today, most sociological specialties do without general theory.

And sociological theory itself has become a fragmented and hyperspecialized subdiscipline without integrating problematics or central paradigmatic debates. Postmodernists make an important contribution to contemporary social thought by dramatically addressing the exhaustion and irrelevance of professionally compartm-entalized social theory. Furthermore, they have confronted some of the most novel and potentially important social conditions ignored by sociological theorists.

However, the outright rejection of global theorizing by Lyotard and others prevents them from conceptualizing the epochal changes that their theories presuppose. In the same way, Baudrillard's dismissal of "history" and the "social" contradict the application of his conception of "simulation" in critical theories of contemporary culture and society.

Still, taken seriously, the postmodern critique forces social theorists to rethink their presuppositions, the meaning of their practices, and the relationship of theory, history, and politics. In particular, it challenges social theorists to incorporate into their own work postmodern questions about new technologies, new configurations of mass culture, new social experiences, new forms of cultural fragmentation, and new social movements.

If this challenge is taken up, the hostile and aggressive metatheoretical parries of the postmodernists might ultimately lead to a renewal of critical social theory and even revive its progressive political project.

PURPOSE OF SOCIAL WORK THEORY

The purpose of theory in social work is four fold:

- Social workers need to understand a number of issues related to the field of human relationships. Theory provides the system of rules, assumptions, and the logical bases for these issues.
- Social workers work with doctors, sociologists, teachers, and other professionals. The contribution of social workers will be ignored if they cannot show a theoretical understanding of their field.
- Social workers, like counsellors, constantly find themselves faced with the need to predict. Reliable prediction is rooted in social work theory. Theory facilitates the capacity to predict.
- Theory provides a framework for general ideas. It permits a broad and cohesive view of complexities that may be involved in any given human interaction. Theories can be used to organize our assumptions and guesses into hypotheses, that can be tested and proved valid, or invalid. This is an important step in the scientific method. In fact, theories arise from experience. Once a theory is formulated, it leads to practical applications.

TYPES OF THEORIES

Many theories are relevant to the study of development. They originate from psychology, sociology, or biology. In this unit you will learn about the most comprehensive, influential, and useful theories that you can use as you do your social work. There is the Psychoanalytic Theory, which will help you be aware of the importance of early childhood experiences, and which will show you the effect that the immediate environment has on behaviour. You will also learn how the Humanistic Theory gives us an encouraging vision of the goals of human development. Lastly, the Cognitive Theory gives us a greater understanding of how our thinking and beliefs affect our actions. These theoretical approaches/models facilitate the understanding of the concerns of one who requires social welfare interventions. Social work needs ways of understanding situations.

They need tools and techniques for helping clients:

- Reinforce their approaches to human relations;
- Reinforce their self-exploratory behaviour;
- Eliminate their specific anxieties or fears; and
- Reinforce their positive self-images and self-evaluations.

IMPLICATIONS OF CULTURE TO GUIDANCE AND COUNSELLING

- The family and school are important agents of socialization. Therefore, we must:
  - Socialize children from birth;
  - Help children develop acceptable codes of conduct, *i.e.*, language, dress;
  - Give children freedom to make their own decisions.
- Culture is dynamic. It changes and we need to adapt to new situations.
  - Talk about abstinence versus the use of contraceptives;
  - Note changes in outlook, possessions, and the general behaviour of students.
    (a) Clothing – shoes, uniform
    (b) Food – do all children come to school with/without?
    (c) Shelter – where do students come from?
    (d) Transport – how do they get to school (*i.e.*, bus or cars), long distances
    (e) Students with luxurious extras (*i.e.*, money, watches, expensive shoes, cars)
    (f) Language, music, *etc.*
- Some cultures have changed but others have survived.
  - Sex education/family life education versus indigenous structures (*i.e.*, instead of telling children a baby comes from the river, we need to tell the truth.).
  - Effect of exposure to TV and other media in influencing change.
- Socialization agents (*i.e.*,. the family, school, church, mass media, and other institutions) should work closely together.
  - Reproductive health/family life education should start within the family, and be supported by the school and by other institutions.
  - Promotion of safer sex, using condoms versus non-traditional practices.
- Attend to problems of disability. There were no institutions for the disabled in the past. Families took care of them. There is a need to

educate both families and children in schools on how to assist individuals.

- Social stratification – the way members of a society are organized, in ranks or class just as to status.
  - Some children carry their social class to the classroom, and their behaviour may be unique (*i.e.*, they make a show of coming in cars, some may resist discipline).
  - Being in a group confers social status. Not being a member of a group can be associated with social stigma.
- Social mobility – one's movement in the social ladder.
  - Children need to know that they can climb up or down the ladder, depending on their determination, behaviour, and their goals in life.
  - Children must be willing to work hard and behave acceptably in society.
  - Education can raise their status in society regardless of gender.
  - Encourage girls to take subjects like mathematics/science, or enter professions that will encourage upward mobility and independence.
  - Encourage girls to aim high so they can be promoted to managerial positions.
  - Encourage girls to participate actively in business. They should think of selfemployment as an option, even if this is dominated by men. Women are usually engaged only in market selling.
- Accept children who come from diverse cultural backgrounds. Identify children who risk dropping out. Assist and support them.

6

Management of Social Work Programmes

TRADITIONAL WAYS OF MANAGING SOCIAL PROBLEMS

Throughout history, men have tried to help one another solve difficulties. In African societies, the wisdom of elders has always played a significant role in assisting members of communities to resolve problems. Today, their advice or counsel still has a big role.

SETTING SCHEDULES AND PROGRAMMES FOR SOCIAL WORK

The nature of the problem determines the schedules and programmes for social work:

- *Establish clear lines of communication*: Before embarking on social work, it is important first to establish clear lines of communication, and delegate authority to the agencies concerned (*i.e.*, health institutions and other agencies that deal with the disadvantaged in society). Only then can social work draw support from the community it serves.
- *Make services accessible to the public*: It is essential to stress the importance of making services accessible to the public. In this way, the public will know where to go for help. Given that social services have limited resources, this inevitably raises questions about how far they should be involved with the early identification of need, and to what extent services can be distributed equitably between geographical areas and different social groups.
- Social services staff need to see themselves, not as a self-contained unit, but aspart of a network of services to the community. In the administration of social services, effective coordination with other services and individuals, and the mobilization of community resources (especially volunteers), are important.
- *Coordination*: Coordination is another important aspect of managing social work. Coordination is about the relationship between staff

within, and outside, the agency. There should be a mechanism for coordinating the activities of field workers with other service groups. Where social work is a single individual's responsibility, it reflects the absence of a formal coordinating mechanism.

STRUCTURE OF SOCIAL WORK WITHIN AND OUTSIDE THE GOVERNMENT

Each country in the sub-Saharan region of Africa has its own organizational structure for social work. Participants from the respective states can best explain the structure of social work within their country.

It is important to note that outside the recognized government structure, there are a number of organizations, such as churches and other non-governmental organizations, which provide social work services. Such non-governmental organizations need to work hand in hand with government structures, to ensure the success of their work.

PROGRAMME EVALUATION

Social counsellors, guidance counsellors, and human service professionals, are increasingly called upon to justify the effectiveness of services. This is an age of accountability and transparency. Tax-payers want to know whether social service programmes are really worthwhile. Programme evaluation is important. It is an attempt to assess the extent to which a programme reaches its objectives.

This can be done at two levels:

1. At one level, social workers can assess the services they provide to each client, to be able to understand the effectiveness of the work, and measure the impact of the programmes on their clients. They can ask themselves the following questions:
   - Is there an improvement in behaviour? If so, what strategies were used?
   - Was there fair recording and record-keeping?
   - How about the accuracy of information and the suggested treatment?
2. At the other level, a social worker might ask:
   - What are our activities?
   - What are our goals, and how can we relate activities to goals?
   - Are we reaching our goals?

APPROACHES IN DOING SOCIAL WORK

Before we discuss the various approaches in doing social work, it is important to note that as a social worker, you first need to understand the nature of the problem of the client, before you decide on the method of intervention.

The intervention you use must be appropriate to the client, and effective for the situation.

Some of the methods of intervention you may use are counselling, family therapy, general interviews, data collection/analysis and report writing, intervention strategies, and referrals. Social work emphasizes four major approaches. They are the casework approach, institutionalization, the group work approach, and the community work approach.

CASE WORK APPROACH

Case work is when you are involved individually with a client who has a problem. It involves interaction between you and your client or a family unit.

Case work incorporates the following methods:

- *Problem-Solving*: The emphasis is on releasing the client's fears and anxieties, and motivating him to deal with his problems. **Example:** A worried student who has failed to join the course of his/her choice but has other alternatives.
- *Functional Casework*: This puts emphasis on giving and receiving help. It is built on the basis that human beings use human relationships, including the relationship with you, to find and strengthen their own purpose, and move towards its realisation. **Example:** A student who wants to join an institution on which she has no information.
- *Crisis-Oriented Short-Term Casework*: This realises the vulnerability of individuals in dealing with personal crisis. Its primary value lies in helping the client deal with his/her emotional upset. In this case, the brevity of the social worker's service, and evidence of its effectiveness, are important. *Example:* Helping someone who has lost a relative, especially if the death was sudden.
- *Task-Centred Casework*: This method incorporates crisis intervention, problemsolving, and functional approaches. It involves identifying the problem, sharing the task of problem-solving with your client, and setting a deadline for achieving your goals. **Example:** A student who is a good athlete but is fearful of competition. You will counsel him, and the trainer will give him more training.

ELEMENTS FOR SUCCESSFUL OUTCOMES IN CASEWORK

- Identifying the specific aims and goals to be achieved, usually short-term definite goals.
- Clarifying what the worker and agency have to offer.
- Structuring the role and what is expected of the client.
- Specifying the tasks which need to be accomplished in order to reach the goals.
- Using time, usually a short specified period.

MAJOR EMPHASIS IN CASEWORK

There are certain problem areas in social casework. You need to focus on those areas to guide you in determining from what social problem your client is suffering. You will have to isolate these factors in a problem situation, and determine how best to work with the client to achieve an equilibrium effectively.

The following are the areas you need to focus on:

- *Individualization*: This aspect of casework recognizes the client as the focus of attention. It maximizes the client's participation in finding a solution to his own problems, without running the danger of showing disinterest, and lack of concern, on your part.
- *Communication*: This aspect recognizes a person's difficulty in asking for help, and you should try to create a climate which is not threatening, and which helps the client discuss his/her problem.
- *Information*: This aspect recognizes the fact that most clients do not know what alternatives are open to them, and how they can avail themselves of these alternatives, let alone how to make informed choices once they are known. You need to provide the client with information which is helpful.

INSTITUTIONALIZATION

In some cases, a handicap, illness, or problem, may be so intense that the client needs to be referred to an institution. The institution should be able to deal with the problem and should provide assistance. There may be a number of people affected by the same illness, which will make it easier to obtain treatment. It is important for all counsellors and social workers to obtain a list of names of institutions that deal with certain problems. This should help you refer your clients to these institutions if a problem is beyond your control. Many countries are now moving away from the idea of institutionalization in favour of community-based outreach programmes. There is the belief that family support and a familiar environment may bring about faster recovery, because even family members receive help and support from the social worker.

GROUP WORK APPROACH

The group work approach refers to a technique where you deal with groups of people either in centres or institutions, as opposed to individual persons or individual families. The group work approach, therefore, involves interaction between a client and a group of people with the same needs. Examples of social services using a group work approach are the institutions for the elderly, programmes for single parents, correctional centres, street gang work, residential or day camping, alcohol abuse support groups, and AIDS support groups.

Value of Working with Groups

- People are enriched by interpersonal experiences structured around collectively defined goals.
- People satisfy peer relationships, and share decision-making tasks pertaining to the group.
- The leader helps individual members to use group discussions and activities to negotiate, and then fulfil, behavioural and developmental contracts.
- Achieve a socially desirable but highly individualistic growth.
- Opportunity for lonely persons to belong to a purposeful social organization, where they have a sense of belonging and identity, and where they share problems and aspirations.

Purpose of Groups

The formation of groups in any society has a purpose. Some of these purposes are:

- *Recreation groups*: The activities are purely for enjoyment. Such groups often operate without a leader, and the community simply provides the premises and some equipment.
- *Recreation-skill groups*: These are instruction- and task-oriented groups, but the emphasis is still on socialization and enjoyment. These have an additional dimension from recreation groups, because they enhance social and recreational learning purposes. Competitive team sports may be an outgrowth of such groups.
- *Education groups*: These are groups for the learning of more complex skills, often in an instructional manner. It may resemble a class where there is interaction and group-planned agendas. Leaders of such groups are able to deal with diverse groups of people. The leader focuses on the group agenda, and creates an atmosphere conducive to learning.
- *Self-help groups*: The emphasis is on personal involvement, and groups are antagonistic to professional leadership. Examples of self-help groups are Alcoholics Anonymous to help alcoholics, Parents Anonymous for parents of the mentally retarded, and so on. Many of these operate as community programmes, and spend much time raising funds. These are usually started when community programmes are absent, or provide inadequate service. While self-help groups reject professional involvement in principle, social workers are instrumental in promoting the creation of such organizations.
- *Socialization groups*: They are viewed as the primary focus of social group work, since their goal is behaviour change, increased social skills in its members, and re-entry into society. Youth groups are

organized to increase social skills, reduce isolation and conflict, and enhance cooperation. They also create developmental opportunities to supplement family and neighbourhood life.

- *Therapeutic groups*: These groups require strong leadership skills in a group setting. They cater for conflict and maladaptive social responses. Therapeutic groups usually require the presence of a therapist, and the group leader is usually a nurse, a social worker, a psychologist, or a psychiatrist. The leader uses the group to assist in direct observation of the patient's behaviour, his perceptions of situations, and expression of feelings. This permits the explicit diagnosis of the patient's interpersonal needs and problems, and sets the stage for the therapist and other group members to intervene directly when recommended.

Basic Requirements in Starting a Group

What are the basic requirements in starting a group?

The following are the things to consider:

- Assess the need.
- Identify the problem.
- Identify the strategy that the group intends to use to achieve a goal.
- When the group can implement its strategies.
- Evaluation of the results achieved.

Principles in Group Work Approach

For any practice to be successful, it must follow certain principles. Just like the case work approach, the group work approach has principles and techniques which are used as guidelines, in order to guarantee success in the delivery of guidance and counselling services.

The guiding principles of the group work approach are the following:

- *Decision-making*: You have to recognize the worth, dignity, and uniqueness of group members, and enable them to assume increasing responsibility and control in group deliberations and planning. Each individual member must be encouraged to support the group's efforts. This will lead to a better level of self-direction.
- *Initial concern*: Particular attention is given to the group's initial concerns and resistance, usually by acknowledging that most beginnings tend to evoke conflicting feelings of hope and uncertainty, or excitement, and fear of the unknown. You should begin by dealing with parts of the total problem, rather than attempt to solve whole problems within a short period of time, as clients might expect.
- *Individualization*: The problems and needs of individual members lead to their participation in the group. Their individual problems and needs may emerge as they seek their identity within the group. Often, group

members require special support, confrontation or reinforcement, for contributions to the group, as a means of acknowledging movement towards change and self-realisation.

CORE CRUELTY PROGRAMME AVAILABILITY AND CHILD MISTREATMENT

While the empirical literature on child maltreatment is substantial, the vast majority of data is obtained from studies conducted in metropolitan areas. Very few have included rural populations or compare rural and urban populations, even though 21 per cent of the U.S. population lives in rural areas. Because urban study findings cannot be easily translated to rural settings, it is necessary for researchers to adequately represent rural populations, especially in studies that affect the well-being of children and their families.

The focus of this study is the state of Iowa. The purpose is to examine Iowan counties in order to determine the relationship between substance use, treatment programme availability, and child maltreatment. The following hypotheses will be addressed in the study: the availability of certified substance abuse treatment programmes will be associated with decreased child maltreatment rates, drug and DUI arrest rates will be higher for counties that do not have certified substance abuse treatment programmes, child maltreatment rates will be higher in counties with high drug and DUI arrest rates, and variation will exist between non-metropolitan/nonadjacent, non-metropolitan/adjacent, and metropolitan counties.

National rates of child maltreatment have decreased in recent years, however, during that same period, rates in Iowa have dramatically increased. In 2001, Iowa's abuse rate was 18.0. In 2005, that rate increased to 20.9 confirmed cases; nearly double the national rate. The 2005 maltreatment rates in Iowa varied widely across counties, with a range of 8.1 in Sioux County to 59.1 in Wapello County. Some professionals suggest Iowa's increased maltreatment rate is related to increased parental substance use, especially methamphetamine.

Approximately ten per cent of confirmed child abuse cases in 2003 were directly related to illicit drug use, and two-thirds of neglect cases had underlying components of parental substance abuse. One aspect of this study will be to further examine the relationship between substance use and child maltreatment. While both rural and urban communities face many of the same challenges, the way in which these problems manifest themselves differ from urban to rural settings. Rural challenges involve a lack of resources, distance issues, and communication problems that may be less problematic for families living in urban areas. For individuals with substance abuse issues, accessing treatment programmes may be a challenge. In some rural areas, the nearest treatment facility can be as far away as 40 miles and the cost of fuel and travel time create major obstacles in these cases.

REVIEW

Child Maltreatment

Limited research exists on the prevalence of child abuse and neglect in rural areas and, while urban explanations may at times parallel rural explanations, it is a fallacy that they are comparable to the extent that research of one population can be generalized to the other. Rural populations must be considered in child welfare studies in order to fully understand child abuse and neglect in this population. At least as far back as 1993, the U.S.

Advisory Board on Child Abuse and Neglect recognized the dearth of information on rural child welfare when it stated, "The safety of children should not be a function of geography". Unfortunately, adequate research of this population continues to be lacking. For the few studies that compare rural and urban child maltreatment, the findings are mixed. English, Marshall, Brummel and Orme found that rereferrals and recurrences of child maltreatment were higher for rural areas than for metropolitan areas, while other researchers suggest that no significant differences exist in rates or changes in abuse or neglect for rural counties when compared to urban and suburban counties. Likewise, Ernst reported increased rates of physical abuse and Menard and Ruback reported increased rates of sexual abuse in rural populations, while Cappelleri, Eckenrode, and Powers reported no urban-rural differences in the rates of sexual abuse or physical abuse. These inconsistent results may be due to methodological issues that are common when studying populations that are difficult to access. Relying on child maltreatment rates, which is commonplace for most rural studies, may not be the most accurate means of obtaining this information.

Substance Abuse

The child welfare system, in both rural and urban locales, is substantially impacted by substance abuse. An estimated nine per cent of children in the United States live with at least one parent who abuses drugs or alcohol and these children are more likely to be victims of maltreatment than children whose parents do not abuse drugs or alcohol. Numerous studies have identified parental drug and alcohol use as a correlate of child maltreatment. Kelleher, Chaffin, Hollenberg, and Fisher found, after controlling for DSM-Axis II and household factors, that drug and alcohol use tripled the risk of maltreatment and Leonard reported that studies in both the United States and New Zealand found significant associations between drug and alcohol use and child maltreatment.

Similarly, other studies reflect these findings and substantiate the relationship between these two variables. While many studies of substance abuse utilize an aggregate measure that includes any substance used for mood-altering purposes, one particular drug has made headlines and appears to have a dramatic impact on child maltreatment. That drug, methamphetamine, is currently a major cause of child abuse and neglect and is a considerable problem in the rural Midwest. Children whose parents abuse methamphetamine are often exposed to toxic chemicals, violence, criminal behaviour, and neglect as well as physical, sexual, and emotional abuse. Similar to child maltreatment, researchers concerned with the problems of substance abuse have focused their attention almost exclusively on urban America. The studies that do exist often use arrest rates or treatment programme usage as a measure of the extent of the problem. Rural living was once considered a haven for those wishing to escape the crime and drug laden problems of the inner cities.

Rural regions were protective areas where children could be raised without the fear urban parents often faced. Drug use was mainly limited to alcohol and tobacco use and the hard-core drugs, such as heroin and cocaine, were seen as urban evils. Unfortunately, this view of rural living is changing. The farm crisis of the 1980s created a rural structure that is becoming similar to inner areas of major cities. The same social forces that molded the inner cities of today are now affecting rural areas: intergenerational poverty, out-migration of more prosperous and younger residents, and an accelerated downward spiral resulting in conditions similar to inner city ghettos. Disparities between urban and rural drug use began to diminish after 1985. That year marked the beginning of a temporary decline in overall drug use; however, rural rates declined more gradually than urban rates.

By 1991, only two percentage points separated the two groups and the two per cent disparity has remained constant since. Studies reveal a disturbing trend in rural substance use with the introduction of methamphetamine and OxyContin. The Drug Enforcement Agency currently considers methamphetamine the number one illegal drug in rural America. Rural regions are ideal for maintaining methamphetamine labs as their proximity allows the producers to avoid detection from the powerful fumes emitted during the manufacturing process.

Additionally, substances used in the production of methamphetamine are readily available for purchase in these areas. Despite the media coverage of the methamphetamine and OxyContin epidemics, use of these substances is only one one-hundredth as common as alcohol use. The National Advisory Committee on Rural Health and Human Services refers to alcohol as "universally, the substance of choice" among youth and adults in both rural and urban areas. However, while the use of alcohol is not exclusively a rural or urban problem, at least one study has found that alcohol use, including use to the point of intoxication, is higher in very rural areas.

Treatment Programmes

Barriers to treatment exist, whether one lives in rural American or urban America, however, the types of barriers vary depending on the geographic area.

A major barrier for those living in rural areas is the apparent lack of available services. Many rural communities do not have adequate substance abuse treatment facilities to deal with the growing problem of rural substance use. Political decisions that determine treatment locales are often based on the number of individuals needing treatment in an area.

Because of the low numbers of individuals spread over vast areas, funding for rural treatment centers are stretched thin. Even for those rural programmes that do exist, services are more limited than in urban areas. Outmigration of professionals has led to a shortage of trained practitioners who can help identify substance abuse and supervise treatment and few providers are knowledgeable of rural culture.

In Iowa, 49 of the 99 counties lack a certified treatment facility and those seeking treatment often must travel to other counties to receive services. Surveys of welfare recipients in rural areas show that lack of transportation is a key barrier to accessing services in these communities. In 2000, one rural state spent 77 per cent of welfare funding on transportation assistance and car repairs so their clients could access support services.

Travel time, combined with the cost of gas and vehicle maintenance, can be the determining factor for those seeking treatment. For many low-income rural residents, the time and cost are just too great. The objective of the present study is to examine the effect substance abuse treatment availability has on child maltreatment in rural and small metro areas. Iowa, the focus of this study, is considered a rural state and is similar in structure to other rural Midwest counties in the United States.

METHODOLOGY

Sample

The ninety-nine counties in Iowa were the item of analysis for this study. The data were accessed using a variety of existing measures, including child maltreatment rates, drug and DUI arrest rates, and poverty and minority percentages. In order to obtain an adequate sample size for the analysis and to obtain an average measure for the four year study period, data for the counties were entered four times each; once for every year from 2002 to 2005, for a total sample size of 396.

Measurement

Child Maltreatment

The primary criterion variable in this study was child maltreatment. Child maltreatment was measured as a continuous variable using child maltreatment rates obtained from the 2005 Iowa Kids Count report. The rates reflect only substantiated cases and do not include all reported cases. Data were collected for four years, from 2002 to 2005.

Urban Influence

The Beale Urban Influence Codes provide a rigorous measure for categorizing rural and non-rural areas. The measure consists of a system of codes that conflates area population with proximity to urban services. The codes range from 1 to 12, with larger numbers being assigned to the most rural and isolated counties. Because the codes are labeled just as to the population of their largest city or town and their proximity to metro and micro areas, they can be categorized into three major groups: 1) metropolitan counties, 2) non-metropolitan counties adjacent to metro areas, and 3) non-metropolitan counties not adjacent to metro areas.

Treatment Availability

Treatment availability was measured as a dichotomous variable with a value of "0" assigned to counties with no licensed substance abuse treatment programme and a value of "1" assigned to those that have at least one licensed programme. The data for this variable were obtained from the Iowa Department of Public Health, Division of Behavioral Health and Professional Licensure, 2007.

Substance Abuse

Substance abuse data were collected from the Iowa Uniform Crime Reporting document. These data reflect drug and alcohol arrests per year by county. Four different offesces related to substance use were included in the UCR report: Drug/Narcotic Violation, Drug Equipment Violation, Driving under the Influence, and Drunkenness.

Drug Equipment Violation is often an offense given when an individual is arrested for Drug/Narcotic Violation. Similarly, Drunkenness is often an offense given to individuals arrested for Driving under the Influence. Using all four arrest offesces would create duplication; therefore, Drug/Narcotic Violation was the measure used to determine drug use and Driving under the Influence was the measure used to determine the DUI arrest variable. Drug Equipment Violation and Drunkenness data were excluded from the analysis.

Other Variables

Minority and poverty status were included in the analysis, as well. These data were obtained from the 1999 Census for each of the 99 counties. Minority status was operationalized as the per cent of the population that was non-White. The percentage of each county's poverty population at the time of the census was included as a continuous variable for the poverty measure.

COMMUNITY WORK APPROACH/COMMUNITY DEVELOPMENT

COMMUNITY DEVELOPMENT

Community development is an integrated development process aimed at improving the overall economic, social, and cultural conditions of a community. It is an attempt to equip people who are unemployed or underemployed, with skills which will bring them a better life. In many African countries, community projects have been initiated by women, to enable them generate income. Different agencies support these efforts, especially if such efforts attempt to empower women to contribute towards economic development. In some countries, such projects for women are financially supported by UN agencies, such as UNDP, UNFPA, and WHO. These include community gardens, dressmaking, handicrafts, block-making, health education, *etc.* Such projects are highly appreciated by women in rural communities who are often the breadwinners.

They form the majority in their communities, since men join the workforce in towns. This is in addition to their normal workload. Community organizations generally include the coordination of existing services, action to expand and modify services, and the creation and organization of new services. Community organizations are involved in many social issues, such as education, housing, health, leisure-time services, alienation of youth, economic and social control, labour relations, minority-group employment, child care, and immunization programmes.

Social issues develop from citizens' interest in, and concern about, the imbalance between the needs of people, and the provisions for these needs. From issues, citizens who become caught up in the cause, develop programmes or action to address those problems. The role of the social worker in community development is important. It is not to tell the community what to do, or what they need. It is to help the community identify their needs, and find ways of satisfying them. This involves a lot of planning, hard work and good communication skills.

Community Work Approach

To be effective in community work, you need to do community analysis. This component of social work can be likened to family assessment in the case work approach. Community analysis is done in two ways: by horizontal and vertical orientations. The horizontal orientations are the structural and functional relationships of the community's various social units and sub-systems with each other. For example, the relationships among racial and ethnic groups, or between capital and labour, within the community.

The vertical orientations are the structural and functional relationships of the community's social units to forces outside the community. Such assessment will assist in learning the outside resources being given to the community. There may be unusual difficulties in making decisions, for example, because the local sawmill is a branch of a company in another town.

A Profile Outline for Community Analysis

A community worker will be assisted in his analysis through these topics:

- Background and setting, including history, geography, and government
- Demography
- Communications
- Economic life
- Government politics, law enforcement
- Housing
- Education

The Planning Cycle

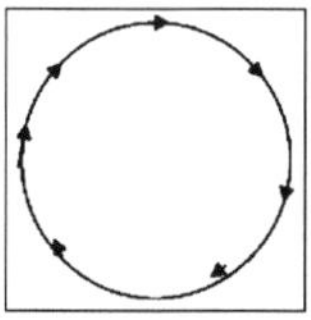

- Identification of Needs
- Assessment of Needs, Identification of Problems
- Priority Needs
- Identification of Resources
- Project Plan, Action Plan, Proposals for Solution
- Implementation
- Follow-Up, Monitoring, Evaluation, Reassessment

In such instances, planners and organizers need to understand the social fabric of society, community sociology, social problems, community psychology, social planning and social policy in relevant areas, such as health, housing, child care, mental health and leisure services. Equally important is the knowledge of social welfare organizations, communication theory, fund-raising, and public relations technology. Finally, skills and business management, social law, and human behaviour are useful tools.

Strategies for Community Development

Quite often, in your duties as a social worker, you have to go beyond the identification of problems to suggesting practical solutions. The strategies you choose will depend on the nature of the group you are dealing with, and the nature of the problem. The following are some of the strategies you can employ.

ORGANISING CREDIT GROUPS

These are groups or associations of women, young people, or men. They come together for the purpose of pooling financial resources. Though the money contributed per month by each member is little, it amounts to a sizeable amount when pooled. This money is then lent to members at an interest.

REVOLVING FUNDS

Unlike the credit group, where the capital is raised by the members themselves, in a revolving fund, the initial capital is secured from another source. This capital is then lent to one person, and after he/she has paid it, it is lent to another. The group members act as supervisors. The funds thus continue to revolve around the group. As a social worker, you have a duty to help them secure funds from relevant agencies.

ENTERPRISE EDUCATION

Are you engaged in any money-generating activity? Does it require special skills? How did you acquire these skills? To stimulate the unemployed, or underemployed, to self-employment, education is often necessary.

This education should seek to build the following:

- *Desire*: You cannot achieve anything unless you have a strong desire for it. Enthusiasm is very important in enterprise education. You can stimulate desire by calling attention to the business opportunities available, and the benefits of selfemployment.
- *Faith*: This can also be taken as confidence. This is the foundation for risktaking, which is important in business. Faith is knowing that what you believe in will come true. You should believe that business ideas will grow into business enterprises. Faith is the basis of all miracles and all mysteries that cannot be analysed by the rules of science.
- *Vision*: This is the mission they want to achieve. They should be able to visualize what they want to achieve. The more specific the vision, the higher will be the chance of achieving it. For example, how much money do you want to earn per month by the end of this year? You have to set off for somewhere if you are to get anywhere.
- *Action planning*: Your clients will need skills to transform their vision into action plans. How do they want to realise their dreams?
- *Specialized knowledge*: Action planning usually leads to a desire to acquire the knowledge and skills necessary for your vision. Accurate information can be acquired through:
  - Your own experience and education
  - The cooperation of others who are skilled, that is, your business partners.
  - You can employ others who are skilled
  - You can acquire this information from relevant books and other reading materials.
  - You can take a special training course.
- *Constructive associations*: In life it is rare to achieve goals without the help of others. Often you need others to realise your ambitions.

You have, therefore, to form a master group. These can be business partners or employees. You need to gather around yourself a skilled, knowledgeable and enthusiastic group. You are very lucky if another person is your wife or husband. This is the most important person in your life. He/she can build you up or destroy you.

- *Starting your own business*: The following are some of the questions which you may need to ask yourself in enterprise education (starting your own business):
  - Do you want to be self-employed?
  - Which business do you want to engage in?
  - How much capital do you need?
  - How do you intend to raise this money?
  - What is the existing market? How many people want your goods or services?
  - Are there other people with whom you have to compete? Are there any other similar undertakings?
  - Where do you intend to locate your business? Is it strategic enough?
  - Do you have the necessary knowledge, skills and information to provide the goods or services? How do you intend to acquire them?
  - You can start planning your business today! Good luck.

VIABLE ECONOMIC ACTIVITIES

You can help in community development by mobilizing the people to participate in activities that pay. Sometimes traditional activities are not economically viable. You have a duty to alert people to alternatives. You can achieve this by working with local leaders and other relevant agencies. Education in the form of seminars, workshops and conferences is of great help. In instances where social work needs the advice of elders, this should be welcomed and encouraged. Problem-solving is not an issue one person can handle alone. It requires the support of all those considered vital in solving a problem. Social work helps to extend guidance services outside the schools, which means children's homes, parents, and communities.

7

Themes and Issues in Contemporary Social Work

PURPOSE OF SOCIAL WORK

The purpose of this part is to analyse key elements of contemporary social work, drawing on themes that were identified in the parts. It represents a condensed version of a complex debate, focusing on specific controversies in social work in the recent past. It starts with a consideration of the politically inspired critiques of social work that were generated in the 1960s and 1970s.

It continues with an analysis of the Barclay Report, concentrating particularly on the debate engendered by the dissenting reports by Pinker and Hadley *et al*. It then moves on to consider the ways in which social work has been challenged by groups of the people it exists to serve, fuelled by the growth of the 'new social movements' from the 1980s onwards. Finally, the part suggests a way in which the various types of social work practice can be understood that provides a conceptual framework for the remainder of the book. The political critique of social work that had particular force from the 1960s on was from the 'radical social work' movement, the outline of which was sketched in the previous part. It rejected what it saw as the pathologising elements of individual casework, notably the common assumption that poverty was the result of personal failure rather than economic forces.

It pressed for the establishment of a form of practice that re-engaged with the economic basis of disadvantage, drawing on ideas of community development and social action that are traceable to the Settlement Movement. Radical social work largely rejected the notion of individual casework, believing that this distracted from the central mission of social work, which it saw as combating poverty and disadvantage. The critique from the right was of a different order, focusing on the fundamental ineffectiveness of social work. Brewer and Lait contended that social work was imprecisely defined, encompassing too broad a range of roles and functions. They argued that it should be much more narrowly focused and defined, and followed Wootton in questioning the essence of social work's claims for professional status, believing that social workers were 'valued but essentially subordinate employees of the traditional health and welfare agencies', whose role was basically to carry out the practical work of such agencies. Brewer and Lait further suggested that the diffuse, over-ambitious and ill-defined aims of social services departments ensured the futility of much practice, and that the poor quality of the education and training offered to social workers further compounded the problems. Their conception of social work had the practitioner occupying a predominantly bureaucratic position, with 'professional' training replaced by a form of apprenticeship.

These criticisms of social work found a ready audience within certain parts of the media and politics, not to mention the medical profession. However, their analysis is contaminated by the prejudiced language in which it is conveyed, with constant disparaging barbs directed to all and sundry within social work and a dismissive tone towards all knowledge that is not based in hard, scientific certainty. For example, in discussion on the selection of students, the authors suggested that 'only graduates in maths, physics or chemistry, with firsts or upper seconds, should be accepted for training, since to attract them one would need to put on courses with intellectual content'. In addition, their insistence that social work training had taken a strongly psychoanalytical direction is largely out of line with the realities of the late 1970s, however true it might have been of the 1950s.

Indeed, their insistence that the influence of radical left-wing academics was such that students were 'having to regurgitate their tedious and irrelevant nostrums to obtain a certificate in applied social studies' appears to contradict their very claim of psycho-analytical dominance within the social work academy. The debate that this critique engendered concerned the essence of social work; it was extended through the process of the Barclay Report, which sought to clarify the role and tasks of social work. As is often the case with large committees, not all the parties to the Barclay Report were able to agree. The majority report contained a strong focus on the elements of 'social care planning' within the social work role, which was contrasted with the element of 'counselling' that the report identified as its other core strand. The most far-reaching recommendation of the majority report was for the creation of what it termed 'community social work', where practice and policy would become more responsive to the needs of a community, defined in terms either of locality or of 'shared concerns'.

In the committee's view, this would require a change of attitude and orientation by social workers. Critical areas of contention were laid out in two contrasting minority reports, one of which was largely the work of Roger Hadley, the other being solely the work of Robert Pinker. Hadley and colleagues advocated for the extension of the notion of community social work, the most controversial of the recommendations of the main report.

They argued that the central role of social work should be to support informal caring networks; in order to do this, they suggested that a community-oriented approach had to be developed.

In their view, such an orientation required four conditions to be met:

- *Localisation*: 'Statutory services must be local enough to operate at street and village level'.
- *Integration*: Three kinds of integration were suggested–Integration within each social services department, integration between the department and other service-providing agencies, and integration between the department and social networks.
- *Wider Roles*: To accomplish this fundamental shift, staff roles had to be defined much less narrowly than before.
- *Greater Autonomy*: 'Local social services teams will need a larger measure of discretion to develop these approaches than they have been formally accorded'.

There had been a number of projects that had explored this sort of practice and the alternative view adopted by Hadley and colleagues was firmly in this tradition. However, this conception of the social work role did not fit comfortably with the increasingly coercive nature of social workers' activities, particularly in respect of child protection. Pinker took a diametrically opposite position, contending that social workers had no mandate for the sorts of activity that could be grouped under the banners either of 'community social work' or 'neighbourhood social work'. The concept of 'community' on which they founded their analysis was not clearly defined, there were fatal ambiguities in the concepts of accountability that were deployed, and unresolved tensions between the principles of 'specialism' and 'genericism' within social work practice. By contrast, Pinker recommended that social work would be more securely defined in a manner that was limited by its statutory remit.

In a memorable turn of phrase he characterised community social work in the following terms:

- It conjures up the vision of a captainless crew under a patchwork ensign stitched together from remnants of the Red Flag and the Jolly Roger–all with a licence and some with a disposition to mutiny–heading in the gusty winds of populist rhetoric, with presumption as their figurehead and inexperience as their compass, straight for the reefs of public incredulity.

While the Barclay Report did not have the impact on social work that had been widely anticipated, it encapsulated an ongoing debate within social work between those who argued for a wider involvement of the occupation in social action and those who took a more limited view of its role and functions. Although framed in different terms and language, this dispute echoed earlier debates about the essential nature of social work.

Given the political climate into which the Report was catapulted, it is little surprise that the more restricted vision of Pinker was to characterise social work practice in the following years. In the 1980s there were challenges to social work from groups–women, Black people, service user groups, the advocacy movement, *etc.*–who had been subject to the services of social workers. These challenges have been usefully summarised by Taylor, who argued that the groups share common purposes, despite their obvious differences, in their focus on issues such as diversity, universalism, power and rights. The tests that these movements have posed for social work served to expose fundamental elements of the occupation's self-image.

- A key underlying theme is that their criticisms highlight the fact that social work has often failed to live up to its more lofty ideals. Given that an important principle of social work has always been its ability to respond positively to the most disadvantaged parts of society, this condemnation highlights a dismal failure within the occupation.
- The groups have also highlighted social workers' inability to work effectively in practice with individual disabled people, black people, gays and lesbians, *etc.*

In combination, these concerns helped to create a climate of uncertainty and doubt within social work, attesting to the fact that it was an occupation in some disarray. The final part of this part will seek to understand how the various themes that have characterised social work through its history can be placed into a conceptual framework that will help to govern the subsequent discussion. Working on the assumption that disputes about the nature of social work are really disputes about the nature and causes of, and solutions to, social problems, the different perspectives on social work therefore represent alternative views on the role that the occupation plays within society.

In this respect Mullaly has differentiated between broadly 'conventional' and 'progressive' perspectives on the role and functions of social work. In the 'conventional' view–which he suggests is, and always has been, held by the majority of the profession–the structure of society is believed to be fundamentally sound. The broad role of social work is therefore either to help people adjust to existing social structures, or to amend those structures in a limited way.

In the minority 'progressive' view the purpose of social work is different, being primarily to contribute to a fundamental social transformation, on the basis that the problems of individuals are caused by inequitable social structures rather than individual inadequacy or weakness. In the foregoing debate about the origins of social work, the efficient administration of relief and most individual casework can be placed within the 'conventional' perspective. Indeed, support for the status quo was a central part of the role of the COS. In addition, there is relatively little in the literature on individual casework that argues for a more radical social vision.

By contrast, the Settlement Movement contained the seeds of a more critical perspective; it is therefore no surprise that many future socialist politicians–including the future Prime Minister Clement Attlee–were active in this movement in their youth. This critical perspective became more explicit in the radical social work movement. An alternative way of conceptualising different perspectives on social work has been devised by Payne. He has suggested that three 'general perspectives' on social work can be identified: 'individualist-reformist', 'socialistcollectivist', and 'reflexive-therapeutic'.

The discipline of social work is held to contain elements of these three perspectives, with one or another being influential at different times. For example, the reflexive-therapeutic perspective was particularly powerful in the USA in the early part of the twentieth century, being imported for British consumption in the years following the Second World War. The socialist-collectivist perspective was especially prominent in the radical social work literature in Britain in the 1970s and early 1980s.

By contrast, most social work in contemporary Britain is more within the individualist-reformist tradition, which has been influentially articulated by Martin Davies, who claimed that, 'although social workers have many roles... they are all subsumed under a general theory of maintenance'. That this has become the dominant perspective is far from being a matter of chance, as it accepts the basic structures of society and sets limits to the social work role that circumscribe its focus.

While these are helpful ways of conceptualising the place of social work, they do both over-simplify some of the inherent contradictions that characterise daily practice. To take Mullaly's split, even if a practitioner were to espouse a 'progressive' view of social work, s/he must necessarily frequently act in ways that support the framework of society: the legislative and statutory basis of social work requires no less. Similarly, it is at least conceptually possible for a social worker to practise in accordance with all of Payne's 'general perspectives' on social work at different times: they are not mutually exclusive.

In reality, the bulk of what a social worker actually does in practice with older people in Britain will fit within the individualist-reformist perspective, simply because the key statutory and policy requirements of the agencies within which most of them operate–carrying out community care assessments, arranging for safe and speedy hospital discharges, *etc.*–lend themselves to this orientation to social work. However, a social worker should not forget that there are other perspectives on which to draw. For example, s/he might recognise that an older person needs additional support to come to terms with loss and bereavement, or that a carer for a person with dementia has a particular need for counselling to come to terms with the changes that dementia engenders.

Both examples are of work that fits within a more therapeutic tradition. Similarly, on different occasions a social worker might perceive the need for collective action, for example by supporting a group of carers to meet, or by enabling the formation of service user groups to argue for better services. This book makes an argument for a broad view of social work, encompassing all three perspectives identified by Payne. It argues that it is unrealistic to construe social work as simply about a process of social reform, as individuals in genuine need require more immediate help to assist them with their problems. However, to perceive social work simply as a succession of individual 'cases' is likely to lead to safe but sterile practice.

Indeed, not all of the problems confronting older people can be seen as relating to the individual; such a conception ignores the collective experiences of older people, and the structured oppression that they experience within society. A skilled social work practitioner must be able to identify the approach that most suits the circumstances with which s/he is confronted, being sufficiently flexible to respond to them in different ways according to their nature and cause. Therefore, to adjust the terminology deployed in this stage, drawing particularly on Payne and Seed, social workers need to be capable of working in three different but complementary approaches:

- Working with individuals, in both problem-solving and therapeutic ways. For the purposes of this book, I have labelled this the individualist/therapeutic approach.
- Working as a go-between, ensuring that resources are mobilised to meet need, with particular stress on the tasks of liaison and coordination. In this book, this has been termed the administrative approach.
- Working with groups and communities, to construct creative and new types of response to problems, including the development of new services and resources. This has been termed a collectivist approach.

This approach recognises that human problems are complex and that the ways of responding to them are manifold. An individualist/therapeutic, an administrative or a collectivist response may be indicated at different times; the practitioner has to retain the capacity to identify what approach is more likely to be effective, and at what time. In addition, and this is particularly true for practice with older people, the functions of agencies need to be constructed in ways that allow for this element of flexibility on the part of the social worker. The way in which social work with older people is currently constructed forces the practitioner into an administrative response, irrespective of need. It is apparent that, in taking this line, I have also defined my position in relation to Mullaly's 'conventional' and 'progressive' orientations. In his terms, this would be within the 'conventional' camp, since it does accept the legitimacy of the present social order.

This is less a statement of personal political beliefs than it is a recognition of the nature of social work practice within British society. Pinker was surely correct in pointing out that social workers have no mandate to work against the system that employs them; in addition, most service users would not necessarily appreciate their concerns being transformed into political tools. However, in the context of social work practice with older people, the approach advocated does move beyond the limits of what has customarily been accepted as normal for this group. There has historically been scant opportunity for the development of therapeutic approaches to practice, and little evidence of collectivist work. It can be argued that these failures are an expression of the low value accorded to older people within society at large as well as within social work.

HISTORY AND PROGRESS OF SOCIAL WORK

The purpose of this stage is to analyse the establishment, growth and development of social work in Britain, from its origins in the nineteenth century to its position at the start of the twenty-first century. It is written on the assumption that understanding the history of social work is helpful when seeking to explore options for its future direction. This is particularly important when the social work role is under question, as it undoubtedly is in relation to work with older people.

Ensuring that forms of practice are developed that pay full attention to its history and potential might form a useful corrective to the overwhelmingly 'administrative' nature of much contemporary social work. As the quotation from Jordan indicates, there are different ways of interpreting the growth and development of social work as an organised activity. Following Seed, three strands in its development are charted. The first of these is the focus on individual casework, which originated in the work of the Charity Organisation Society. The second is the role of social work in social administration, particularly involving various forms of relief from poverty.

Although much of this originated from the Poor Law, it was also promoted in some of the work of the COS. The third is the focus on social action, which has been particularly identified with the growth of the Settlement Movement, both in Britain and the United States. Although these three strands will be addressed separately for analytical purposes, they have often been interconnected. If one examines the origins of social work, for example, many key figures spanned these themes. For example, Octavia Hill was closely associated with both the COS and the Settlement Movement, while Canon Barnett was originally a supporter of the COS before establishing the first settlement at Toynbee Hall in East London as an example of what he then considered to be the most effective way of bringing about social change.

Both Hill and Barnett actively engaged in more general processes of social reform, meaning that they were at different times 'case-workers, group workers and reformers'. The close complementary working of the Poor Law and charity was a vital prerequisite for the effective operation of the COS, while some practitioners–notably hospital almoners—brought together casework and financial administration. These links and connections have reappeared throughout the history of social work, albeit in a range of different guises.

INDIVIDUAL CASEWORK

Most historical accounts identify the COS as the initiator of the social theory that led to the formation of the occupation of social work. A particular element of the work of the COS was its focus on individual casework. As this part will demonstrate, this has been perhaps the most consistent theme running through the entire history of social work.

This part will therefore examine the ways in which individual casework developed, starting with its origins in the COS before moving to consider how it flourished in the years immediately following the Second World War into the present day. One of the key contributions of the COS to social work was its clear–if perhaps partial and misguided–view of the cause of many social problems in Victorian Britain.

London, as graphically portrayed by Bosanquet was seen as beset by a 'mass of chronic pauperism, beggary and crime', behind which lay 'an appalling amount of genuine misfortune'. In the view of the COS, existing services for the relief of poverty actually made matters worse, due to the inadequacy of the Poor Law combined with the counterproductive impact of the vast growth of charitable organisations.

In the view of the COS, this combination stripped people of the will to fight against the circumstances in which they found themselves; by not making any distinction between those who did and did not merit support, it was held that the system in effect encouraged all people to throw themselves onto the combined ministrations of the Poor Law and charity rather than maintain their independence. The COS maintained that this weakened the family and hence had a profoundly negative impact on society at large. To put their social theory into effect, the COS established systems and structures that enabled action in accordance with its principles.

First and foremost, it insisted on proper coordination of charitable endeavour to avoid overlap and competition between organisations. To support this, an understanding was reached about the respective roles and purposes of the two arms of welfare, charity and the Poor Law. Charity was to be the first port of call for people in need, with the Poor Law and its institutions functioning as a general safety net beneath the charitable institutions. The next priority for the COS was to establish an organisational structure and a system to assist people who appeared to have some level of need. While the COS did not originally intend to provide charity directly, but rather to coordinate the charitable provision of other organisations, District Committees of the COS soon became established to provide relief on their own account.

The critical task was to oversee a process whereby a judgement could be made concerning the eligibility of applicants for support. This was accomplished by judging whether an applicant was considered to be 'deserving' or 'undeserving' of assistance. Even though the terminology used by the COS changed in later years, a moral dimension is clearly evident; this has had a continued impact on social work.

It is in this process of investigation where the roots of social work practice can be clearly divined. If charity was to be properly directed, there needed to be a full, 'scientifically' organised examination of the circumstances of individuals and families who presented for a service. The basic techniques of 'casework' that the COS instigated have continued applicability. For example, judgements had to be based on a detailed assessment of the applicant's circumstances, requiring home visits. The COS termed this 'taking down the case', a process that is clearly analogous to the preparation of assessments in contemporary practice.

The COS issued guidance about how the process of 'taking down the case' should be organised; again, this role is broadly analogous to the guidance routinely issued by governments and employers to assist organisations and managers come to grips with changes in policy and practice. Following the assessment, a judgement was then to be made concerning an individual's eligibility to receive a service, which has its exact parallel in the existence of defined 'eligibility criteria' in current practice.

If services were to be provided, they could be of many different types, as is evident in the case histories that the COS cited in support of their work. The COS did not simply dispense financial charity, but also sought to find creative ways of maintaining and enhancing people's independence as such approaches were more in line with their governing philosophy.

Although there was considerable variability between District Committees in terms of the number of people served and the quality of the investigations undertaken, the number of cases which the COS investigated was surprising to many, indicating that the organisation was uncovering a large amount of unmet need within society. However, its general approach was not popular, as is evident from the defensive tone throughout Bosanquet's history.

While the COS took pride in the efficiency of its system, for many others it appeared harsh in the extreme. In addition, the COS was markedly hostile to other organisations involved in the provision of charity, as well as to other perceptions of the causes of poverty. It was apparently difficult to criticise the work of the COS–even in relatively mild terms–without provoking an antagonistic response; for example, the differences of view between the COS and Canon Barnett were addressed in a peculiarly arrogant and defensive manner. In addition, the success of the COS in fulfilling its mission was also called into question, despite the robust way in which it sought to protect its position. Throughout its period of peak influence–up to the outbreak of the First World War in 1914—it was never able to escape from a paradox that it had itself created: 'The fact remained that the "unassisted" might be those who most needed help but least deserved it... while those helped, the respectable and provident, ought least to have needed help'. In addition, it was claimed that the perceived harshness of the COS approach actually promoted rather than curbed 'unscientific' charitable activity.

It was also argued that the COS had not actually managed to classify the deserving and undeserving poor accurately, and that the charity that was dispensed was quite inadequate to combat need. As Webb concluded: 'the administration of the Poor Law... supplemented by charitable assistance according to the tenets of the COS.... had next to no effect either on the poverty or on the misery of the poor'. These were powerful criticisms, which the COS struggled to combat successfully. In addition, the tide of opinion was shifting against the belief that the relief of poverty and distress was primarily an individual responsibility.

In British society, following the cataclysm of the First World War, there was a much stronger level of acceptance that the provision of welfare was a matter for the state as much as the individual and the family. However, the influence of the COS on the development of social work was vast; in fact, it effectively created the occupation of social work, as well as defining many of its core tasks. The COS also recognised that effective work required a level of training of those people undertaking it. Indeed, one of its most significant legacies to social work was the development of systematic programmes of education and training for the role of the social worker.

With a diminution of the influence of the COS, a separation therefore appeared between the practice of individual casework and the social theory from which it originated. This was certainly a difficult time for social work in Britain, as it sought to establish a role and function that was separate from the specific ideas of the COS. One of the effects of the separation of social work methods from a broader social theory was a fragmentation in the occupational processes that sustained it. For example, different branches of social work–psychiatric social workers, hospital almoners, *etc.*–operated separate systems of education and training, and in effect created parallel routes into the occupation. The search for an alternative rationale for social work was a preoccupation for much of the next part of its existence. The importation of a collection of ideas from the USA was to have a particular importance in this respect. The first of these was the detailed codification of the process of 'social diagnosis' undertaken by Mary Richmond, which was an early attempt to establish a common base for all social work practice.

Richmond asserted that: 'in essentials, the methods and aims of social case work were or should be the same in every type of service'. Central to this was the act of assessing needs, which should be based on a systematic process of gathering 'social evidence' from a range of sources–the individual, family members, and outside sources such as schools, doctors, employers, *etc.* The key contribution of Richmond to the development of social work was in the detailed, 'scientific' organisation of data that she propounded, which represented a major step forward along the path first outlined by the COS. The second major import stemmed from the popularity of psychologicallybased theories in American social work from the 1920s onwards.

Cormack and McDougall suggested that the introduction of treatment methods deriving from related disciplines did little to suggest that a social worker possessed unique expertise and was hence worthy of professional status; it appeared that a social worker was doing nothing that could not equally well be accomplished by many other occupations–and even mature people of good sense lacking any qualification at all.

Nevertheless, the adoption of psychologically-oriented insights increased the focus of social work on the workings of the mind, as is apparent from the content of one of the most significant post-war textbooks on social casework in Britain. The attraction of 'universal applicability' for social work approaches was obvious, particularly given the occupation's fragmentation in the first half of the twentieth century. A focus on social casework informed by psychological theories offered the prospect of unifying these disparate elements. Indeed, the first 'generic' training course for social workers was established for precisely this purpose.

The increased confidence that this gave to the social work world should not be underestimated–it suffuses all the contributions to Morris' seminal text. For example, Younghusband is somewhat patronising to the pioneers of social work practice who managed to operate without the knowledge of 'unconscious motivations, behaviour patterns, the transference situation, client–worker relationships, social maladjustment, obsessional behaviour, the need to express feelings of guilt and aggression, reactions to deprivations in childhood' that were the stock in trade of the 'modern' practitioner. She is clear that social work practice had developed for the better as a result of the increased knowledge that social workers had of the innermost workings of people.

In addition, she is in little doubt of the greater levels of skill and knowledge that could be required of the social worker. The scope of the social work task, as Younghusband defined it, was greatly increased–indeed, it was ambitiously framed. However, there was an element of unreality in her description: only a small minority of people could receive the sort of service she identified. It was difficult for social workers in statutory agencies to accommodate these requirements into their daily work, as Rodgers and Stevenson made clear. Even in voluntary organisations, the ideals of individual casework were difficult to put into practice.

However, the way in which the social work task was theorised represented an elaborate updating of its key elements. However, it was this very ambition that caused one of the most notable attacks on the developing occupation of social work. In her book Social Science and Social Pathology Barbara Wootton excoriated what she saw as social work's obsession with methods drawn from psychiatry and psychology. The essence of her critique was that the fascination with psychology and psychiatry created a 'fantastically pretentious façade' for the occupation, resulting from 'a tendency to emphasise certain aspects of social work, while playing down others that are potentially at least as valuable'.

She identified the rhetoric that accompanied descriptions of social work practice as particularly worrying, and mocked the idea that social work could actually achieve the sorts of change its advocates appeared to propose. Her preferred remedy was that social work should rediscover a more modest focus on helping people by acting as what she termed a 'middleman': mobilising, organising and coordinating the services of a huge range of other professional colleagues, and by guiding people through the mass of legislation and policy that could affect them. In this way, Wootton suggested that the social worker could once again be essential to the effective functioning of the welfare state. While this was a witty and stimulating critique, Wootton's analysis did not engage fully with the reality that confronted social workers.

Her conception of the limited role of social work offered little that could assist, for example, an abused child, a person with a mental health problem, or people who had experienced bereavement, all of whom would require an approach that was more in line with that suggested by the advocates of individual casework. In addition, Wootton's perception of the role of social work did not accord with the reality of what practitioners actually did–vividly conveyed by Rodgers and Stevenson—but related more closely to the rhetoric of those whose role it was to promote the development of social work. In reality, practice already contained much that drew on social work's administrative origins. Younghusband certainly recognised that social workers required knowledge of resources and the ability to coordinate them effectively, even if she downplayed this aspect of the social work role.

In that sense, Wootton's critique was built on somewhat insecure foundations. However, it strongly influenced subsequent attacks of social work from the political Left and Right. These will be addressed in a forthcoming part. With the benefit of hindsight, the 1950s represented the period where individual casework was most highly prized within social work. However, as we have seen, one key problem with this formulation was that it did not equate to much of the actual practice of people employed as social workers, particularly those working within statutory settings. For such people, there remained an emphasis on the efficient administration of relief; this will be the focus of the next part. In addition, it moved the occupation a long way from its origins as a social movement; the idea that social work can be seen as a movement interested in securing social change is the focus of the part after that. In terms of work with older people it had relatively little impact; the role of social worker has always had more of an element of administrative requirements.

SOCIAL WORK AS SOCIAL ADMINISTRATION

As various commentators have noted social work has its earliest roots–even pre-dating the formation of the COS–in the work of the Poor Law relieving officers, whose duty was to administer the system that had first been created through the Poor Law Act of 1601. The importance of their role was given additional stimulus by the Poor Law Amendment Act of 1834, which emphasised the element of deterrence through the formal introduction of the concept of 'less eligibility'. This meant that the conditions of relief would consciously be made no better than was available to the lowest paid worker, in order not to make such relief more attractive to those who might be eligible for it and hence discourage their desire to engage in productive labour. The Poor Law was administered on a local level by Boards of Guardians, which gave rise to considerable variation in the way in which it was managed across the country.

All Boards of Guardians required some basis of making judgements about the eligibility of applicants to forms of relief, which were generally financial. Relieving officers were widely employed to accomplish this end in the early years of the nineteenth century. By contrast with the COS or the Settlement Movement it was not generally argued that these officers required a formal period of education and training to accomplish their tasks: as a result their quality was variable. Although a National Poor Law Officers' Association was formed in 1884, seeking to improve the status and quality of the occupation through better professional training, this had little effect on the low public esteem in which it was held. However, the 1929 Local Government Act did manage to achieve some degree of change for this group of staff, as the responsibility for managing the Poor Law transferred to the direct control of local government, with the relieving officers redesignated as public assistance officers.

In their location, as well as in some of their work, the influence of these staff on the development of social work is considerable. Elements of social administration were also contained in the role of workers within the COS. For example, although much assistance was other than financial, direct financial support was provided in some instances.

In addition, the role of hospital almoners contained elements that were explicitly concerned with financial administration, which was a staple of their work until the establishment of the NHS in 1948. As noted in the previous part, even where the rhetoric of casework most affected social work in the 1950s it was accepted that the social worker needed to have a good understanding of the range and scope of resources that could be made available to an individual or family. Indeed, the conception that the social work role was, at least in part, concerned with humanising the administration of social services was well accepted. This general perception lasted through reorganisation in the early 1970s, which coincided with a rapid increase in the numbers of qualified social workers.

In reality, irrespective of the rhetoric of individual casework much of the practice of social workers was concerned with responding to the minutiae of people's lives in a practical and pragmatic fashion. Throughout this period, there is little doubt that the administrative elements of the social work role far outweighed the elements that derived from casework, particularly in respect of older people.

It was in recognition of this that very little practice with older people was actually carried out by qualified staff until the passage of the National Health Service and Community Care Act 1990.

Even though this legislation increased the numbers of qualified staff employed to work with older people, care management–the dominant form of social work practice with older people–particularly emphasised the administrative role of the practitioner. The social work role was increasingly restricted to the act of assessment, leading to the establishment of care packages and the rapid closure of the 'case'.

Arguably, these trends have made social work with older people into a particularly dispiriting enterprise for many practitioners. Although the 'administrative' elements of social work have a long history, it is the development of 'casework' that has been more frequently cited as the main contributor to the development of the occupation of social work. However, the origins of social work in social administration are apparent, and this focus for practice remains evident. This is in direct contrast with the conception of social work as a form of 'social action', the subject of the following part, which is relatively little in evidence.

SOCIAL ACTION IN SOCIAL WORK

The earliest example of social work as a form of collective social action in Britain can be found in the work of the Settlement Movement, established by Canon Barnett in the 1880s.

The Settlement Movement was underpinned by a number of beliefs that it shared with the COS. Both were based on similar moral principles, even though different forms of practice stemmed from these principles; a belief in the value of education and example underpinned the values of both. In addition, both accepted that financial assistance was insufficient to combat problems within communities and individuals. Similarly, both had their origins in the sense of obligation of the more privileged to those less fortunate than themselves, and shared a strong belief in the purpose and value of education, establishing training courses in conjunction with universities.

Gilchrist and Jeffs have indicated that the movement was based on three linked ideas:

- The need to develop scientific research on the causes and effects of poverty.
- That the 'settlers' could help to broaden the lives and horizons of people and communities through education.
- That they could also enhance leadership within local communities.

As this outline indicates, its practice differed from the work of the COS. For example, it was not predicated on resolving immediate individual needs, but rather sought to work through the community and the group to improve general social conditions. Critically, the vision of Canon Barnett was different from that of the COS on one key point, relating to the social theory that underpinned the Settlement Movement.

Barnett came to believe that the root causes of poverty and distress could be located in social structures more than in the defects of individual character; he termed the action that followed this diagnosis 'practical socialism'. His vision was that people of education–the movement attracted women as well as men—could establish a relationship with people of a different class to their mutual benefit.

The residence requirement for 'settlers'was critical for this; while most worked outside the community for their paid employment, they spent other time undertaking forms of community service and development. To the modern reader, there seems at least as much unifying as dividing the COS and the Settlement Movement–and some early pioneers like Octavia Hill supported both—but the division was deeply felt by the COS at least. The explanation for this can be located in the clarity of the COS vision: if the analysis on which it was based was accurate, then only one possible set of responses could logically follow.

Any divergence from this path was treated almost as apostasy. Although the Settlement Movement initially expanded quite quickly in Britain–and with even more speed in the USA–its growth did not outlive the main establishing pioneers.

By 1914 there were 46 settlements; these were a mixture of women-only, men-only and mixed establishments. However, as the education and training of 'settlers' developed, the pioneers tended to be replaced by 'professionals', who saw their role as consolidating the innovations that they inherited, rather than devising new ones. As a result, as Seed pointed out, the nature of the movement gradually changed, losing much of its radical edge.

With the decline in significance of the Settlement Movement paralleled by the advance of individual casework, there was little connection in social work practice in the middle years of the twentieth century to the strand of social action and community development that had motivated Canon Barnett and his followers.

Indeed, the 1950s and early part of the 1960s represented the almost total eclipse of collective action as part of social work. However, a coherent critique of the contemporary state of social work was mounted from the late 1960s onwards, focusing on the failures of a practice that 'pathologised' the individual while ignoring the material and social causes of poverty and disadvantage. The establishment of the radical journal Case Con in 1970 was a key moment in this process, providing a focal point for an alternative conception of the potential of social work.

This was more fully articulated in a variety of texts in the late 1970s and early 1980s, of which Bailey and Brake, Jones and Simpkin are a representative sample from the UK.

They are part of a movement that became known as 'radical social work' after the title of Bailey and Brake's important text. Although there were differences amongst the proponents of radical social work, particularly in the way in which they addressed issues of inequality that were other than class-based, they shared an understanding of the causes of human problems that sought to shift the focus of social work intervention in a profound way, moving away from an individual to a collective response to problems.

While influential within the academy and within certain areas of practice, ultimately radical social work as a 'movement' foundered on some barely recognised contradictions. For example, while its analysis of social problems was a necessary corrective to the highly individualised understandings within 'casework', it was much less effective in guiding social workers towards alternative models of practice.

As Cohen observed, the emphasis on structural causes of disadvantage did not necessarily enable individuals to address the specific problems that they encountered. In addition, the radical social work agenda appeared to assume that social workers had more capacity to challenge and change policy than was realistic, given their occupational location. Certainly, employers did not expect their staff to foment revolution, despite the apparent inducement so to do within some radical social work material! This was particularly true from the 1980s onwards, a difficult period for the development of more progressive forms of social work. Finally, the early analyses of the radical social work movement were heavily class-based, with relatively little attention devoted to issues of race, gender, disability, sexuality, *etc.*

This meant that it did not connect sufficiently well with groups of people–practitioners and service users alike–who could have been allies. It is perhaps significant that the radical social work movement was relatively short-lived, failing to surmount either the challenges provided by the changed social and political climate of the 1980s or the different sorts of critique mounted by Black people, women and disabled people.

It had less impact on social work than it had intended, but the sorts of analysis that it engendered have proved to have a continuing influence. Its impact on social work with older people was particularly limited. As an attempt to re-focus social work onto its potential to operate as a social movement it was only partly successful, but it certainly helped to draw attention to various issues–the impact of poverty, the potential of community–that had been long neglected.

8

Social Work for Social Welfare and Rights

SOCIAL WELFARE SERVICES

Because our communities face a variety of problems, countries have realisd that there is a need for social welfare services. This refers to formally organized, and socially sponsored institutions, agencies and programmes, to maintain or improve economic and social conditions, health or personal competence in some, or all, parts of the population. The provision of welfare services is called social work. Let us look at the aims of social work services.

AIMS OF SOCIAL WORK SERVICES

- Enhance problem-solving and capacities of people to cope;
- Assist children, young people and adults with social problems;
- Provide rehabilitation services for individuals in prison, the physically handicapped, parents and their communities;
- Assist the community to initiate useful programmes for people using available community resources;
- Link people with systems that provide them with services, resources, and opportunities;
- Promote the effective operation of these systems;
- Carry out research (*i.e.*, case study, survey, observation, *etc.*); and
- Contribute to the development and improvement of social policy.

THE BASIC PRINCIPLES OF SOCIAL WORK

William E. Gordon (1962), the philosophical foundations of the social work profession are based on several propositions.

These form the basic principles of social work:

- The individual is the primary concern of society.
- There is interdependence between individuals and society.
- Individuals have social responsibility for one another.
- There are human needs in each person, yet each person is essentially unique and different from others.

Many countries have established social services through their Departments or Ministries of Social Welfare Services. These formal structures initially assumed major responsibility for personal and social services. Later, the expansion of such services included rehabilitation and community development programmes. Recently, there has been an influx of refugees in many countries, and there is a need for the further expansion of social welfare services. Because of an increase in crime and juvenile delinquency, there is a need to provide social work correctional services within departments or ministries. Big industries, too, provide their workers with services, so that they have advice on their social or health-related problems.

VULNERABLE AND MARGINALIZED GROUPS

These are groups that require strong social welfare services in your country:

- The children and young people;
- The elderly;
- The disabled and handicapped;
- The unemployed;
- The needy families; and
- The sick and injured.

CHILDREN AND YOUNG PEOPLE

Many children live under conditions of poverty with inadequate housing, clothing, supervision and love. One contributing factor to this is the migration of families from rural to urban areas, where they face not only economic difficulties, but also a lack of the traditional support system offered by the extended family unit. Urban migration results in cultural diffusion, and a loss of the values and norms that used to govern society. There is also a trend for the traditional family structure to break down. This has grave consequences, especially for the children and youth, who comprise more than 50 per cent of the population in most African countries.

Some by-products of the lack of a family support system and guidance for youth are teenage pregnancy and AIDS-related cases. These are increasing, despite advanced health services and modern methods of family planning. For the benefit of the children and young people, governments provide a variety of institutions, such as schools, colleges and universities, where young people can be socialized.

But because these institutions are becoming increasingly expensive, many children are deprived of such opportunities. Except where education is free, some governments help brilliant, but disadvantaged children, and young people, through bursaries and scholarships, to continue and complete their education. To help children and young people, some countries also offer foster care. Some have children's villages.

Most of the institutions which offer help to young people belong to non-governmental organizations such as the church. The need for social services to help children and young people cannot be overemphasized. They need all the help and guidance they can get, especially in the face of the challenges that life offers them. There is the lure of drugs, or premarital sex, both of which lead easily to sexually transmitted diseases including HIV (AIDS). The choices the young make may have grave consequences for their lives and their future. This is why support and counselling are important. It is important that the young receive adequate social services.

THE ELDERLY

Traditionally, the family insured a person throughout life. Young family members had to provide for the elderly. However, because of an increase in paid employment, young members of the family migrate to towns and cities. The result of this is that the number of people, upon whom the elderly can depend, has become smaller. Industrialization has attracted the young, and the not-so-young, to urban areas leaving the elderly relatively alone. It must be noted, however, that this does not mean that extended family obligations are not observed. During such events as births, marriages and deaths, members of the extended family still return home, and discuss their needs and plan together.

This shows that the elderly still hold a special position in the traditional family structure. Times are changing, and it will not be long before the elderly are left to fend for themselves. This is why it is becoming important among the working population to have a fund established to provide for them when they retire and no longer work. Such insurance includes retirement benefits, provident funds, and pension benefit schemes. Other personal social services are provided by both governmental and non-governmental organizations providing social services for communities. There are only a few old people's homes in Africa.

The belief remains that the extended family system continues to work, and is encouraged to provide and care for the elderly. Our career education programmes must support and encourage the ties that exist between the young members of society and the old. They must teach respect for the elderly. Everyone should be taught to consider the offers of financial institutions, such as retirement benefits, life policies, *etc.*, to reduce dependency later in their lives. Of particular importance is girl's education in this regard, because women have a longer life span than men.

THE DISABLED AND HANDICAPPED

The disabled and the handicapped have the same needs as others. They need friendship, a satisfying job, an adequate income, recreation and comfortable housing. Unfortunately, the prevailing social attitude towards them is unhealthy.

This stems from the stigma attached to the family with a disabled or handicapped member. Some families do not have the love and patience needed for such a child. Originally, a disabled person was the sole responsibility of the family. Now, many governments recognize their rights, and make efforts to provide formal and informal education services for them. These services are provided by cooperative efforts between voluntary agencies and ministries. Natural disablement is common. Counselling for the disabled is important, since some disabled people have problems in accepting themselves as they are. Some need to build up their self-image.

A handicapped girl usually worries that she may not find a husband. This reduces her self-image even further. Families whose children attend a school where there is a handicapped child also need counselling. It is important that these families teach their children to accept, and understand, the disabled or handicapped child who goes to their school. There are many countries which have institutions where children/people with the same disability live together, to receive formal or informal education and training. They have institutions like schools for the blind, deaf, mentally handicapped, or vocational rehabilitation centres for the handicapped, *etc.*

THE UNEMPLOYED

Some may say that unemployment is not a social worker's concern. Unemployment in Africa continues to be a problem. Among those affected are the rural migrants to urban areas, the rural unemployed and underemployed (unskilled), young school-leavers, the retrenched, and recently the educated unemployed. Young school-leavers leave school without proper skills to do any kind of work. They need special attention, as most of them leave school with high expectations that the government will provide them with jobs.

There is also the retrenched worker who needs crisis counselling. This means that not only career counselling is required, but also social counselling. Often, a retrenched person is desperate when he loses his job. He does not know what to do. It is like death. And his family is affected by the loss. In many countries, career or vocational counselling for workers is done by the Ministry of Labour, while the Ministry of Education is responsible for the school-going population. However, the social worker remains in contact with all types of people in your area, whether they require career/vocational counselling, or whether they are the school-going population requiring help.

You will listen to their needs and concerns, and work with other ministries to solve their problems. In some cases, you will need to provide career information, or information about where the client can register for a job. You may need to improve the client's job-seeking skills. You may also need to work with the family of the unemployed, as the burden of feeding, housing and clothing their family members still rests with them, even though they are jobless. The family of the unemployed likewise needs counselling, and this may include advice on financial matters, to help them embark on a small business enterprise.

NEEDY FAMILIES

As a result of the rapid population growth experienced by many countries in Africa, the proportion of needy families has increased. The family unit in Africa is primarily responsible for its own welfare. Many governments play a limited role when it comes to providing for needy families. One reason for this is that they have difficulty in identifying needy families. Usually, the government depends on the Department of Social Services to identify these needy families. This is why the Department encourages such people to come forward and register with them.

These could be old people in the community, the widowed, and children, who need money to go to school or buy food. Natural disasters have also contributed to an increase in needy families. These include drought, a cyclone, or a similar natural calamity. These are shocking experiences. In such cases, people not only need counselling but help with their basic needs like shelter, clothing, and food. The refugees are another group of needy people. They also need a lot of help and support.

CHILD WELFARE SYSTEM AND EMPLOYEE SECURITY

The tragedy of a rural child welfare social worker meeting her death during the process of carrying out her job duties is an unfortunate reality. Recently a child welfare worker in rural Kentucky was killed as she was in the process of providing supervised visitation for a young child and her family. It is understood by those who decide on the pursuit of achild welfare social work career that interactions with angry and sometimes violent clientele can and often will happen.

While attempting to protect children and support families, child welfare social workers face a growing threat to their safety. Shields et al. maintained that child welfare social workers charged with the task of questioning clients about private family and personal matters are at greater risk of personal injury. In a discussion of child abuse risk assessment models, English and Pecora indicated that there is practical use for a tool to determine the severity, frequency, and prediction of child abuse by high risk parents.

To date there is no tool to assist in the assessment of danger to child welfare workers who are intervening in the lives of high risk populations. Scalera observed that factors contributing to increased concern for worker safety are a collapse of family structure; poor housing conditions or homelessness; unemployment; lack of affordable health care; and substance abuse. These findings are in accord with the findings of English and Pecora who considered overall risk factors with regard to perpetrators of child abuse and found that economic status also had an independent effect on the urgency or "risk status" of child abuse cases.

EVALUATION

Sole Problems and Characteristics of Working in Rural Areas

Dillon highlighted the growing violence towards child welfare social workers in a New York Times object entitled "Social Workers: Targets in a Violent Society".

Dillon called attention to the violence faced by child welfare social workers and discussed several incidents of child welfare social worker death and injury during the course of the worker's duties. He maintained that the majority of child welfare social worker deaths occurred in rural areas which had witnessed a 21 per cent increase in violent episodes towards child welfare social workers over a three year period.

Although rural areas comprise 83 per cent of the land in the United States, little social work research focuses on the unique problems social workers face when working with the rural population. Material discussing the issues facing child welfare social workers is scant. Scalera over 12 years ago discussed the issue with regard to New Jersey child welfare social workers.

To date these are the only accessible sources of information regarding the issue. Templeman et al., highlighted how a lack of literature results in a "one-size-fits all urban-centrist" phenomenon which is detrimental to the safety of rural child welfare social workers. The Templeman study identified two distinct needs which are unique to rural families: "mechanisms to minimize isolation and increase access to specialized services".

Rural Poverty and Substance Abuse

Almost 8 million Americans live in poverty in rural areas despite the economic growth of the last decade. Rural job growth and earnings continue to fall behind metro areas obstructing the ability to move welfare recipients into gainful employment. Rural families have culturally unique characteristics which include an isolationist mentality leading to a lack of understanding and utilization of formal resources.

Because many rural social services clients are isolationist, they often reside in isolated areas affecting the child welfare social worker's emergency response times, and the client-professional relationship. Templeman contended that rural client characteristics often impact child welfare social worker recruitment and retention rates. They expand on this trend by pointing out that decreased funding, high per-unit cost for services due to low population density, restricted mobility of families, and increased mileage cost contribute to the difficulty of transferring urban models normally taught in contemporary schools and departments of social work to rural models that are rarely taught.

The lack of knowledge of rural models appears to lessen the retention rate of rural child welfare social workers due to a breakdown of understanding rural clientele. These barriers additionally contribute to increased worker safety concerns as child welfare social workers have more interaction with families outside of the agency than other social services professionals. Studies performed by Burns give credence to an increase in substance abuse and mental health issues experienced by high risk parents in the rural social welfare system.

The rise in methamphetamine use and production within rural settings has created further safety concerns for child welfare social workers. A study in a rural Midwest county found that nearly 25 per cent of daily child maltreatment reports involved parent methamphetamine abuse. Lowe reported that methamphetamine use and production is spreading throughout the rural Appalachia Ohio counties and that caseworkers need to ensure their own safety when conducting home visits. Caseworkers, who participated in the Statewide Training Assessment for the Ohio Child Welfare Training Programme, reported that they sought out training and educational materials on methamphetamine labs in an effort to protect themselves as well as their clients.

Child welfare caseworkers reported in an Ohio Statewide Training Assessment that they feel an increased sense of danger when they cannot take another worker into the field with them. They cited three reasons which prevented taking an additional worker into the field: small agencies in which two workers in the field led to inadequate coverage in the agency; agencies which would not approve overtime if two workers responded to a report after hours; and supervisors who were unaware of danger and would not approve for two workers to respond. Additionally, caseworkers cited a lack of cell phone coverage or lack of cell phone availability and an increased sense of danger.

Worker Perception of Safety in the Rural Workplace

One in every ten rural workers is pushed, shoved, or hit by one or more agency clients each year. While 97 per cent of the respondents of this study reported being screamed or cursed at on at least one occasion in the previous 12 months, one-third of the workers reported being threatened with death at least once in the year prior to the study. Macdonald et al. maintained that 84.4 per cent of the respondents who reported feeling unsafe with clients were the front-line staff.

These authors observed that child welfare social workers felt just as intimidated by threats of violence as actual acts of violence. Newhill found an occurrence rate of 75 per cent for child welfare social workers, topped only by criminal justice workers and drug/alcohol workers. The results of these studies are echoed by Ringstad who found 86 per cent of social workers experienced some type of violence during their career. Despite the high rates of occurrence, Macdonald found that nearly 25 per cent of workers did not report an incident of violence.

Responses of Rural Child Welfare Social Workers

The annual conference of the National Association of Social Workers in West Virginia provided a venue for gathering information regarding the responses of child welfare social workers regarding the question of safety at work. The authors designed the workshop as a focus group from which information could be used to influence policy development at the agency, local, state, and national levels. There was no plan to meet the qualitative research definition of focus group as defined by Sherman and Reed in this workshop.

Therefore the term focus group in this respect is a loose application. Information was collected in the form of summary notes rather than verbatim transcripts. Participants were also asked to complete a questionnaire regarding their years of experience in child welfare, demographic information, and the types and numbers of child welfare social work safety trainings that they have participated in. They were also asked to rate the trainings that they attended and provide an estimate of the numbers of events that they had experienced in which they felt that their personal safety was threatened while performing their job duties.

They were encouraged to expand on these events if they felt comfortable in doing so. Of the 34 participants, 33 were women between the ages of 25-60. The mean number of years worked was 9.9 with a standard deviation of 7.4. With regard to threats to personal safety, 88.6 per cent indicated that they had experienced at least 1 situation where they felt compromised. Information gained from the surveys and subsequent focus group summary notes revealed that participants had been: shot at with bows and arrows; hit by beer bottles; threatened with hand guns and knives; pushed and shoved; received death threats; beaten in front of the court house; the recipient of a bomb threat; and threatened with disembowelment upon the client's release from prison.

Participants emphasized that they usually travel to remote locations often alone and do not have adequate assistance during their sessions. Many participants voiced a concern about going alone on calls at night during their "on call" duties which all stated that they were required to engage in. Participants indicated that often their agencies are small and under funded. That, in tandem with their superiors' lack of understanding about the potential for violence from a particular family is often the recipe for a dangerous client encounter.

Participants also discussed the potential for bodily harm from dogs, chickens, pigs, raccoons, rats, cat, possums, goats, snakes, and roosters which many rural families have on their property. Issues regarding general health concerns surfaced during the session with regard to having been spat on from a client reported to have HIV and issues with lice, fleas, and roaches in client homes as well as sitting in chairs where clients have urinated. Several participants indicated that their clients had tried to get into their cars upon leaving a threatening scene, had lunged at them, run them off of the road, and had threatened to harm the worker's family members.

Incidents involving physical violence towards family members are especially threatening in rural areas due to small population size which allows for more familiarity about family members and where they reside. Large urban populations often reside in areas that are condensed by high rise dwellings as opposed to the smaller rural populations residing in larger areas of land mass making criminal acts often easier to hide.

Regarding the vast miles that workers have to travel, participants stated that they had encountered issues in snow and ice storms, floods, mud and mudslides, and the hazard of having to cross a creek with no bridge to a client's home. Participants voiced a concern about discovering that some clients had a history of violence which was either downplayed or undisclosed by the client.

Participants also discussed the possibility of injury from falling through wooden porches, holding onto rotten hand rails, and falling down steep stairs. Finally, participants indicated that they were often threatened by their clients in the form of the client threatening to file slander charges against them and calling the governor's and their supervisor's office to file complaints.

Rural Child Welfare Social Worker Trainings

With regard to safety training of the 34 participants, 31.4 per cent indicated that they had participated in safety trainings upon hire; 5.7 per cent indicated that they participated in safety trainings quarterly; 11.4 per cent indicated that they had participated in a safety training at least one time yearly; and 51.4 per cent maintained that they had never participated in safety trainings.

Of the 49.6 per cent who did participate in safety trainings only 11.4 per cent felt that the trainings were "somewhat important to their work". With regard to the safety training being "feasible to use in their work", approximately 46 per cent of participants engaging in safety training believed the trainings to be a feasible component to their work responsibilities.

Regarding the "ease of learning the safety techniques" 40 per cent of participants who participated in safety trainings felt that the techniques were easy to learn. Participants were asked if the techniques that they learned were easily utilized in a threatening situation. Only 36 per cent of those who participated in training felt that the techniques would be useful in a threatening situation. Finally, participants were asked how "easily the trainings were worked into their work schedules".

Approximately 35 per cent of participants felt that the trainings were practical with regard to their work schedules. These statistics reveal that these rural child welfare social work participants overwhelmingly never received any type of safety trainings related to their jobs. Although participants who were offered trainings felt that the information was important and easily learned, they appeared to be disenchanted with the feasibility of the techniques to work in a threatening situation.

Clearly, participants felt that the trainings offered to them were not easily worked into their schedules. This finding could have ramifications for agencies with regard to making trainings an important if not mandated part of child welfare social worker orientation.

Safety Issues in Social Work Education Child Welfare Field Practicums

In a study conducted by Messinger gay and lesbian social work students reported the general feeling of lack of safety and anxiety during their field placements. The students related this feeling to working with clients and within the agency atmospheres in general. Gelman found 30 per cent of foundation-year MSW students were concerned about safety issues in the field practicum.

Another 74 per cent of the students were concerned about the quality of supervision they would receive and that they might be put into situations without sufficient preparation or support. These results are congruent with the Delphi study, which found a strong consensus from respondents that safety issues needed attention in field settings. In a national survey of field directors, 42 per cent of social work programmes reported having at least one student threatened by a client during the field experience.

Yet only 12 per cent of the agencies had formal safety policies against assaults and threats. The study found that nearly one-third of social work programmes provide safety training to students. The majority of programmes had mandatory safety training with half of the programmes integrating safety training into existing course curriculum. Two-thirds of the field directors did not feel that the safety training offered by their social work programmes was adequate.

A study of violence with field placements in 1993, found that more than half of students reported their field sites did not have safety policies. Only half of the students in the study reported that their social work programmes provided safety information in relation to practice. In a similar study, students believed that field instructors are responsible for explaining safety concerns and risks concerning field placements. The study pointed out that students want field instructors to make them aware of safety procedures, formal or informal.

Current Solutions to Enhance Child Welfare Social Worker Safety

Scalera advocates for child welfare social workers to have a mandated buddy system when clients have a history of violence or a conviction involving the use of a weapon. He argues that the use of the buddy system demonstrates a commitment and a sense of entitlement that promotes worker safety. The participants at the annual National Association of Social Work conference in West Virginia also discussed safety options during the focus group session.

Their recommendations included: finding out when a client is to be released from prison; ask clients to remove barriers from exits or ask if this could be done by the worker; carry mace or pepper spray; try to stand in a client's home if possible; back your car up so that the front is facing an exit; leave purses and bags in the car if possible; carry a dog whistle; carry a regular whistle; carry dog biscuits; obtain prior information about the family and environment; do a risk assessment on violence before a home visit; use a buddy system; increase cooperation with law enforcement; leave an increasingly tense situation; build a good repairé with the client and family; obtain a concealed weapon permit for off duty times; leave the home before the client; make a call list of colleagues pertinent to a case and let them know your location before you leave; take off jewelry; put long hair into a clasp or rubber band; take a clipboard and if it is necessary to sit down it can be used; be respectful and ask the client's permission before taking any action; take few if any notes during a conversation, keep eye contact; use verbal de-escalation; take note of your instincts; use an interview room at the agency if possible; know when the client is frustrated; make sure that the agency lobby and interview rooms are secure; create alliances with family members; use flea collars in the cuffs of slacks and in car floor boards; use four wheel drive vehicles; use antennas designed to work in remote locations for cell phones; know where to find gas, food, and restrooms en route to a client's home; always keep an emergency cell phone charger in the car; have on hand disinfecting wipes; diaper wipes; lice spray; disinfectant spray; garbage bags; mentholated rub; extra clothes and shoes; flashlight and batteries; spare glasses or contact lenses; shovel; rock salt; and cat litter. The participants also indicated that the worker should always lock their car doors, and if possible have an electronic opener and carry a spare set of keys in their pockets.

CHILDREN'S RIGHTS

Children's rights are the human rights of children with particular attention to the rights of special protection and care afforded to the young, including their right to association with both biological parents, human identity as well as the basic needs for food, universal state-paid education, health care and criminal laws appropriate for the age and development of the child.

Interpretations of children's rights range from allowing children the capacity for autonomous action to the enforcement of children being physically, mentally and emotionally free from abuse, though what constitutes "abuse" is a matter of debate. Other definitions include the rights to care and nurturing. "A child is any human being below the age of eighteen years, unless under the law applicable to the child, majority is attained earlier." Cornell University, a child is a person, not a subperson, and the parent has absolute interest and possession of the child, but this is very much an American view. The term "child" does not necessarily mean minor but can include adult children as well as adult non-dependent children.

There are no definitions of other terms used to describe young people such as "adolescents", "teenagers," or "youth" in international law, but the children's rights movement is considered distinct from the youth rights movement. The field of children's rights spans the fields of law, politics, religion, and morality.

RATIONALE

As minors by law children do not have autonomy or the right to make decisions on their own for themselves in any known jurisdiction of the world. Instead their adult caregivers, including parents, social workers, teachers, youth workers and others, are vested with that authority, depending on the circumstances. Some believe that this state of affairs gives children insufficient control over their own lives and causes them to be vulnerable.

Louis Althusser has gone so far as describe this legal machinery, as it applies to children, as "repressive state apparatuses". Structures such as government policy have been held by some commentators to mask the ways adults abuse and exploit children, resulting in child poverty, lack of educational opportunities, and child labour. On this view, children are to be regarded as a minority group towards whom society needs to reconsider the way it behaves.

However, there is no evidence that such views are widely shared in society. Researchers have identified children as needing to be recognized as participants in society whose rights and responsibilities need to be recognized at all ages.

HISTORIC DEFINITIONS OF CHILDREN'S RIGHTS

Consensus on defining children's rights has become clearer in the last fifty years. A 1973 publication by Hillary Clinton stated that children's rights were a "slogan in need of a definition". The notion of children's rights is still not well defined, with at least one proposing that there is no singularly accepted definition or theory of the rights held by children. Children's rights law is defined as the point where the law intersects with a child's life.

That includes juvenile delinquency, due process for children involved in the criminal justice system, appropriate representation, and effective rehabilitative services; care and protection for children in state care; ensuring education for all children regardless of their origin, race, gender, disabilities, or abilities, and; health care and advocacy.

TYPES OF RIGHTS

Children's rights are defined in numerous ways, including a wide spectrum of civil, cultural, economic, social and political rights. Rights tend to be of two general types: those advocating for children as autonomous persons under the law and those placing a claim on society for protection from harms perpetrated on children because of their dependency. These have been labeled as the right of empowerment and as the right to protection.

One Canadian organization categorizes children's rights into three categories:

1. *Provision:* Children have the right to an adequate standard of living, health care, education and services, and to play. These include a balanced diet, a warm bed to sleep in, and access to schooling.
2. *Protection:* Children have the right to protection from abuse, neglect, exploitation and discrimination. This includes the right to safe places for children to play; constructive child rearing behaviour, and acknowledgment of the evolving capacities of children.
3. *Participation:* Children have the right to participate in communities and have programmes and services for themselves. This includes children's involvement in libraries and community programmes, youth voice activities, and involving children as decision-makers.

In a similar fashion, the Child Rights Information Network, or CRIN for short, categorizes rights into two groups:

1. Economic, social and cultural rights, related to the conditions necessary to meet basic human needs such as food, shelter, education, health care, and gainful employment. Included are rights to education, adequate housing, food, water, the highest attainable standard of health, the right to work and rights at work, as well as the cultural rights of minorities and indigenous peoples.
2. Environmental, cultural and developmental rights, which are sometimes called "third generation rights," and including the right to live in safe and healthy environments and that groups of people have the right to cultural, political, and economic development.

Amnesty International openly advocates four particular children's rights, including the end to juvenile incarceration without parole, an end to the recruitment of military use of children, ending the death penalty for people under 21, and raising awareness of human rights in the classroom. Human Rights Watch, an international advocacy organization, includes child labour, juvenile justice, orphans and abandoned children, refugees, street children and corporal punishment. Scholarly study generally focuses children's rights by identifying individual rights.

The following rights "allow children to grow up healthy and free":

- Freedom of speech
- Freedom of thought
- Freedom from fear
- Freedom of choice and the right to make decisions
- Ownership over one's body

Other issues affecting children's rights include the sale of children, child prostitution and child pornography.

Difference between Children's Rights and Youth Rights

"In the majority of jurisdictions, for instance, children are not allowed to vote, to marry, to buy alcohol, to have sex, or to engage in paid employment." Within the youth rights movement, it is believed that the key difference between children's rights and youth rights is that children's rights supporters generally advocate the establishment and enforcement of protection for children and youths, while youth rights generally advocates the expansion of freedom for children and/or youths and of rights such as suffrage. Also, many people who support youth rights, are concerned with adolescents and not children.

Parental Rights

Parents affect the lives of children in a unique way, and as such their role in children's rights has to be distinguished in a particular way. Particular issues in the child-parent relationship include child neglect, child abuse, freedom of choice, corporal punishment and child custody. There have been theories offered that provide parents with rights-based practices that resolve the tension between "commonsense parenting" and children's rights.

The issue is particularly relevant in legal proceedings that affect the potential emancipation of minors, and in cases where children sue their parents. A child's rights to a relationship with both their parents is increasingly recognized as an important factor for determining the best interests of the child in divorce and child custody proceedings. Some governments have enacted laws creating a rebuttable presumption that shared parenting is in the best interests of children.

MOVEMENT

The Children's Rights Movement is a historical and modern movement committed to the acknowledgment, expansion, and/or regression of the rights of children around the world.

While the historical definition of child has varied, the United Nations Convention on the Rights of the Child explains, "A child is any human being below the age of eighteen years, unless under the law applicable to the child, majority is attained earlier."

There are no definitions of other terms used to describe young people such as "adolescents", "teenagers" or "youth" in international law. Thomas Spence's The Rights of Infants is an early English-language assertion of the natural rights of children. In the USA, the Children's Rights Movement was born in the 1800s with the orphan train. In the big cities, when a child's parents died or were extremely poor, the child frequently had to go to work to support himself and/or his family. Boys generally became factory or coal workers, and girls became prostitutes or saloon girls, or else went to work in a sweat shop. All of these jobs paid only starvation wages. In 1852, Massachusetts required children to attend school. In 1853, Charles Brace founded the Children's Aid Society, which worked hard to take street children in. The following year, the children were placed on a train headed for the West, where they were adopted, and often given work.

By 1929, the orphan train stopped running altogether, but its principles lived on. The National Child Labour Committee, an organization dedicated to the abolition of all child labour, was formed in the 1890s. It managed to pass one law, which was struck down by the Supreme Court two years later for violating a child's right to contract his work. In 1924, Congress attempted to pass a constitutional amendment that would authorize a national child labour law.

This measure was blocked, and the bill was eventually dropped. It took the Great Depression to end child labour nationwide; adults had become so desperate for jobs that they would work for the same wage as children. In 1938, President Franklin D. Roosevelt signed the Fair Labour Standards Act which, amongst other things, placed limits on many forms of child labour. Now that child labour had been effectively eradicated in parts of the world, the movement turned to other things, but it again stalled when World War II broke out and children and women began to enter the workforce once more.

With millions of adults at war, the children were needed to help keep the country running. In Europe, children served as couriers, intelligence collectors, and other underground resistance workers in opposition to Hitler's regime. In the early twentieth century, moves began to promote the idea of children's rights as distinct from those of adults and as requiring explicit recognition. The Polish educationalist Janusz Korczak wrote of the rights of children in his book How to Love a Child; a later book was entitled The Child's Right to Respect.

In 1917, following the Russian Revolution, the Moscow branch of the organization Proletkult produced a Declaration of Children's Rights. However, the first effective attempt to promote children's rights was the Declaration of the Rights of the Child, drafted by Eglantyne Jebb in 1923 and adopted by the League of Nations in 1924. This was accepted by the United Nations on its formation and updated in 1959, and replaced with a more extensive UN Convention on the Rights of the Child in 1989.

From the formation of the United Nations in the 1940s and extending to present day, the Children's Rights Movement has become global in focus. While the situation of children in the United States has become grave, children around the world have increasingly become engaged in illegal, forced child labour, genital mutilation, military service, and sex trafficking. Several international organizations have rallied to the assistance of children.

They include Save the Children, Free the Children, and the Children's Defence Fund. The Child Rights Information Network, or CRIN, formed in 1983, is the group of 1,600 non-governmental organizations from around the world which advocate for the implementation of the Convention on the Rights of the Child. Organization's report on their countries' progress towards implementation, as do governments that have ratified the Convention. Every 5 years reporting to the United Nations Committee on the Rights of the Child is required for governments.

While there is a long history of children's rights in the U.S., scholars contend that there is no "golden age". Many children's rights advocates in the U.S. today advocate for a smaller agenda than their international peers. Groups predominately focus on child abuse and neglect, child fatalities, foster care, youth aging out of foster care, preventing foster care placement, and adoption. A longstanding movement promoting youth rights in the United States has made substantial gains in the past.Anti-Children's Rights propagandists often raise the spectre of Rights without Responsibilities.

The Children's Rights Movement assert that it is rather the case that children have rights which adults, states and government have a responsibility to uphold. The UK maintains a position that UNCRC is not legally enforceable and is hence 'aspirational' only-albeit a 2003 ECHR ruling states: "The human rights of children and the standards to which all governments must aspire in realizing these rights for all children are set out in the Convention on the Rights of the Child.". 18 years after ratification, the four Children's Commissioners in the devolved administrations have united in calling for adoption of the Convention into domestic legislation, making children's rights legally enforceable.

Several countries have created an institute of children's rights ombudsman, most notably Sweden, Finland and Ukraine, which is first country worldwide to install children at that post. In Ukraine Ivan Cherevko and Julia Kruk became first children's rights ombudsmen in late 2005.

The United Nations Convention on the Rights of the Child has outlined a standard premise for the children's rights movement and has been ratified by all but two nations-the United States and Somalia. Somalia's inability to sign the Convention is attributed to their lack of governmental structure. The US administration under Bush has opposed ratifying the Convention because of "serious political and legal concerns that it conflicts with U.S. policies on the central role of parents, sovereignty, and state and local law." However, the new administration may be taking another look at it.

INTERNATIONAL LAW

The Universal Declaration of Human Rights is seen as a basis for all international legal standards for children's rights today. There are several conventions and laws that address children's rights around the world. A number of current and historical documents affect those rights, including the 1923 Declaration of the Rights of the Child, drafted by Eglantyne Jebb and her sister Dorothy Buxton in London, England in 1919, endorsed by the League of Nations and adopted by the United Nations in 1946. It later served as the basis for the Convention on the Rights of the Child.

Convention on the Rights of the Child

The United Nations' 1989 Convention on the Rights of the Child, or CRC, is the first legally binding international instrument to incorporate the full range of human rights—civil, cultural, economic, political and social rights. Its implementation is monitored by the Committee on the Rights of the Child. National governments that ratify it commit themselves to protecting and ensuring children's rights, and agree to hold themselves accountable for this commitment before the international community.

The CRC is the most widely ratified human rights treaty with 190 ratifications. Somalia and USA are the only two countries which have not agreed to the CRC. The CRC is based on four core principles, namely the principle of non discrimination, the best interests of the child, the right to life, survival and development, and considering the views of the child in decisions which affect them. The CRC, along with international criminal accountability mechanisms such as the International Criminal Court, the Yugoslavia and Rwanda Tribunals, and the Special Court for Sierra Leone, is said to have significantly increased the profile of children's rights worldwide.

Enforcement

A variety of enforcement organizations and mechanisms exist to ensure children's rights and the successful implementation of the Union. They include the Child Rights Caucus for the United Nations General Assembly Special Session on Children. It was set up to promote full implementation and compliance with the Convention on the Rights of the Child, and to ensure that child rights were given priority during the UN General Assembly Special Session on Children and its Preparatory process.

The United Nations Human Rights Council was created "with the hope that it could be more objective, credible and efficient in denouncing human rights violations worldwide than the highly politicised Commission on Human Rights." The NGO Group for the Convention on the Rights of the Child is a coalition of international non-governmental organisations originally formed in 1983 to facilitate the implementation of the United Nations Convention on the Rights of the Child.

Many countries around the world have children's rights ombudspeople or children's commissioners whose official, governmental duty is to represent the interests of the public by investigating and addressing complaints reported by individual citizens regarding children's rights. Children's ombudspeople can also work for a corporation, a newspaper, an NGO, or even for the general public.

United States law

Children are generally afforded the basic rights embodied by the Constitution, as enshrined by the Fourteenth Amendment to the United States Constitution. The Equal Protection Clause of that amendment is to apply to children, born within a marriage or not, but excludes children not yet born. This was reinforced by the landmark US Supreme Court decision of In re Gault. In this trial 15-year-old Gerald Gault of Arizona was taken into custody by local police after being accused of making an obscene telephone call.

He was detained and committed to the Arizona State Industrial School until he reached the age of 21 for making an obscene phone call to an adult neighbour. In an 8–1 decision, the Court ruled that in hearings which could result in commitment to an institution, people under the age of 18 have the right to notice and counsel, to question witnesses, and to protection against self-incrimination. The Court found that the procedures used in Gault's hearing met none of these requirements. There are other concerns in the United States regarding children's rights. The American Academy of Adoption Attorneys is concerned with children's rights to a safe, supportive and stable family structure. Their position on children's rights in adoption cases states that, "children have a constitutionally based liberty interest in the protection of their established families, rights which are at least equal to, and we believe outweigh, the rights of others who would claim a 'possessory' interest in these children." Other issues raised in American children's rights advocacy include children's rights to inheritance in same-sex marriages and particular rights for youth.

STANDARDS FOR SOCIAL WORK PRACTICE WITH FAMILY CAREGIVERS OF OLDER ADULTS

STANDARD 1. ETHICS AND VALUES

Social workers practicing with family caregivers of older adults shall adhere to the ethics and values of the social work profession, using the NASW *Code of Ethics* as a guide to ethical decision making.

Interpretation

The primary mission of the social work profession is to enhance human well-being and to help meet the basic needs of all people, with particular attention to the needs of people who are vulnerable and oppressed.

This mission is rooted in a set of core values that constitutes the foundation of social work and relates closely to social work with family caregivers of older adults:

- *Service*: Social workers apply their knowledge and skills to support the well-being of family caregivers of older adults and to address challenges faced by family caregivers.
- *Social Justice*: Social workers act on individual and systemic levels to ensure access to needed information, services, and resources for family caregivers of older adults and to facilitate family caregivers' meaningful and comfortable participation in decision making.
- *Human Dignity and Worth:* Social workers treat family caregivers of older adults in a respectful and caring manner. They promote family caregivers' self-determination, with sensitivity and respect for the self-determination of older adults when confronted with conflicting values and goals.
- *Importance of Human Relationships:* Social workers engage family caregivers, to the extent possible, as partners in goal identification, progress, and achievement. They strive to strengthen relationships between family caregivers and older adults so as to maintain and enhance the well-being of the family system.
- *Integrity:* Social workers use the power inherent in their professional role responsibly, exercising judicious use of self and avoiding conflicts of interest. Their practice with, and on behalf of, family caregivers of older adults is consistent with the profession's mission and ethics.
- *Competence:* Social workers practice within their areas of competence and continually strive to enhance their knowledge and skills related to family caregiving and aging. Competence also requires that social workers recognize the importance of, and attend to, their own self-care.

The very term *family* is, in fact, rooted in ethical values. For the purposes of these standards, *family* refers to family of origin, extended family, domestic partners, friends, or other individuals who support an older adult and whose primary relationship with the older adult is not based on a financial or professional agreement.

Social work practice with family caregivers of older adults begins with honouring the uniqueness of each family system. Effective practice with family caregivers of older adults requires social workers to identify their own values and perspectives regarding aging and family caregiving, including their personal experiences as family caregivers or with aging family members.

Social workers have an ethical responsibility to assess how their own experiences influence their practice with family caregivers of older adults, to ensure they are not imposing their own values on family caregivers of older adults. Differences in the wishes, perceptions, and capacity of older adults and family caregivers can present complex ethical and legal challenges to social workers.

Social workers must know and comply with federal, state, local, and tribal laws, regulations, and policies related to older adults, such as reporting requirements for elder abuse and neglect, guardianship, and advance directives.

Obtaining informed consent, maintaining confidentiality, and protecting privacy are critical. Careful application of ethical principles is especially important when older adults or family caregivers have limited decision-making capacity or are experiencing or perpetuating mistreatment. Collaboration with colleagues can also help resolve ethical dilemmas.

STANDARD 2. QUALIFICATIONS

Social workers who practice with family caregivers of older adults shall possess a degree in social work from a school or programme accredited by the Council on SocialWork Education; shall comply with state-based licensing and certification requirements; and shall have knowledge, skills, and professional experience in aging and family caregiving.

Interpretation

Social work degree programmes provide education and training in social work values, ethics, theories, practice, policy, and research. This training is essential for any individual engaging in the practice of social work. Social work licensing and certification laws vary by state. It is each social worker's responsibility to ensure compliance with the licensing and certification laws of her or his respective state.

Social work practice with (or on behalf of) family caregivers of older adults requires specialized knowledge and skills as outlined in these standards. Ideally, social workers attain such knowledge and skills during their degree programmes through coursework and field practice experience related to aging and family caregiving.

Specialty practice certifications may also indicate expertise in areas relevant to practice with family caregivers of older adults, such as gerontological social work, geriatric care management, case management, or health care. Whether through certification, continuing education, or professional experience, social workers should continually enhance their skills and knowledge related to aging and family caregiving.

As the aging population grows and family caregiving becomes increasingly central to health care and social service delivery, social workers will increasingly interface with older adults and family caregivers, regardless of practice specialty or setting.

Social workers specializing in areas other than aging and family caregiving should seek supervision, consultation, and continuing professional development, as described in these standards, to ensure they have the requisite knowledge of systems of care and skills for practice with older adults and family caregivers (or to make responsible referrals to other social workers with expertise in this area).

STANDARD 3. KNOWLEDGE

Social workers shall acquire and maintain a working knowledge of current theory, practice, sociohistorical context, policy, evidence-based research, and evaluation methods related to aging and family caregiving and shall integrate such information into practice.

Interpretation

Social work with family caregivers of older adults is a specialized practice area requiring focused preparation and continuing education. Social workers apply knowledge about aging, resilience, disability, health conditions, and caregiving to enhance the well-being of family caregivers of older adults. Social workers also support family caregivers in navigating health care and social service systems, accessing resources, and identifying service gaps and barriers.

Knowledge essential to social work with family caregivers of older adults includes, but is not limited to, the following areas:

- Aging
  - Concepts and theories associated with aging, such as cohorts and lifespan development
  - Physiological and cognitive processes associated with healthy aging
  - Grief, loss, death, dying, and bereavement
  - Effects of ageism on medical and social service delivery to older adults
- Physical health
  - Physiological and cognitive processes associated with acute and chronic conditions and medication use and misuse
  - Psychosocial effects of acute, chronic, and life-limiting illness
  - Psychosocial effects of physical and cognitive disability
- Mental and behavioural health
  - Depression, anxiety, and other mental health conditions
  - Addictive behaviours and their effect on the family system
  - Elder abuse, neglect, and exploitation
- Family caregiving experiences
  - Family systems, interpersonal dynamics, and the complexity of caregiving relationships
  - Interdependence in care partnerships (*i.e.*, between caregivers and care recipients)
  - Family caregivers' central role in health care delivery
  - Growth and rewards associated with family caregiving

  - Physical, emotional, and financial challenges associated with family caregiving at various points in the individual lifespan and family life cycle
  - Signs of caregiver strain
  - Reengagement and healing after death of care recipient
- Resources
  - Health care, long-term care, social service, and housing systems and programmes
  - Policies, eligibility requirements, and financial concerns affecting family caregivers and older adults
  - Resources available to family caregivers and older adults, such as respite care, family medical leave, and assistive technology
- Professional social work role
  - The multifaceted social work roles and functions related to family caregiving and aging
  - Interdisciplinary collaboration
  - Appropriate professional boundaries and use of self, including managing countertransference when social workers are personally involved in family caregiving outside of the workplace
  - Signs of, and strategies to address, ethical dilem-mas, compassion fatigue, burnout, secondary traumatization, and professional grief

STANDARD 4. CULTURAL AND LINGUISTIC COMPETENCE

Social workers shall provide and facilitate access to culturally and linguistically appropriate services to family caregivers of older adults, consistent with the *NASW Indicators for the Achievement of the NASW Standards for Cultural Competence in Social Work Practice*.

Interpretation

The increasing cultural and linguistic diversity of family caregivers and older adults requires social workers to strive continually for cultural and linguistic competence. Social workers' recognition and affirmation of cultural and linguistic diversity are critical both to the formation of therapeutic alliances with family caregivers and to cooperative working relationships with colleagues.

Such diversity includes, but is not limited to, race, ethnicity, socioeconomic class, biological sex, gender identity, sexual orientation, religion, age, health status, preferred language, migration background, documentation status, degree of acculturation, and literacy (including health and financial literacy). It can also include vocational affiliations, such as participation in the military or involvement in veterans' services. Cultural competence begins with each social worker's cultural self-identification. Cultural self-awareness is fundamental to recognizing and addressing how one's own cultural values, beliefs, experiences, and practices affect interactions with family caregivers and colleagues. Social workers who practice such self-assessment can then recognize how cultural identity, in its multifaceted expressions, is central to the resilience of the individuals, families, and communities with which they interact.

Specifically, social workers need to support family caregivers' resilience by appreciating and affirming the cultural values, beliefs, and practices of family caregivers with whom they work, especially the ways in which culture influences perceptions and practices related to aging, illness, and disability; physical and psychosocial pain; health care treatments; providing care to, or receiving care from, family members; help-seeking behaviours; health care, financial, and other decision making; and death and dying.

Social workers also need to recognize that culture varies within families. These differences may manifest in multiple ways, such as different perceptions of caregiving responsi-bilities or varying levels of fluency in the dominant language of the country of residence. In such instances, social workers should honour the differences within the family system and facilitate maximal participation of all members with whom they interact—by using professional interpreters rather than relying on family caregivers to interpret for older adults, for example.

Cultural and linguistic factors influence not only practitioner-client relationships but also organizational structures and societal structures and dynamics. Social workers should comprehend how systemic or institutional oppression related to cultural and linguistic diversity (such as ageism, racism, or sexism) affects family caregivers' role in care, access to and utilization of resources, health care outcomes, and well-being.

Identification of ageism in policy, the media, and systems of care is especially useful in helping families contextualize the challenges they face—and, sometimes, in identifying and addressing their own ageism. Action to eliminate ageism and other forms of institutional oppression on organizational, community, and broader levels is essential to optimizing family caregiving roles and reducing economic, health, and social disparities experienced by family caregivers and older adults.

STANDARD 5. ASSESSMENT

Social workers shall assess family caregivers of older adults on an ongoing basis, gathering comprehensive information to develop and amend plans for care or services.

Interpretation

Biopsychosocial assessment is the foundation of social work practice and is conducted in collaboration with the family system. Assessment is a complex function requiring openness to a wide variety of information, both verbal and non-verbal, presented by the family system in the context of the social environment.

Using empathy, client-centered interviewing skills, and methods appropriate to clients' capacity, social workers engage family caregivers of older adults in identifying their strengths, resources, and concerns.

Because assessment guides intervention, social workers need to complete initial assessments in a timely manner and then reassess and revise service plans in response to caregivers' shifting needs and altered goals. Use of standardized assessment instruments, such as caregiver burden scales, can aid social workers in identifying and responding to caregivers' concerns. Social work assessments may vary based on practice setting and specialty.

Comprehensive biopsychosocial social work assessments of family caregivers of older adults may include the following domains, as they pertain to service needs:

- Family characteristics and dynamics
  - Motivating factors in seeking social work services, if applicable
  - Family structure and roles, including the ways various family members provide care and identified decision-makers (both legally and informally designated)
  - Communication patterns, conflict management styles, and alliances within the family system, especially history of relationships between caregiver(s) and older adult receiving care
  - Living arrangements
  - Vocational history (*e.g.*, work, school, or voluntee-ring) and lifespan development
  - Language preferences and proficiency levels
  - Degrees of literacy, including health and financial literacy
  - Cultural values, beliefs, and practices (including spirituality and religion) related to caregiving and aging

  (a) Psychosocial strengths, protective factors, and points of resilience
  (b) Family system experiences, including genera-tional patterns, related to illness, disability, loss, and death throughout the life cycle
  (c) Family's relationships with community and religious organizations
  (d) Experiences specific to populations such as immigrants and refugees, survivors of violence or trauma, child or adolescent caregivers, and people who are homeless, and family system's responses to those experiences
- Risk assessment
  - Physical, cognitive, and psychosocial functioning of older adults receiving care
  - Older adults' desire and capacity for independence
  - Degree of adherence to plan of care, including medications

- Household environment and need for adaptive equipment, home modification, or alternate living arrangements
- Family caregivers' self-care capacity (physical, emotional, and cognitive)
- Family caregivers' perceptions of older adults' capacity for independence and tolerance of safety risks
- Family caregivers' physical, emotional, and cognitive capacity to fulfill caregiving responsibilities
- Family system's psychosocial supports, both formal and informal, and barriers to access
- Family system's financial resources and barriers to access
- Family system's ability to navigate health, long-term care, and social service systems
- Advance care planning, including use and compre-hension of advance directives and other legal documents
- Family system's behavioural and mental health functioning, including history, coping styles, crisis management skills, and risk of suicide or homicide
- Risk of abuse, neglect, or exploitation by or of family caregivers, and underlying causes for such mistreatment

- Goals and effects of family caregiving
  - Caregivers' goals for care of their older family member(s)
  - Indicators of caregiver burden, such as depression, anxiety, deteriorating health, financial insecurity, and social isolation
  - Impact of health conditions and caregiving on emotional intimacy and, if applicable, sexual relationships between family caregivers and older adults
  - Impact of caregiving on caregivers' other relation-ships and responsibilities
  - Family caregivers' need for physical assistance, emotional or social support, respite, financial resources, or other services
  - Changes in policies and programmes needed to support family system

STANDARD 6. SERVICE PLANNING, DELIVERY, AND MONITORING

Social workers shall collaborate with family caregivers of older adults to plan, deliver, and monitor individualized services that promote caregivers' strengths and well-being. Care plans shall be based on assessments and have measurable objectives.

Interpretation

Social work services should be designed to meet the biopsychosocial needs of family caregivers of older adults and should be delivered in a manner that ensures confidentiality in accordance with the NASW*Code of Ethics*. Service planning, delivery, and monitoring draw not only on ongoing, comprehensive social work assessments but also, if appropriate and available, on the input of other service providers involved in supporting the family system.

Collaborative engagement of family caregivers of older adults throughout the service planning, delivery, and monitoring process is critical to ensure that services are mutually agreed upon, appropriate to caregivers' circum-stances, clearly communicated, and delivered in a timely manner.

Care plans should include short-and long-term goals centered on family caregivers of older adults. Service frequency and duration may be affected by practitioner role and setting parameters but, ideally, should be in accordance with the needs and goals identified in the assessment.

Care plans also vary by the social worker's scope of practice and may incorporate the following services:

- Education and coaching (*e.g.*, wellness promotion, disease management, and differentiating normal age-related changes from behaviours that may warrant professional evaluation)
- Lifespan and advance care planning
- Individual counseling and psychotherapy drawing on a variety of modalities (*e.g.*, psychodynamic or cognitive-behavioural)
- Couples and family counseling
- Family-team conferences
- Group interventions (*e.g.*, caregiver or bereavement support groups)
- Interventions addressing grief, loss, end-of-life issues, and bereavement
- Mediation and conflict resolution
- Crisis intervention
- Client advocacy and systems navigation
- Team, organizational, and interorganizational care planning and collaboration
- Resource information and referral (*e.g.*, medical, psychosocial, financial, and legal resources)
- Case/care management and care coordination
- Planning for service termination or discharge, including planning for cessation of family caregiving roles and supports associated with that transition

STANDARD 7. ADVOCACY

Social workers shall advocate for the needs, decisions, and rights of family caregivers of older adults. The social worker shall engage in social and political action that seeks to ensure that family caregivers of older adults have equitable access to resources to meet their biopsychosocial needs.

Interpretation

Effective advocacy involves helping family caregivers of older adults identify and define their strengths, needs, and goals, and to communicate those needs and goals to service providers and decision-makers.

Social workers strive not only to promote family caregivers' self-advocacy, but also to enhance the capacity of communities to integrate family caregivers' contributions. Creativity and flexibility are central to successful advocacy efforts with, and on behalf of, family caregivers of older adults.

Social work advocacy takes place on both micro and macro levels and may involve the following activities:

- Adaptation of organizational policy, procedures, and resources to facilitate service provision to multicultural clientele
- Advocacy with other service providers and organiza-tions to improve family caregivers' access to high-quality services
- Identification and development of strategies to address service gaps, fragmentation, discrimination, and other barriers that affect family caregivers of older adults
- Inclusion of family caregivers of older adults in advocacy efforts and in programme design, planning, and evaluation
- Analysis of historical and current local, state, and national policies as they affect family caregivers of older adults, especially historically marginalized or underresourced populations
- Education of the public, the media, corporations, and policymakers regarding the strengths, contributions, needs, and concerns of family caregivers of older adults
- Advocacy to foster age-friendly community capacity and to enhance the contributions of family caregivers of older adults
- Use of multiple media, including written materials, oral presentations, and computer technology, to achieve advocacy goals

STANDARD 8. COLLABORATION

Social workers shall promote interdisciplinary and interorganizational collaboration to support, enhance, and create services delivered to family caregivers of older adults.

Interpretation

Multiple service providers and organizations are often involved in supporting family caregivers of older adults. Collaboration within care teams and organizations, as well as among organizations and service delivery systems, is essential to continuity of care for family caregivers of older adults. Social workers play an integral role in fostering, maintaining, and strengthening such partnerships.

As members of teams and organizations serving older adults and family caregivers, social workers shall demonstrate the following abilities:

- Differentiate social work perspectives, values, and interventions from other disciplines
- Describe and support the roles of other disciplines and organizations involved in supporting family care-givers of older adults
- Articulate and fulfill the missions and functions of their employing organizations
- Communicate effectively with all professionals, direct care workers, and volunteers involved in supporting family caregivers of older adults
- Advocate for family caregivers' integral role in team communications and service planning, delivery, and monitoring
- Communicate family system information in a respectful, objective manner while protecting clients' confidentiality and privacy
- Promote the strengths, contributions, needs, and goals of family caregivers of older adults
- Facilitate communication between family caregivers and providers/ organizations involved in supporting the family system
- Share team leadership in planning and providing services to family caregivers of older adults
- Create organizational culture that promotes effective, coordinated services for family caregivers of older adults
- Foster and maintain partnerships across disciplines, organizations, and the service spectrum to enhance access to and continuity of care for family caregivers of older adults
- Integrate a strengths perspective in programme and organizational administration to maximize and sustain human and fiscal resources on behalf of family caregivers of older adults
- Manage personal and interpersonal processes at the intraorganizational, interorganizational, and community levels to optimize services for family caregivers of older adults

STANDARD 9. PRACTICE EVALUATION AND IMPROVEMENT

Social workers serving family caregivers of older adults shall participate in ongoing, formal evaluation of their practice to maximize family caregivers' well-being, assess quality and appropriateness of services, improve practice, and ensure competence.

Interpretation

Evaluation entails soliciting and integrating internal and external feedback on the process and outcomes of social work practice with family caregivers of older adults. Practice evaluation is vital to ensuring that services provided to family caregivers of older adults are appropriate, effective, timely, and efficient in helping family caregivers achieve their goals.

Such goals may include reduction of stress, enhanced ability to fulfill caregiving responsibilities, improved balance between caregiving responsibilities and other commitments, or increased time and strategies for self-care. Moreover, outcomes from evaluations are increasingly used for position justification, performance review, practice standards, goal setting, and research efforts. As in all phases of practice with family caregivers, caregiver involvement is essential, as is protecting the privacy of the family system and other service providers.

Evaluation practices may include the following activities:

- Solicitation and incorporation of feedback from family caregivers of older adults regarding the extent to which social work services helped caregivers identify and achieve their goals
- Strategic planning to reach measurable objectives in programme, organizational, or community development for family caregivers of older adults
- Development of programme budgets that take into account diverse sources of financial support for family caregivers of older adults
- Application of appropriate tools such as clinical indicators, practice guidelines, family caregiver satisfaction surveys, and standardized performance assessments
- Measurement of both process and outcome objectives
- Use of external practice or programme evaluators, as appropriate
- Practitioner, programme, and organizational self-evaluation
- Use of peer review, supervision, and consultation with other social workers and across disciplines
- Incorporation of evaluation practices in the service transfer or termination process
- Participation in social work research, including qualitative research
- Application of evaluation and research findings (including evidence-based practice, when available) to enhance practice and programme outcomes
- Dissemination of evaluative data to clients, payers, and other professionals on request, and with consideration for privacy rights

STANDARD 10. DOCUMENTATION

Social workers shall document all practice with family caregivers of older adults in the appropriate client record. Social work documentation may be recorded in writing or electronically and shall be completed, maintained, and disclosed in accordance with regulatory, legislative, statutory, and employer requirements.

Interpretation

Clear, concise, and ongoing documentation of social work practice facilitates clear communication with other service providers and organizations, thereby promoting continuity of care and services. Documentation also serves as a foundation for practice and programme evaluation and for creating new service delivery models on behalf of family caregivers of older adults. The purpose of documentation is not to supplant but, rather, to foster strong working relationships with, and services for, family caregivers.

Thus, documentation should reflect family caregivers' involvement in, and concordance with, all phases of social work practice: assessment; service planning, delivery, and monitoring; practice evaluation and improvement; and termination or transfer of services. Social workers can ensure their practice centers on family caregivers by incorporating in their documentation caregivers' own words, stories, goals, and feedback.

Social work documentation should reflect the following elements:

- Dates, times, and descriptions of contact with family caregivers, other members of the family system, and other service providers or organizations
- Initial and subsequent psychosocial assessments of family caregivers
- Concerns and services discussed with family caregivers
- Plan of care, services, or treatment
- Services provided, including education offered and written information presented to family caregivers
- Outcomes of service provision
- Referrals to or from other providers, organizations, or resources, including rationale for referrals
- Supervision or consultation sought or provided to enhance practice with family caregivers

The client record should also include the following elements:

- Follow-up and recommendations from external providers or organizations
- Written permission, when appropriate, to release and obtain information
- Compliance with confidentiality and privacy rights and responsibilities
- Receipts and disbursements related to client service provision
- Rationale for termination or transfer of services

STANDARD 11.WORKLOAD

Social workers shall advocate for a workload that allows for efficient, high-quality service delivery to family caregivers of older adults. The size of the social work staff shall represent both the scope and complexity of the organization and the nature and numbers of the populations served.

Interpretation

Social workers, social work managers, and organizations have joint responsibility for establishing and maintaining a workload that allows for adequate and appropriate interventions and monitoring of services and outcomes. A workload consists of any social work function, such as direct practice, administration, policy, research, or education, performed for the purpose of the social work position. The workload also reflects the needs and goals of the population served and may include social work coverage outside of regular office hours.

STANDARD 12. PROFESSIONAL DEVELOPMENT AND COMPETENCE

Social workers practicing with, or on behalf of, family caregivers of older adults shall assume personal responsibility for their professional development and competence in accordance with the NASW*Code of Ethics*, the *NASW Standards for Continuing Professional Education*, and state licensure or certification requirements.

Interpretation

Aging and family caregiving are rapidly expanding specialties that cross all practice settings. Social workers must engage in ongoing professional development to maintain competence in their practice with family caregivers of older adults. Employing organizations should encourage and support social workers' participation in professional develop-ment activities.

Such activities may include receiving or providing continuing education, training, supervision, or mentoring, as well as participating in peer review, research, and publication activities. Numerous opportunities for professional development exist within NASW, other professional organizations, schools of social work, and organizations providing services to or on behalf of older adults or family caregivers at the local, state, national, and international levels.

Professional development activities relevant to practice with family caregivers of older adults may address the following topics:

- Developments in social work theory, practice, and research
- Policies and legislation affecting family caregivers of older adults
- Community resources available to family caregivers of older adults
- Issues and experiences specific to aging, family systems, caregiver health and wellness, disability, grief and loss, death and dying, elder mistreatment, and ethics
- Cultural and linguistic competence
- Assessment of professional and personal strengths, learning needs, and goals as related to social work practice
- Professional and personal self-care

WOMEN'S RIGHT AND ITS OBSTACLES

THE CONSTITUTIONAL POSITION

While the Constitution of India adopted in November 1949 contains articles mandating equality and non-discrimination on the grounds of sex, several laws that clearly violate these principles continue to exist, especially in the area of personal laws or family laws. Most of these laws, which contain provisions that are highly discriminatory against women, have either remained static or have changed in retrogressive ways.

The Indian state has, however, made no effort to change these laws or introduce new legislation in conformity with Constitutional principles. In fact, the Indian government seems to have chosen to ignore these principles completely and acts as if they did not exist. The only personal laws in India that have been reformed to some extent have been the Hindu personal laws. Personal laws have been retained for reasons of political expediency and electoral gain and to deny equality to women.

The only justification put forth by the state, however, has been that it does not want to interfere in the personal matters of a minority community. In fact, while signing the Convention on the Elimination of All Forms of Discrimination Against women on 30 July 1980, the Indian government made a unilateral declaration that "with regard to Articles 5(a) and 16(1)... the Government of India declares that it shall abide by...these provisions in conformity with its policy of non-interference in the personal affairs of any community without its initiative and consent." But the government ratified the Women's Convention on 9 July 1993 without reservations and is therefore obligated to implement the entire Convention. While some reforms have been introduced in the criminal laws, ostensibly to deal with the issue of violence against women, these reforms have been half-hearted and inadequate.

There is also an almost complete absence of laws dealing with the majority of women workers, who work in the rural unorganized sector. It is significant to note that even the changes brought about in the criminal laws during the last decade were largely due to massive and sustained campaigns by women's groups and others. These campaigns forced a reluctant state to give more rights to women. On several occasions, however, the Indian government has paid lip service to the cause of women while acting in a totally contradictory manner.

The Rajiv Gandhi government, for instance, after passing the Muslim Women's (Protection of Rights on Divorce) Act of 1986, which deprived divorced Muslim women of their right to maintenance, actually came out with a "National Perspective Plan" for Women that recommended, among other things, a complete overhauling of the discriminatory laws and the passing of a common civil code by the end of the century, that is, by the year 2000. As anticipated, no action to change any laws as recommended in this plan has yet taken place.

The government thus seems to have formulated this plan only to put up a false front that it was interested in advancing women's rights.

The most significant barrier to women's rights in India, therefore, is a hostile state that is not actually interested in giving them any rights. Other factors that have adversely affected women's rights in India include the lack of implementation of laws by the state law and order machinery and the gender bias pervasive in the judiciary at all levels. In spite of the amendments to the rape and dowry laws during the 1980s, these laws have not been enforced or implemented by the state and its administrative machinery. Further, though certain challenges to personal laws as being discriminatory and violative of the right to equality are pending before the Supreme Court of India, the Supreme Court and other courts have in the past mostly interpreted laws relating to women in an extremely narrow, conservative, and anti-women manner without taking into account the women's perspective and their situation in India. Illiteracy and poverty also have a major role to play. Most Indian women have no access to the courts or knowledge of the laws and, because of the dismal conditions in which they live, they cannot afford to fight for their rights in a hostile social and economic environment.

These are the reasons at the domestic level that are primarily responsible for inhibiting the growth of women's rights in India. After outlining the Constitutional position, this document briefly discusses various personal laws and analyses whether they are violative of the Indian Constitution or can be justified on the basis of freedom of religion. It discusses the reforms brought about in the Hindu personal laws, which were based on the concepts of equality and non-discrimination against women, and the objections to these reforms raised by Hindu fundamentalists, which were very similar to the objections raised by Muslim fundamentalists at the time of the Shah Bano decision by the Supreme Court of India in 1985. Following this is a brief discussion of how Indian courts have interpreted personal and related laws in the context of the Constitution.

Thereafter the document deals with the other factors responsible for denial of women's rights in India, primarily the inadequacy of criminal laws and their lack of implementation because of the anti-woman and grossly negligent attitude of the law and order machinery, including the reaction of the police and the courts to cases of violence against women.

The document concludes by showing how the stand of the Indian government is violative of both the provisions of the Constitution at the national level and the obligation of India to uphold the provisions of international conventions and treaties which it has signed or ratified. The Indian Constitution has a "Fundamental Rights" stage that guarantees various rights. The rights of special importance to women are the Right to Equality in Article 14 and the Express Prohibition Against Discrimination in Article 15. Article 14 mandates that "the state shall not deny to any person equality before the law or the equal protection of the laws within the territory of India."

Article 15(1) prohibits discrimination against any citizen by the state "on grounds only of religion, race, caste, sex, place of birth or any of them." Article 15(3) also allows for special provision for women and children by clarifying that "Nothing in this Article shall prevent the state from making any special provision for women and children." This article has been used by courts to justify reservation in favour of women and to justify a provision, Section 497(1) of the unamended Indian Criminal Procedure Code of 1898, which gave special treatment to women and children and prescribed leniency in granting them bail. In addition, Article 16(1) mandates equality of opportunity for all citizens in matters relating to employment or appointment to any office under the state.

Article 16(2) clarifies that "no citizen shall, on grounds only of religion, race, caste, sex, descent, place of birth, residence or any of them, be ineligible for, or discriminated against in respect of, any employment or office under the State." Article 19 guarantees the basic freedoms of speech and expression, movement, and peaceable assembly, and the right to form associations or unions. Another important right is the protection of life and personal liberty provided in Article 21, since this right has been very widely interpreted by the courts and has been held to include the right of privacy and the right of an individual to live with dignity.

These Fundamental Rights in Chapter III of the Constitution are obviously enforceable in a court of law. Chapter IV of the Constitution of India contains principles of law known as the "Directive Principles of State Policy," which, though not enforceable, are supposed to be fundamental in the governance of the country. It is also supposed to be the duty of the state to apply these principles in making laws. These principles direct the state, in Article 39(a), to ensure that all citizens, men and women equally, have the right to an adequate means of livelihood. In Article 39(d), the state is directed to ensure that there is equal pay for equal work for both men and women. The Equal Remuneration Act passed by the Indian Parliament in 1975 does provide that men and women will be paid equally for doing the same work or work of a similar nature.

This act also states that there will be no discrimination against women at the time of recruitment or later at the time of promotion. In Article 39(e) of the Constitution, the state is directed to secure that the health and strength of workers, men and women, and the tender age of children are not abused and citizens are not forced by economic necessity to enter occupations unsuited to their age or strength. Article 42 of the Directive Principles directs the state to make provisions for securing just and humane conditions of work and for maternity relief. The Maternity Benefit Act of 1961 was ostensibly passed to achieve this purpose. Another very important article of the Directive Principles of State Policy aims at ending the regime of personal laws and states that "the State shall endeavour to secure for the citizens a uniform civil code throughout the territory of India."

PERSONAL LAWS

Personal laws in India deal with marriage and divorce, maintenance, guardianship, adoption, wills, intestacy and succession, joint family, and partition, and can broadly be characterized as "family laws." These laws are basically divided along religious lines, whether or not they are based on religion. Thus Hindus in India are governed by the Hindu Marriage Act of 1955, the Hindu Succession Act of 1956, the Hindu Guardianship and Minorities Act of 1956, and the Hindu Adoption and Maintenance Act of 1956.

Indian Muslims are governed by the Shari'a Act of 1937, the Muslim Women's Dissolution of Marriage Act of 1939, the Muslim Women's (Protection of Rights on Divorce) Act of 1986, and uncodified Muslim personal laws. Christians are governed by their own Christian Marriage Act, the Indian Divorce Act, and the Indian Succession Act, while Parsis, too, have codified laws of marriage and divorce and of succession.The main characteristic of all the personal laws is that they are antiwomen, anti-liberal, and anti-human. It is ironic that while all Indian women suffer from the same or similar discrimination at home or within their families, the family or personal laws applicable to them are different and subject them to varying degrees of discrimination.

We are thus confronted with a strange situation that while a Hindu, Christian, or Parsi woman can sue her husband for bigamy under the criminal law code for punishment of up to seven years imprisonment, Indian Muslim personal law allows a Muslim man to marry up to four times. One of the main arguments advanced against reform of personal law has been that such reform violates the right of all Indian citizens to freedom of religion. If one examines Article 25 of the Constitution which gives all persons freedom of conscience and the right to profess, practice and propagate religion. Article 25 therefore clearly states the parameters within which the right freely to practice, propagate, and profess religion is limited.

It in fact defines the content of secularism by stating that the right to freely propagate and practice religion is not an unlimited right but is subject to the constitutional rights of equality and freedom from discrimination. It also enables the state to regulate any economic, financial, political, or other secular activity associated with religious practice. The state has also been empowered to make any laws for social welfare and reform which may interfere with the right to freedom of religion.

A bare reading of this article shows clearly that the Constitution restricts the scope of the right to freedom of religion. The question, however, of enacting a common civil code has never been on the agenda of the government, in spite of the fact that from time to time various committees, women's organizations, and others interested in women's rights have asked for a uniform secular family law based on equality. In fact, until the judgement of the Supreme Court in Shah Bano's case, several women's groups and others were actively working towards a uniform civil code based on equality that would apply to all Indian women regardless of their community. After witnessing the opposition to a uniform civil code from sections of the Muslim population, however, women's groups and others have been demanding reforms in the personal laws of the different communities. A look at the various reforms in Hindu personal laws shows that they have come about due to the separation of family laws from religion.

In fact, the progressive changes that have been brought about in Hindu personal law have nothing to do with religion, but were instead based on the concept of equality and had nothing to do with smritis (old Hindu texts) and the laws of Manu (an ancient law-giver who prohibited divorce). Prior to Independence, the British rulers also followed a policy of retaining and not reforming the family laws applicable to Hindus, Muslims, and Parsis. In fact, during this entire period the personal laws of various communities remained static, and the British system of courts relied heavily on religious pundits and the ulama for interpreting the personal laws applicable to Hindus and Muslims.

In several instances, this resulted in further communalizing the law. Family laws were therefore extremely backward at the time of Indian Independence and needed to be extensively amended. Changes, however, took place only in Hindu law. This law was codified and separate acts dealing with marriage and divorce, adoption and maintenance, succession and minority, and guardianship were passed. The concept of monogamy was introduced for the first time in the Hindu Marriage Act of 1955. Concomitantly, certain limited grounds of divorce were introduced into Hindu law for the first time.Prior to the change, while a man was free to marry an unlimited number of times without getting divorced, the woman could not do so and once married had to remain married until she died.

The passing of the Hindu Marriage Act with its provision for divorce was opposed by conservative members of Parliament who were members of Hindu communal organizations like the Jan Sangh and the Hindu Maha Sabha. These members claimed that the bill had been passed to "wound the religious feelings of the Hindus" and was "against the fundamental principles of Hinduism." It is interesting that one Hindu fundamentalist member of Parliament at that time, V.M. Trivedi, actually proposed an amendment to the effect that if the wife agreed that she did not object to her husband's having a second wife, this condition should not apply. Strangely enough, the fundamentalists demanded that a uniform civil code be introduced and stated that Hindus were being discriminated against since the bill did not apply to Muslims. It was only because the government of the day was in favour of reforming and codifying Hindu law that the Act was passed despite fierce opposition.

In fact the Minister of Law in Parliament at the time, while introducing the bill, said it was a measure of great social importance to do good to women because men had been enjoying disproportionate rights and privileges as compared with women and the government could not, in the name of preserving the sanctity of any ancient culture, try to treat women differently in the present time and conditions. The Minister also pointed out that ancient Hindu law had already been altered from time to time. Similarly, the Hindu Succession Act was passed in 1956, giving more property rights to women, including the complete right of disposal of their property. Previously women could not sell or alienate their property and had only what was known as a "limited estate" in their property.

This bill did not grant equal rights of inheritance to women. In fact, at that time the All India Women's Conference, a women's organization allied to the Congress Party, objected to the Hindu Succession Act on the grounds that "The Bill, although a step in the right direction, falls far short of what is required due to the fact that it excludes from its application the Mitakshara joint family property. As the Mitakshara Law with its various sections prevails over more than two-thirds of India, a substantial number of women will be debarred from inheriting property on the same terms as their male relatives, thus leading to discrimination on grounds of sex which is contrary to the provisions of the Indian Constitution." The Hindu Succession Act, however, contained several retrogressive features in addition to not conferring equal property rights on women.

In section 4(2), "laws providing for the prevention of fragmentation of agricultural holding" were left out or exempted from the application of the act. This meant that in the name of "prevention of fragmentation of agricultural land," Hindu women could be deprived of their right to property. Further, section 23 stipulated that if a woman inherited a house in which members of the family were living, she had no right to ask for a "partition" of the house and could only reside in it if she was not married or had been separated. The act also provided that if a female Hindu died intestate and left behind no children or husband, her property would devolve on her husband's heirs. The only exception to this rule was that property inherited by a woman from her parents would revert, in the absence of a son or daughter (or their son or daughter), to the heirs of her father.

These provisions have not been altered or amended to date. The passage of this act was also vehemently opposed by orthodox Hindu members. The Hindu Guardianship and Minority Act was also passed at this time, though it made no radical departure from old Hindu law. The father is the natural guardian of the child under this act and only in the absence of the father can the mother be the natural guardian. A proviso, however, gives the custody of the minor child who has not completed the age of five years to the mother.

A suggestion during the Parliamentary debates at the time the act was being discussed, that custody of the minor child remain with the mother till the age of fourteen years, was not accepted. Only in respect to illegitimate children has the mother been given the privilege of being the natural guardian. The Hindu Adoption and Maintenance Act provided a Law of Adoption only for Hindus. No other community in India has the right to adoption. This was the first act that allowed Hindu daughters as well as sons to be adopted. Hindus earlier believed that only a son should be adopted as only the son inherited the property of the father.

It is interesting that even at the time of its passage conservative Hindu members of Parliament protested various features of this act; one conservative member actually said, I am again entering my protest against this kind of communal legislation. You are going against your Constitution and the Directive Principles. Though they are not justiciable as per the Fundamental Rights, still you solemnly enacted them for the purposes of giving guidance to the Parliament and the state Legislatures. It is not proper on the part of the Government which has been responsible for ushering in that Constitution to enact this law in defiance of the Directive Principles. They say that there shall be a uniform Civil Code for all the citizens of India. Have it for everybody. As Mahamahopadhyaya Kane himself said, why run after the Hindus only.

The preceding discussion shows that the subject of reform was hotly debated in the 1950s. All sorts of arguments, including cries that religion was in danger and that reforms were against secularism and against the Constitution of India were put forward to stop any reform from taking place. After the 1950s these laws have remained largely static; only some changes like divorce by mutual consent and on the grounds of cruelty and desertion were introduced in 1976. No reforms were brought about in the laws of other communities. As far as the Christian law of marriage and divorce is concerned, it is extremely backward, since both the Christian Marriage Act and the Indian Divorce Act were framed by the British rulers on the then prevailing English law of marriage and divorce, and no changes or reforms have been brought about in these laws.

The Indian Divorce Act recognizes only adultery as a ground for divorce for men. The wife is subject to even harsher grounds of divorce and can ask for divorce only if the husband has changed his religion and married another woman or has been guilty of adultery along with bigamy or rape, sodomy, bestiality, cruelty, or desertion.

This act, besides being archaic, obviously discriminates against women on the grounds of sex alone. No reforms have been brought about in this law in spite of demands from various liberal Christian and women's organizations. This is because the orthodox Christian clergy have been opposed to these reforms and the government policy of "no interference in the religious affairs of the minorities" has been a convenient tool to avoid reform. As far as Muslim personal law is concerned, not only has the law remained static, there has been a steady retrogression, which culminated in the introduction of the Muslim Women's (Protection of Rights on Divorce) Act of 1986.

This act restricts the right of Muslim women to maintenance only to the iddat period, approximately three months after divorce, and stipulates that thereafter her own family and the Waqf board would be responsible for her maintenance. As stated earlier, the act debars Muslim women from claiming maintenance under the general criminal law under Section 125, Code of Criminal Procedure. It further states that, where the woman herself maintains the children, maintenance is to be paid by her former husband for a period of two years from the dates of birth of such children. This act clearly violates the right to equality and discriminates against Muslim women on the ground only of religion.

The history of how this act came to be passed is interesting. For over a century, since 1898, a provision in the Criminal Procedure Code of India provided for maintenance for neglected and deserted wives and children unable to maintain themselves. This provision has been applicable to all Indian women, irrespective of their religion. In 1974, the Criminal Procedure was amended to include within the definition of "wife" a divorced wife.

This had become necessary since divorced wives were often in urgent need of maintenance and the Code of Criminal Procedure provided a relatively speedy remedy, even though the amount of maintenance was more in the nature of a dole and was and is restricted to a maximum sum of ₹ 500 per person per month. Fundamentalist and orthodox Muslim opinion, however, opposed the inclusion of a "divorced wife" in the definition of a "wife," as they argued that under Muslim personal law, a divorced wife could only receive maintenance for the iddat period.

The government succumbed to this opinion and added a section to this law that stated that, if the woman had received "the whole of the sum which, under any customary or Personal Law, applicable to the parties, was payable on such divorce," she was not entitled to any maintenance. Even after this amendment, however, the Supreme Court in a series of judgements held that a divorced Muslim woman was entitled to adequate maintenance and that the provision in the Criminal Penal Code was meant for destitute women and to prevent vagrancy.

In 1985 the famous Shah Bano judgement on the right of a divorced Muslim woman to get maintenance was pronounced by the Supreme Court. The case was filed by Shah Bano, who had been thrown out of her house by her husband after thirty years of marriage. When she asked for maintenance in the Court of the Judicial Magistrate, she was divorced by her lawyer husband who maintained that he had already given her her mehar (dowry) and maintenance and was not liable to pay any further amounts. The Magistrate awarded a princely sum of ₹

25 per month to Shah Bano and this sum was enhanced to ₹ 179.20 per month by the High Court. Not willing to pay even that amount, the husband appealed to the Supreme Court, saying that he was not liable to pay any maintenance beyond the *iddat* period just as to his personal law. The Court held that the provisions regarding maintenance were applicable to all communities, that Section 125 of the Criminal Procedure Code had been enacted in order to provide a quick and summary remedy to a class of persons unable to maintain themselves, and, further, that the religion professed by the party cannot have any repercussion on the applicability of such laws.

The Court also quoted certain provisions of the Qur'an and stated that it imposes an obligation on a Muslim husband to make provision for or to provide maintenance to the divorced wife.It further held that mehar/dowry was not a sum payable on divorce by the husband but was a sum payable in consideration of the marriage. The Court also stated that it was a matter of deep regret that Article 44 of the Constitution had remained a dead letter. It stated that, though the article provides that the state shall endeavor to secure for its citizens a uniform civil code for the country, "there is no evidence of any official activity for framing a common civil code for the country" and that a beginning has to be made if the Constitution is to have any meaning.

This judgement was vehemently criticized by fundamentalist Muslims, who described the judgement as an unacceptable interference in Muslim personal law. The Muslim Personal Law Board, which was an intervenor in the Court, and other Muslim religious leaders and organizations launched a huge campaign alleging that Islam was in "danger," and that the government should introduce a bill exempting Muslim women from Section 125 of the Criminal Procedure Code. While various reasons have been advanced for the support the funda mentalists could master on this occasion it is in some respects easy to understand how economically poor and socially oppressed illiterate minority populations can react to the highly emotional cry of "religion in danger."

Some Indian Muslims were also forced to take this stand as Hindu fundamentalists, represented by the Vishwa Hindu Parishad, the Rashtriya Sewak Sangh, and the Bharatiya Janata Party, decided to use the issue as a convenient whip against Muslims and demand a uniform civil code that in their understanding probably meant a Hindu civil code. But it would be wrong to state that the entire Muslim population supported the fundamentalists.

Women's groups also carried out massive campaigns in support of the Shah Bano judgement as it was a vital issue for them that the Supreme Court had upheld a deserted and destitute divorced woman's right to maintenance, whatever her religion. The women's groups and other liberal organizations carried out a campaign throughout the country, convening meetings and holding demonstrations and mass signature campaigns. Women blocked traffic outside Parliament in Delhi for hours when the bill was introduced in Parliament to deny divorced Muslim women their right to maintenance. Fifteen women's organizations held a demonstration in Delhi on 6 March 1986 to protest the government action. In Bombay, thirtyfive women's organizations led by the Women's Liberation Movement held a rally demanding a secular civil code; 1,500 Muslim women demonstrated in Delhi in April 1986; one organization alone collected the signatures of 100,000 women, 20,000 of whom were Muslim.

The government, however, paid no attention to the women's voices and, though it had initially supported the Shah Bano judgement through the speech of its Minister of State for Home Affairs in the Lower House of Parliament (Lok Sabha), completely changed its stand and introduced the Muslim Women's Act containing all the provisions which the fundamentalists desired. It is mostly believed that the government changed its stand because it felt it could not afford to alienate the Muslim fundamentalist leaders who were valuable vote banks.

This opportunist stand of the Indian government sealed the fate of millions of Muslim women in India. As far as the other personal laws were concerned, attempts had earlier been made to introduce a uniform Indian Adoption Act as well. This, too, was opposed by orthodox Muslims, including the Muslim Personal Law Board, who claimed that adoption was against the Qur'an and that any change in Muslim personal law would impinge on the secular character of the Constitution. It is important to note that even an optional law governing adoption was vehemently opposed by funda mentalists, who claimed that members of their community should not have the option to adopt even if they wanted to. Fundamentalist leadership and other politicians have always used religion to promote their own vested interests and to preserve the status quo regarding women's rights, preventing reform in the family laws relating to women.

Courts on Personal Law

As far as the courts are concerned, other than a few judgements like Shah Bano, they have been mainly concerned with preserving the status quo. It was only in the 1950s that the courts showed a determination to uphold the reforms passed in the Hindu Law. In the 1950s there were some challenges to certain laws prohibiting bigamy that had been passed in some states prior to the Hindu reforms. In State of Bombay v. Narasu Appa Mali, the Bombay High Court held that the "Bombay Prevention of Hindu Bigamous Marriage Act was a measure of social reform and the state was empowered to legislate with regard to Article 25(2) (b), notwithstanding the fact that it may interfere with the right of a citizen to freely profess, practice, and propagate religion."

Similarly, in Srinivasa v. Saraswati Ammal, it was held that the freedom to practice religion was not an absolute right as Article 25 itself states, but that it is subject to the other provisions of Part III of the Constitution. It was further held that Article 25(2) empowered the legislature to enact a law providing for social welfare and reform and that religious practice, therefore, may be controlled by legislation if the states think that it is necessary to do so in the interest of social welfare and reform. Both cases also made a sharp distinction between religious belief and practice.

In the former case it was held that what the state protects is religious faith and belief and quoted with approval an American case, Davis v. Beason, in which it had been held that "laws are made for the Governments of action and while they cannot interfere with mere religious beliefs and opinions, they may with practices." The court held that it was difficult to accept the proposition that polygamy is an integral part of the Hindu religion.

In the latter case also the court quoted another American case, Reynolds v. U.S., in which religious belief and practice were distinguished, to show that the freedom to practice religion is not an absolute right, though it went on to justify the Madras Hindu (Bigamy and Divorce) Act of 1949, on the basis of Article 25(2). The two courts also held that there was no discrimination between Hindus and Muslims in spite of the fact that Muslims could marry more than once, because the classification between Muslim and Hindu was based on a reasonable and rational consideration and thus did not offend Article 15 of the Constitution.

Thus in these cases the courts were mainly concerned with justifying the reforms in the laws. Later challenges to various personal laws have not been upheld, even though the laws challenged blatantly discriminate against women. In a challenge to Section 10 of the Indian Divorce Act, the Madras High Court refused to hold that the said section was in violation of Articles 13, 14, and 15 of the Constitution of India. Section 10 of the Indian Divorce Act applies to Christians in India; as stated earlier, under this section adultery is the only ground of divorce for the husband whereas the wife has to prove that the husband was guilty of adultery plus another ground. The wife challenged that this section violates Articles 13 to 15 of the Constitution of India as it discriminates against women on the grounds of sex.

The court held that adultery by a wife is different from adultery by a husband. Since a wife can bear a child as a result and the husband will have to maintain the said child, this difference in the result of their acts was said to show that the classification is not based on sex alone. In another judgement the Supreme Court of India refused to strike down a provision of the Indian Penal Code which allows a husband to prosecute the man with whom his wife has committed adultery and provides for punishment up to five years fine or both. The court held that this section was not in violation of Articles 14 or 15 as it makes a rational classification between men and women by a rather strange reasoning.

The court also held that since under the section the wife is not liable to be prosecuted for the offense of adultery, "no grievance can then be made that the section does not allow the wife to prosecute the husband for adultery." The court further stated that "the offence of adultery, as defined in Section

497, is considered by the legislature as an offence against the sanctity of the matrimonial home, an act which is committed by a man, as it generally is. Therefore those who defile the sanctity are brought within the net of law." This judgement shows the conservative and outdated attitude of the judges since they refused to acknowledge that this archaic provision of law is blatantly anti-woman and treats her as the property of her husband Only in a couple of cases has the judiciary seen the woman as an independent human being who is capable of making her own decisions. In a landmark judgement, a judge of the Andhra Pradesh High Court held that the remedy of restitution of conjugal rights "violates the right to privacy and human dignity guaranteed by and contained in Article 21 of our Constitution."

The restitution of conjugal rights is an old English remedy retained by the Indian legislature in both the Hindu Marriage Act and the Special Marriage Act of 1954, which is the only optional civil law of marriage and divorce. It was pointed out by the judge that the purpose of the remedy was through the judicial process to coerce the unwilling party to have "sex" against the person's consent and free will, since conjugal rights necessarily connote "the right which husband and wife have to each other's society" and "marital intercourse." The judgement further stated that a decree for restitution of conjugal right constitutes the grossest form of violation of an individual's right to privacy. It "deprives a woman of control over her choice as to when and by whom the various parts of her body should be allowed to be sensed" and "when and how her body is to become the vehicle for the procreation of another human being."

This judgement is significant because it makes a clear break from the earlier judgements and upholds the right of an Indian woman to live with dignity, and lays stress on an individual's happiness and the woman's right to decide when and with whom she wants to live. The Supreme Court, however, in a later judgement held that there were sufficient safeguards in Section 9 of the Hindu Marriage Act, which allows a spouse to sue for restitution of conjugal rights, to prevent it from being a tyranny, as only financial sanctions could be applied under the law to the earning spouse who willfully refused to obey the decree for restitution of conjugal rights. The Supreme Court also held that the decree "serves a social purpose as an aid to the prevention of break-up of marriage." In upholding the remedy, the Supreme Court totally ignored the effect that such a decree could have on an Indian woman, who, under the threat of judicial and social pressure and financial sanctions may well be forced to go back to the matrimonial home and, because of her vulnerable position in it, be forced to have sex and live a life of misery in an atmosphere she obviously abhors.

This judgement is thus a denial of the fundamental right of every human being to privacy and a right to decide at least with whom they want or wish to live. It is also relevant to mention that several of the earlier judgements of various High Courts had taken the extremely backward view that a Hindu woman's duty is to live with her husband in the matrimonial home.

The said judgements completely overlook the fact that marriage is supposed to be a voluntary union and the state cannot force two people to remain married. As far as bigamy is concerned, the Indian Supreme Court has held that in order to prove bigamy it is essential for the prosecution to prove that the second marriage has been solemnized with proper ceremonies and in due form. In Bhurao v. State of Maharashtra, the court held that "if a marriage is not a valid marriage, it is not a marriage in the eyes of law.

The bare fact of a man and woman living as husband and wife does not, at any rate normally, give them the status of husband and wife even though they may hold themselves out before society as husband and wife and the society treats them as husband and wife." In this case, the court held that, since the prosecution had failed to establish that the second marriage had been performed in accordance with the customary rites as provided by the act or in accordance with the essential requirements for a valid marriage under Hindu law, bigamy was not proved. In subsequent cases the Supreme Court has held that both the marriages must be valid and strictly proved just as to the law governing the parties in order for the offence to be proven. It is obvious that if a person wants to commit bigamy he is not likely to do so openly, as he knows that he is about to commit an offense. The Supreme Court has thus sided with the bigamist by taking too technical a view, and a complainant has to prove factually that the second marriage was performed strictly in accordance with all the requirements of a valid marriage under the law. In fact in many cases husbands have married again without bothering to take a divorce and give maintenance. Most such marriages are performed secretly and it is impossible to find evidence about where and how they were performed since marriages need not be registered just as to Hindu law.

Crimes Against Women

On 9 April 1992, a Minister of State of Home Affairs in the Government of India admitted in the Lok Sabha that there was a sharp rise in atrocities against women, by almost 104 per cent during the last decade. In fact, government statistics over the past few years have shown a phenomenal rise in crimes against women. It is also a wellacknowledged fact that these statistics represent only the tip of the iceberg, since most violence against women is not reported to the police.

Violence against women in India has assumed terrifying proportions, both within the family and outside. In the family the woman is often subjected to all forms of domestic violence, harassment for dowry, and sometimes rape. Outside the family she is subjected to rape, molestation, and sexual harassment at work, among other forms of violence. Further, new forms of violence like female feticide and a regeneration of older forms like sati have taken place. This increase in crime reflects the worsening status of Indian women, which also shows itself in the falling sex ratio, rising unemployment, and wide-scale discrimination and harassment at work.

One of the main problems is that, though many changes have taken place in the criminal laws, through the ceaseless efforts of women's groups and others, the government has made little effort to implement the laws. These laws have either remained unused or been flouted with impunity, often by the law and order machinery itself.

In fact when a woman victim of violence goes to a police station she comes face to face with a police force that is corrupt and inefficient, and that basically has an anti-woman attitude. If the woman is poor, the police are very likely to throw her out on the street or mistreat her themselves. The catalyst for change in the laws relating to rape involved a policeman who raped a girl in the police station. A young girl, Mathura, was raped inside a police station by one policeman and molested by another.

Mathura had gone to the police station at night for interrogation along with her boyfriend on a complaint filed against both by her brother. The boyfriend and brother were told to go outside after interrogation while Mathura was taken to a bathroom at the rear of the police station and raped. Mathura sustained no bodily injuries and no semen was found on her pubic hair or in vaginal smears when she was medically examined twenty hours later. The policeman's clothes however, were stained. It is said that the case was investigated at all only because Mathura immediately told her brother and friend about the rape and a huge crowd had gathered outside the police station demanding justice. The Sessions Court held that Mathura had voluntarily had sexual intercourse with the policeman. The High Court, however, reversed the findings and held that "mere passive surrender" did not mean that the sexual act was voluntary. The Supreme Court of India, however, held that, since Mathura had not raised any alarm, her allegations were untrue. This decision of the Supreme Court generated massive protest marches organized by various women's organizations and groups.

Three eminent professors of law from Delhi addressed an open letter to the Chief Justice of India. Women members of Parliament and various women's groups demanded changes in the laws relating to rape. One of the demands was that, if sexual intercourse is proved and the woman, who is alleged to have been raped says that she has not consented to the act, the onus of proof should be shifted to the accused to prove that the woman consented. Some women's groups felt that given the social backwardness of Indian women they would never make an allegation of rape.

This demand was partly conceded. Widespread amendments to the law on rape were enacted. By these amendments, a special category of rape known as "custodial rape" was introduced. Under this amendment, rape by a man in a position of authority over a woman is considered more serious than ordinary rape. In this category were included rape by a policeman in a police station or of a woman in his custody or on the premises of a police station; rape by a public servant of a woman in his custody; rape by a person on the staff or management of a jail or remand home or any other place of custody of any woman inmate; rape by a person in the management of a hospital; rape of a pregnant woman; rape of a girl under twelve years of age; and gang rape. The punishment prescribed for this category of rape was made more severe—rigorous imprisonment for ten years or a life sentence.

Punishment by way of imprisonment for an ordinary case of rape was also increased to a minimum of seven years. In a major concession to women's groups, the onus of proof was shifted in cases of custodial rape after the fact of sexual intercourse had been proved. Increasing punishment to a minimum of seven or ten years has not made much difference in the actual sentences that rapists have to serve. On many occasions reduced sentences have been given by the courts, ostensibly for special reasons. In one case, because the doctor who had conducted the medical examination testified that the girl was used to sexual intercourse, the court reduced the sentence for three policemen who had raped her to five years.

When a women's group and others filed a review petition, the court justified the reduction in sentence by saying that when they spoke of "conduct" of the victim they meant her conduct in not logging the first information report till five days after the event. It often happens in India that the victim does not report the crime for a few days, because rape victims are often viewed with suspicion and their families are reluctant to report the matter to the police. Courts have also recognized this tendency in the past. Later rape judgements have also been retrogressive with the judges in one case saying that if there was no injury on the rapist's penis in a minor rape case, rape was not proved. Judges have also differed about the kind of corroboration required in a rape case. In certain cases the court has held that the victim's testimony should ordinarily be accepted, and in other cases the court has insisted on direct evidence or circumstantial evidence in corroboration.

It is important to note that in the Indian situation doctors are often not available, particularly in rural areas, and a rape victim is therefore sometimes not medically examined at all. Among other problems that rape victims face is that the police do not investigate the case properly. They also do not collect basic evidence as they are required to do. Often the sheet on which the rape took place, the clothes of the victim, and other evidence like fingerprints are not collected by the police.

The medical examination is often carried out after a long waiting period. This results in loss of valuable evidence. The medical examination of the victims is also often cursory, and the doctors are sometimes obviously biased. Other victims of domestic violence face similar problems when they complain to the police. Even in big cities like Delhi, the police do not ensure that a victim who has obviously been beaten is medically examined. Instead, they try to dismiss the whole incident as a domestic brawl and often try to send the woman back to the matrimonial home. Even cases of dowry deaths are deliberately not properly investigated.

This has been noticed in cases even by the Supreme Court of India. In the early 1980s, another struggle was launched by women's organizations to change the laws relating to dowry. As a result, the Dowry Prohibition Act of 1961 was amended in 1984 and again in 1986. In the 1986 amendment a provision was made for the appointment of dowry prohibition officers. These officers were meant to prevent dowry from being given or taken and to see that all the provisions of the act were complied with. Only a couple of states, however, have appointed dowry officers.

There has been a complete lack of will on the part of the union and state governments to check the rampant custom of dowry. Other amendments were also brought about in the Indian Penal Code. A section that defined a special kind of murder, dowry death, was introduced.

This amendment provided that when a woman dies by burning or other bodily injury or under unnatural circumstances within seven years of marriage, and it can be shown that she was subjected to cruelty or harassment by her husband or any of his relatives in connection with dowry, such deaths will be known as "dowry death." The person, the amendment stated, "who commits a dowry death shall be punishable for a prison term not less than seven years but which may extend to life." Another amendment to the Evidence Act provided that, once it was shown that a person harassed a woman for dowry prior to her death, the court should presume that such a person had caused the death.

Another amendment to the Penal Code made cruelty to a woman a criminal offense and it has been found that many victims of domestic violence lodge their complaints under this section, at least in the cities. These changes in the dowry laws, however, did not make any attempt to change the basic structure of inheritance and other property laws. Thus, though the giving and taking of dowry, which was largely perceived as the woman's share in the property, was made illegal, women were not given equal inheritance rights. Thus the phenomenon continued to occur, except that dowry was usually used and retained by the husband and his family. The Indian woman, too, has no right to date in the matrimonial property at the time of breakdown of the marriage unless she can prove that she has contributed towards buying it.

All this makes her financially dependent on her husband and makes it extremely difficult for her to opt out of a violent home. On the other hand, her own family does not encourage her to come back, since after she has been given her share, a married woman is supposed to belong to her husband's family.The inaction on the part of the Indian state in not reforming personal law is against the Fundamental Principles of the Constitution, which clearly elevates the Fundamental Rights to equality and freedom from the right to freedom of religion. India is also a party to the Universal Declaration of Human Rights 1948.

It has ratified the International Convention on Civil and Political Rights and has signed the Convention on the Elimination of All Forms of Discrimination Against Women. The International Covenant on Civil and Political Rights in Article 18(3) also subjects the freedom to manifest religion or belief to limitations prescribed by law which are necessary to protect public safety, order, health, or morals or the fundamental rights and freedoms of others.

Thus even this Covenant states that, where religious practices impinge on the fundamental rights and freedoms of others, they can be restricted. India is bound by the terms of this Covenant.

Its action in taking divorced Muslim women out of the purview of the prescribed law, that is, Section 125 of the Code of Criminal Procedure, can easily be argued to be violative of its obligation under the Covenant. Also, at the time of signing the Women's Convention, although India undertook "to refrain from acts which would defeat the object and purpose of the treaty," India in total disregard of this obligation passed the Muslim Women's (Protection of Rights on Divorce) Act of 1986, which actually deprived Muslim women of a pre-existing right. Further, the Indian government's decision of non-interference in the personal affairs of any community is incompatible with the purpose and object of the Women's Convention to improve the status of women. This is also violative of provisions of the Indian Constitution, and the state cannot justify inaction regarding women's rights on this basis. The state is bound by the provisions of the Constitution to which it owes its existence, but by consistently listening to the most orthodox and obscurantist sections of the Indian population, namely, the religious leaders and their allies who are interested in preserving patriarchy, the state is perpetrating a fraud on the women of India.

9

Social Work and Human Rights

SOCIAL WORK

While much of the material in this book can be applied to a broad range of human service professions such as teaching, medicine and the other health-related professions, the primary focus of the book is social work. In this regard,'social work' needs some clarification, as this term has different connotations in different national and cultural contexts. In some societies, most notably Australia and North America,'social worker' implies a fairly narrowly defined group of workers who have high professional qualifications, and excludes many others working in the human service field.

In other societies the term has a much wider application, covering human service workers from a variety of backgrounds, with varying levels of educational qualifications. In some societies, such as the United Kingdom, social work has been seen as the implementation of the policies of the welfare state through the provision of statutory services, with relatively little role in community development or social change.

In other societies, however, such as in Latin America,'social work' has much more radical or activist connotations: it is concerned with bringing about social change, progressive movements for social justice and human rights, and opposition to prevalent forms of bureaucratic and political domination. In some contexts, such as the United States, individualised therapeutic roles for social workers are dominant, while in other contexts, particularly in'the developing world' or'the south', social work has a much stronger community development orientation.

Even in societies that might superficially seem very similar, such as Australia and New Zealand, there can be significant differences in how social work is constructed and in what counts as good practice. Given the importance of grounding social work in its cultural, social and political context, it is inevitable that social work will be constructed differently in different locations. This has considerable benefits for social work as it allows for a diversity of interests and practices. But it also poses problems, in that readers of the social work literature will be seeking to apply that literature in different contexts where the very idea of social work is contested. It is also a recipe for ambiguity and misunderstanding when social workers meet across cultural and national boundaries. This book accepts a broad view of the nature of'social work' and is not confined to specific professional, social control, conservative, radical, therapeutic or developmental formulations.

The term is meant to be understood in its broadest sense and to include all those working in the social services or community development, including those seeking social change. The aim of this book is to show that a human rights perspective such as that developed in the following stages provides a unifying framework within which the various activities identified as'social work' can be incorporated, while still allowing for cultural, national and political difference. There is a strong tradition in social work of identifying a core value position for the profession.

Social work writers have consistently emphasised the importance of this value base; social work is not seen as a neutral, objective or'value-free' activity, but rather as work which is grounded in values and which makes no apology for adopting partisan stances on a range of questions.

In formulating this value base, the idea of human rights is often implicit, through phrases such as'the inherent worth of the individual', the 'right to self-determination', and so on. Such statements serve to locate human rights, though perhaps in a fairly limited form, as having a central role in social work, though characteristically there is usually little explication of the nature of these'rights', the contested nature of rights, what they mean in practice, and how adopting such rights as central actually affects what social workers do in their day-to-day work.

Professional codes of ethics also tend to imply some commitment to an idea of human rights, since it is often from an implied human rights position that the ethics of social work are derived.

This again is a piecemeal approach to human rights and does not really confront the idea of human rights head on. Indeed it might be suggested that the construction of human rights contained in documents such as codes of ethics and introductory texts often treats human rights as if they are self-evident and non-problematic, a position which even the most cursory examination of the extensive literature on rights would show to be misguided and simplistic.

RIGHTS AND SOCIAL DEVELOPMENT

If this meeting had been held a hundred years ago, we would no doubt have been presented with a most extraordinary account of the situation of the world. Some speakers might have celebrated a long, unbroken period of peace and prosperity in Europe. Others would have underlined spectacular advances in science and technology that opened up new vistas of unparalleled progress and well-being for mankind. Observers would have noted that the world had shrunk and that railroads, shipping-lanes and the telegraph were uniting people far and wide. Commerce and industry had greatly increased among nations bringing the peoples of the world closer together.

Responsible statesmen had been able to craft treaties and agreements that would make a repetition of the predatory or dynastic wars of yesteryear very unlikely. The world had been divided up into spheres of influence, and an equilibrium had been reached that would guarantee stability and peace for the coming generations. Europe had assumed its mission civil is a trice and its manifest destiny to bring the light and benefits of civilization and progress to the lesser breeds of humanity. It was the age of smug, self-glorifying imperialism. Queen Victoria, Bismarck and Teddy Roosevelt sat, literally, on top of the world.

But even then there were doubters and challengers. Industrial capitalism had created a dissatisfied and restless working class, which was demanding certain basic rights: decent working conditions, minimum wages and the freedom to associate and organize.

Peasants were abandoning poor and backward rural villages to flock to the cities, whereas others fled from famines, and religious and political persecution across international borders and oceans. While a burgeoning urban middle-class flaunted its lifestyle and levels of consumption, masses of illiterate, unemployed and undernourished populations subsisted at the margins of bourgeois society.

Women were demanding equal rights, and citizens were claiming a place of their own in emerging democratic polities. More dramatically, the peoples of the colonial empires had begun to question the inevitability of having to carry the white man's burden and were preparing for the long march towards freedom. During the previous half-century, remarkable men of vision had theorized about the internal contradictions of the world capitalist system and had prophesied its revolutionary downfall. Indeed, revolutionary groups and movements were already at work trying to bring this about.

Does all this sound familiar a century later? Has the world really changed as much as we are led to believe? Has the end of history been finally achieved or are we witnessing the lull before the next storm? Is it merely a coincidence that the Short Twentieth Century, as historians like to call it, begins and ends in Sarajevo? This short twentieth century has been full of contradictions and extremes. We can understand Yehudi Menuhin when he states: If I had to sum up the twentieth century, I would say that it raised the greatest hopes ever conceived by humanity, and destroyed all illusions and ideals. Although if we agreed completely with the last part of the statement we might not be sitting here today.

THE IMPACT OF GLOBALIZATION ON SOCIAL DEVELOPMENT

In 1995, UNRISD prepared a report for the World Summit for Social Development. The title of this document, States of Disarray: The Social Effects of Globalization, is revealing, because even then it was already clear that the dynamics of the international system after the end of the Cold War had brought in its wake, among other things, a number of very acute structural and systemic problems that had not received sufficient attention by governments and international bodies during the preceding years. The Social Summit itself had been convened to address issues that were not being dealt with adequately by existing institutions, and the debates at the Summit and concurrent meetings focused on global tendencies that required the urgent attention of the international community. UNRISD's publication pointed out the major challenges at the end of the century.

The report indicates, for example:

- At the international level, social organizations have been overtaken by translational corporations and international financial institutions. At a national level, many state institutions have been eroded or eliminated. And at a local level, the imperatives of market forces and globalization have been undermining communities and families. [P]ower has been transferred to institutions that have consistently ignored the social implications of their actions while passing responsibility for absorbing the damage either to non-governmental agencies or to communities and families that have themselves been so weakened that they are in no position to respond.

On the occasion of the Summit, UNRISD also invited a number of scholars to debate their visions of social futures.

It is instructive, some years down the road, to recall some of the major findings of these academics:

- The impact of the globalize economy on social, cultural and political life is, of course, a principal topic of this fin de siècle. Globalization has both positive and negative implications. It liberates entrepreneurial energies and contributes to the accumulation of wealth. But it also generates inequalities poverty and unemployment. Globalization stimulates migrations and competition, but it also arouses xenophobia, discrimination and often, violence.
- The effects of the new technologies on the restructuring of social relations are paramount, and the global economy cannot be understood without them. Particularly affected by these changes are labour markets, which are no longer what they used to be: the nature of work is changing rapidly. At least in the Western industrial countries, manual labour is disappearing and the so-called services sector is

generating increasing employment.Work is no longer a long-term relationship with a fixed employer to be negotiated through a union contract. It has become flexible, in today's jargon, which means that workers have to give up security, benefits and fixed wage rates to return to the old happy-go-lucky ways of early industrial times.Work at decent rates of pay is increasingly hard to come by, says Ralph Dahrendorf, while uprooting people becomes a condition of efficiency and competitiveness.

- A concomitant phenomenon that commands the attention of analysts and provides grist for the polemical mills of academe, is the withering away of the state. Not of course as Karl Marx prophesied, but rather as an accompaniment of the neo-liberal global free market. The dismantling of the welfare state is on the agenda everywhere, Dahrendorf reminds us Still, the nation-state is not about to disappear, argues Eric Hobsbawm, because it carries out some necessary, though nowadays diminished, functions such as security, the political organization of the citizenry, and the redistribution of wealth. Hobsbawm sees little promise in some proposed alternatives to the territorial state, such as free-market ultraliberalism and the ideology of small is beautiful, that is, the substitution of larger political units by smaller ones. The territorial state, augurs Hobsbawm, will continue to play a major role in relation to social development.
- In response to the decreasing political legitimacy of states, some scholars propound a return to community; not the old, traditional and conservative communities relics of a pre-modern era that backward-looking romantics tend to idealize, but rather, a composite concept of responsive community, a group of people who share affective bonds and a culture, based on open participation, dialogue and truly shared values. Communitarians see community as a constructive alternative to the overbearing state and the free-ranging markets, or rather, as a compromise between these two apparently mutually exclusive options.
- This globalize runaway world, which in the West at least may lead to a post-scarcity society, requires a new kind of life politics based on reflexive modernity, who more recently has become a staunch proponent of the polemical Third Way in politics.

It has become fairly evident by now that free-market economics and globalization, if left to themselves, are not able to provide solutions to some of the contemporary world's most serious problems; and that, on the contrary, they contribute to aggravate tendencies that may in the long run spell catastrophe for millions of human beings Can these issues be addressed by making occasional minor adjustments to the excesses of the workings of the market, such as splitting up the Microsoft empire into two smaller ones, phasing out the use of fluorocarbons in refrigerators and hair-spray cans, or taxing the flow of overnight speculative capital from one stock-exchange to another? Sometimes indeed, major transformations are achieved by an accumulation of smaller changes, but often, in history, the reverse is also true: plus ça change, plus ça reste le même.

While the major global tendencies are clear, there is no widespread consensus on the world's priorities at the turn of the millennium. Should the economy just keep growing and create more wealth? Are environmental concerns paramount? Do we have to stop the population explosion ? Must employment top the list? Is the eradication of poverty the major concern? But what about human rights and fundamental freedoms? Is not democratic governance the basic pre-condition for all other concerns? And how important is the need for conviviality and tolerance in a world prone to conflicts and violence? In an ideal world, we might reach agreement on a ranking of world priorities.

But as our planet is a highly diversified congeries of societies and cultures, and each has its own perceptions of right and wrong, of the tasks ahead and how these issues must be addressed. Even when priorities have been identified and agreed upon, there is still no agreement as to how these ought to be met, and the best of intentions may flounder with a lack of political will, or when there is simple incompetence and neglect.

That the idea of social and human development should remain the step-child of international priorities is unfortunate, but that the concept of development can still be wielded without reference to human values and social goals is inexcusable. What I refer to is of course the widespread habit of confusing development with economic growth, and measuring economic achievement principally in terms of gross national product and other macroeconomic indicators.

THE CONCEPT OF HUMAN NEEDS

Several decades ago, reflecting broad disillusionment with growth-centred measures of development, there was much talk of a basic-needs–oriented approach to development, and there has been some interesting theoretical work on this topic. The concept of basic needs, however, was criticized by scholars from the poorer countries, who suggested that it was being used to lock developing countries into persistent poverty, while allowing richer countries to continue on a growth-oriented track Basic needs were soon replaced by human needs or simply by the concept of needs, and scholars tended to agree that basic or not, all human beings have to satisfy material, cultural, social and spiritual needs somehow, and it is the purpose of development strategies and policies to contribute to the satisfaction of these integrated packages of needs

While the needs approach to development seems to have fallen out of favour in the councils of the mighty, there is still a strong debate on the wider objectives of growth strategies and policies, beyond maintaining a certain growth rate or raising a country's gross domestic product.

There seems to be agreement that whatever the final uses to which the outcomes of the economic growth process might be put, the process itself is necessary to create wealth, which in turn is considered by many an end in itself. This is a dubious assertion that not everybody would agree with because the massive accumulation of riches by a few is not necessarily compatible with the improvement of living standards of the many.

Nor is it imperative to cut down the world's remaining tropical forests so that a middle-class urban family can comfortably furnish its apartment. It boils down to a question of values, and the larger and more commonly debated issue is: So, it is okay for economies to grow, but to what uses shall the fruits of growth be put and who shall benefit?. Leaving aside for the moment the questionable thesis that, thanks to an invisible guiding hand, the sum of individual benefits amounts to collective well-being, this is of course a question of values as well.

Classical political economists have shown that human beings, who live in society and share in certain cultural values, work in order to satisfy their human needs. Work is neither a malediction thrust upon humanity by a wrathful god, nor is it the inescapable lot of the suffering poor to enrich the rich. Work is part of human nature, and it is or should be essentially creative and satisfying, except when, due to social and economic conditions, it is alienating. Marx, it is not work itself but alienating work that must be overcome. Work that is alienating or exploitative is a common phenomenon of modern times, although it has existed throughout human history, because of the conditions imposed by world capitalism.

But in the era of globalization, we have reached a period when work need no longer be alienating; yet it still is, for millions of people. And the lack of work is alienating for those millions who are unemployed or underemployed. Will economic growth do away with alienating work? This is not likely, even though globalization has, by all accounts, changed the nature of work. Even the World Bank is now concerned that high growth rates have not been able to do away with poverty and unemployment.

In an era of global transactions, mega mergers and macro strategies, perhaps it is necessary once again to turn the world upside down, or rather downside up. It cannot be stressed often enough that development is not to be confused with economic growth. There can be growth without development, and although many may not agree with this, there can also be development without growth. What I mean is that the well-being of people who live on the lowest levels of the social pyramid can change for the better even in the absence of macroeconomic growth rates. But how can this be achieved? We must turn to some old ideas and values that curiously seem to have gone out of fashion in recent decades. These are simple and well known, and it is surprising that at the beginning of the third millennium we are again debating them as if nothing had been learned from the history of the last two centuries. The first idea is that development must serve the needs of the people, especially those who have less. This means that needs must again be factored into development strategies, and these must be so designed to address the issue squarely: not as a hoped-for secondary fall-out or an afterthought, but as the centrepiece of development thinking.

Secondly, development however defined, and definitions abound while consensus is lacking must be considered not only as a process of accumulation or change, but rather as a collective good, to the extent that it addresses the common needs of specific social and cultural groups. I refer not only to the old problem antique of the commons, but also to the more thorny issue of the relationship between individual or corporate enterprise and the well-being of the group, whether this group is a small peasant village, an indigenous tribe, an urban neighbourhood, a geographical region or a nation. Examples and illustrations abound. Hydroelectric power projects from the Amazon to Aswan used to be promoted as the passport to modernization and development. They are now considered to be white elephants and costly failures: costly in environmental and social as well as financial terms. Take the continuing debate on the Three Gorges Dam on the Yangtze River. Development cannot be reduced to kilowatt-hours of energy, or for that matter, output of steel or automobiles, without taking into consideration the impact on the daily lives of peoples, their environment, their survival, their identities and those of future generations.

In Uganda, for example, a local environmental organization said that World Bank funding should not go towards building a large hydroelectric dam when smaller scale renewable energy, like wind and solar energy, would more likely benefit the nation's rural poor. The NGO said the Bank relied on a false premise that economic growth spurred by the project will trickle down to the poor, and argued that the institution was not taking into account how corruption and social inequalities would inhibit the poor from benefiting from the dam. Another example: the state of Chiapas produces one third of Mexico's total energy, yet the people of Chiapas are among the country's most deprived, and among the lowest on the United Nations Development Programme's human development index.

I can quote a personal anecdote. Almost half a century ago, I worked as a budding government employee in south-eastern Mexico on making the construction of a giant multipurpose dam acceptable to the local indigenous population. We considered ourselves to be harbingers of progress, and it was an exciting experience for a young committed applied anthropologist. It involved, among other things, moving hundreds of peasant families to new locations.

Years later I returned to the area and saw that the project had been a disaster: social disorganization, economic inequality, environmental destruction, waste, corruption, bureaucratic bungling, the whole list of what not to do with a development project. Could it have been done differently? Perhaps, but given the social and political constraints, it was not. Therefore this was a cultural, social, institutional problem, not a financial or a technical one. At that time, it was common to hear arguments about the so-called social and cultural obstacles to development. Nowadays we know better, of course. Very often, development is itself the social and cultural obstacle. We should not forget that

Thirdly, let us assume that society and not the economy is a self-regulating mechanism, and therefore it requires the knowledgeable and committed participation of its members in devising and managing institutions for the collective good. One such institution is, of course, the state, but it is not the only one. The trouble with the state in the twentieth century was that, to put it bluntly, we could not live without it but we could not live with it either. Can we do better during the twenty-first century? I think it should be clear by now that people-centred development requires not only people who participate, but also people-oriented institutions, including a people-oriented state. Allow me to say a few more words about these three simple and not very original ideas. Except for the most basic of all physiological functions all human needs are socially constructed, as are the ways in which all needs are satisfied, because humans are social and cultural animals. The way needs are formulated, defined, expressed, gratified or deferred, becomes in all human societies a culturally determined process.

And all past and present human societies have instituted mechanisms whereby such needs may or may not be satisfied through a host of mores, customs, norms and relationships. When needs are felt, expressed and recognized but not satisfied, or not sufficiently or adequately satisfied, then human beings possess the faculty of doing something about it. When they are hungry, they should work harder, just as to some advisers, but they can also try to immigrate to greener lands, or plunder a warehouse or storm the Bastille.

When they feel the need to participate, they can sit in a community assembly, sing at a prayer meeting, dance in a disco, form a political party, stage a protest or start a revolution. How they react in each case becomes a social and cultural issue, and not infrequently, a political drama. We could draw up a long list of how needs and needs-satisfaction are embedded in the sociocultural matrix of space and time.

HUMAN NEEDS AS HUMAN RIGHTS

What might be emphasized is that most human needs have been framed in modern times as legitimate rights to which citizens can aspire, and which society at large has an obligation to respect and provide for. Johan Galtung has suggested that most of the human rights that appear in international legal documents respond in fact to some basic human need. Throughout history, people have struggled sometimes violently and against formidable odds to obtain need-satisfaction, from the slave revolts of antiquity to trade union organization drives in industrial capitalism, to national liberation struggles and the tearing down of the Berlin wall in our days. These struggles resulted in needs becoming rights, which in turn became the legitimate and legal framework for political and social action in modern nation-states. We live in an age of rights in which, as Norberto Bobbio reminds us, the current increasingly widespread and intense debate on human rights can be interpreted as a prophetic sign of humanity's moral progress, given that it is so widespread as to involve all the peoples of the world and so intense as to be on the agenda of the most authoritative international judicial bodies.

The International Covenant on Economic, Social and Cultural Rights, adopted by the General Assembly in 1966, recognizes the right of everyone to an adequate standard of living for himself and his family, including adequate food, clothing and housing, and to the continuous improvement of living conditions. It also recognizes the fundamental right of everyone to be free from hunger, and obligates the States Parties to the Covenant to take adequate measures for the fulfilment of this right.

As everybody recognizes, this is a large order, and it has led to important debates regarding the concept adequate and the measures and steps, including specific programmes, that states are required to take in order to acquit themselves of this obligation. It is quite clear that we are dealing here implicitly with development strategies based on the international formulation of human rights, which derive from the recognition of specific human needs. What we have here is a concept of development anchored in the dyad of human rights human needs. To what extent does market-driven growth address this challenge? It is well known that the laws of demand and supply can fix the market price of bread, but they do nothing to alleviate hunger and famine. Should not development strategies be expected to provide a response? And if they are expected to do so, as I believe they must, how should these be formulated and by whom?

Let us also remember that the United Nations General Assembly adopted in 1986 a Declaration on the Right to Development, which stipulates that:

- The human person is the central subject of development and should be the active participant and beneficiary of the right to development.
- All human beings have a responsibility for development, individually and collectively, taking into account the need for full respect for their human rights and fundamental freedoms as well as their duties to the community, which alone can ensure the free and complete

fulfilment of the human being, and they should therefore promote and protect an appropriate political, social and economic order for development.

- States have the right and the duty to formulate appropriate national development policies that aim at the constant improvement of the well-being of the entire population and of all individuals, on the basis of their active, free and meaningful participation in development and in the fair distribution of the benefits resulting there from.

It is significant that during the 1980s the members of the UN saw fit to address development as a human right. As so many international declarations before it, however, this one did not generate any a great deal of activity seeking its immediate implementation. Moreover, human rights specialists did not quite know how to translate the principles set out in the Declaration into practical measures, and as far as I can tell, national development strategies were not generally adjusted to follow these principles. To the contrary, it appears that development strategies were subordinated to overall growth objectives in the emerging global marketplace. Is it not time now to return to the principles of the UN Declaration and attempt to adjust development strategies to the integrated and indivisible package of human rights?

THE FREE MARKET ECONOMY AND SOCIAL DEVELOPMENT

Granted that sustainable development strategies must be based on investment in future growth, and not on quick fixes to immediate demands, yet we have learned from brutal experience during the twentieth century that betting on a bright but distant future by deferring immediate needs is a recipe for political and human disaster. But betting on the invisible hand of the market and ignoring the needs and rights of the socially excluded is just as dangerous and morally unacceptable. In UNRISD's volume, Social Futures, Global Visions, Emma Rothschild shows that in eighteenth-century Britain, the father of laissez faire, Adam Smith, was not opposed to government regulation and intervention in favour of socially valued ends, to which he devoted some of his writings, which are ignored by today's economic libertarians. Rothschild laments the lessons of a road not taken. Are we not repeating the unlearned lesson?

Allow me to refer again to the situation in my country. As a result of a violent social revolution early in the century, Mexico adopted radical land reform legislation to satisfy the demands of the exploited and oppressed peasantry. Land and liberty was the rallying cry of the revolutionary peasants who were led by the legendary Emiliano Zapata. While it took several decades to implement the agrarian legislation, results have been mixed. Renewed land concentration took place during the latter part of the century. Small peasants and landless labourers were unable to make ends meet, thus fuelling increasing migration flows into urban areas and the United States; and recent government policies have been biased against peasant-based development.

As part of Mexico's triumphal entry into the era of globalization during the 1980s and 1990s, the government decided to scrap the remnants of land reform altogether, expecting that land reprivatization, foreign investments in agriculture and agribusiness, and the miracles of the global market would raise productivity and international competitiveness to new heights. This was achieved to a certain degree, but the designers of this structural modernization as it was euphemistically named, forgot an essential element in their strategy: namely, the fate of millions of poor farming families and communities.

Here we have a case in which the state deliberately opts out of a constitutional obligation. During the early part of the century, rural development strategies were based on an understanding of the relationship between peasant needs and social rights, which was mediated by a corporatist and paternalistic state. Later, this link was broken and, in the absence of a strong civil society as a countervailing power and the inability of the state to fully assume its responsibility, agrarian issues were neglected and sidetracked. All presidential candidates in the July 2000 electoral process paid lip service to the need for taking up again the just demands of the peasantry, but the free market strategy to which the Mexican government is committed has left millions of poor peasants who, contrary to what the theory predicted, did not become competitive entrepreneurs overnight with many unsatisfied needs, many unrecognized rights and few expectations that either the market or the state will do anything about it. This goes a long way to explaining why Emiliano Zapata rides again in the mountains of southeastern Mexico.

THE ROLE OF COMMUNITIES

The second simple idea we mentioned before is that human rights belong not only to individuals as isolated atoms but to human beings who live their lives in specific social and cultural contexts and are part of all kinds of networks. For most people in the world, the immediate context of their daily lives is family and community. Human needs are fulfilled in these collective human environments: food, shelter, security, education, work, leisure, participation, creativity, spirituality are all conditioned by culture. Peoples behaviour is as much, if not more, determined by the need for belonging and identity as by the desire to accumulate or consume.

Nobody has understood this better than the advertising and merchandising industries, who now cater increasingly to so-called consumer niche markets, thereby changing the nature of culture and of cultures. Moreover, the idea of development itself is a cultural artefact, which is why it can no longer be simply wielded as a purely technical or instrumental construct, but must be regarded as one more element in the processes of cultural change, a problem cogently addressed in UNESCO's report on culture and development, Our Creative Diversity.

What I wish to underline is that despite the rampant individualism that the carefully crafted Western consumer culture tries to foist upon the rest of the world, millions of people around the globe are tied by tradition and volition to communities and collectivities that provide meaning to the lives of individuals and have, indeed, a life of their own. While identity politics is much decried nowadays because of extremist phenomena, it is no less true that communities can provide solutions to many of today's problems. This is what the communitarians put forward, such as Amitai Etzioni who argues in favour of a community-centred approach to social development.

Are communities better equipped to deal with human needs and human rights than market mechanisms? While the question is still open, some practitioners argue that both community and market have a role to play. The currently fashionable Third Way politics holds that the good society is one that strikes a balance between government, markets and the civil society. This is not exactly new nor particularly earth-shaking, but it does stress the fact that development cannot be left to markets alone.

The good society of course is one in which human needs and human rights are equitably taken care of While in the countries of the North this requires rethinking the welfare state, rebuilding human capital, providing opportunities for employment and regulating transfer payments to the underprivileged, in the South the challenge is considerably greater In fact, it is immense. One of the great illusions of the last couple of decades has been that market forces by themselves can pull the poorest countries and the poorest populations in all countries out of the morass they are in. The World Bank reports that worldwide the number of poor and extreme poor has remained stable, amounting to almost half the total population of the world. But the issue is not only poverty of individuals in statistical terms but rather the problematique of structural inequality and collective social exclusion.

Amartya Sen has developed the idea of capability sets, which represents a person's freedom to achieve functionings relevant for one's own well-being. While he recognizes the problem of entrenched deprivation related to issues of class, community, caste and gender, he does not pursue this line of enquiry, which has been followed by other scholars. Charles Tilly shows that durable inequality is categorical, that is, certain categories of people are persistently involved in the transmission of inequality from generation to generation. It is the social and economic structures of inequality which lead to its reproduction. No amount of human capital building or attitude changes will do away with categorical socioeconomic inequalities; this requires more authoritative interventions at the structural levels.

We may conclude from the foregoing that development policies designed to alleviate poverty, overcome social exclusion and reduce persistent categorical inequalities, must focus on the needs and rights of specific categories or groups in society. But they must do so in areas which make a difference: that is, productive activities, and the ownership and control of the means of production and the fruits of labour; the organization of the workplace, decision-making processes, the legal framework enabling autonomous participation, respect for cultural differences and social identities and, of course, democratic governance.

May I be allowed once again to provide an example from my part of the world. Indigenous peoples, for example, the 50 million in Latin America, are the perennially poor, the persistently deprived, the systematically excluded, the eternally marginalized and discriminated against. In Geneva the UN Working Group on Indigenous Populations has been working since 1983 on a Declaration of Indigenous Rights which is still, at this time, bogged down in the Human Rights Commission. What do indigenous peoples want? Not only equal rights with everybody else, because formally they have enjoyed these rights in most countries since the beginning of the nineteenth century.

What they claim, nowadays, is legal recognition as differentiated collectivities, territorial rights, cultural rights, and local and regional autonomy within the framework of the right of peoples to self-determination. Not all of this is accepted by existing states, and political conflicts over these issues have erupted all over the region, in Chile, Brazil, Colombia, Ecuador and Mexico.

The peace accord of 1996, which put an end to a brutal 30-year long civil war in Guatemala, includes provisions for the rights and culture of the Maya people the country's demographic majority. One of the reasons why a peace accord has not been achieved in Mexico is that the national government backed away from the idea of indigenous autonomy, which it had previously negotiated with the Zapatista Liberation Army.

The economic and social development of Latin America must include the indigenous populations not only as a faceless and nameless statistical category of persons in poverty or extreme poverty, but as peoples requiring specific solutions to their historically rooted collective needs, solutions that can only be based on the recognition of group rights without which individual rights cannot be fully guaranteed. The holders of such rights may vary from the vast rather amorphous concept of an indigenous people to the residents of specific territories to local communities. Convention 169 adopted by the International Labour Organization in 1989 goes far in setting out the current rights of indigenous peoples.

It states that:

- Special measures shall be adopted as appropriate for safeguarding the persons, institutions, property, labour, cultures and environment of the peoples concerned.

In applying the provisions of this Convention:

- The social, cultural, religious and spiritual values and practices of these peoples shall be recognised and protected, and due account shall be taken of the nature of the problems which face them both as groups and as individuals;

And governments shall:

- Establish means for the full development of these peoples. own institutions and initiatives, and in appropriate cases provide the resources necessary for this purpose.

Furthermore:

- The peoples concerned shall have the right to decide their own priorities for the process of development as it affects their lives, beliefs, institutions and spiritual well-being and the lands they occupy or otherwise use, and to exercise control, to the extent possible, over their own economic, social and cultural development.
- The improvement of the conditions of life and work and levels of health and education of the peoples concerned, with their participation and co-operation, shall be a matter of priority in plans for the overall economic development of areas they inhabit. Special projects for development of the areas in question shall also be so designed as to promote such improvement.
- Governments shall take measures, in co-operation with the peoples concerned, to protect and preserve the environment of the territories they inhabit.
- The rights of ownership and possession of the peoples concerned over the lands which they traditionally occupy shall be recognised.
- The rights of the peoples concerned to the natural resources pertaining to their lands shall be specially safeguarded. These rights include the right of these peoples to participate in the use, management and conservation of these resources.

Fourteen states had ratified this Convention by July 2000, and it should be clear that its provisions can be implemented only if the group rights of indigenous peoples are recognized in all activities related to social and economic development.

These considerations lead to some ideas regarding the role of people-oriented institutions, including the state. Adam Smith notwithstanding, in today's globalized world there is no invisible hand that guides free markets to socially desired decisions. If these occur at all, they are the by-products, not the major outcomes of laissez faire. There are, on the contrary, many visible fingers punching computer keyboards to obtain the best results of global transactions for the world's power elites.

HUMAN RIGHTS

Human rights are almost a form of religion in today’s world. They are the great ethical yardstick that is used to measure a government’s treatment of its people. A broad consensus has emerged in the twentieth century on rhetoric that frames judgement of nations against an international moral code prescribing certain benefits and treatment for all humans simply because they are human. Within many nations political debates rage over the denial or abuse of human rights.

Even in prosperous, democratic countries like Canada much public discourse is phrased in the rhetoric of rights. Legal documents to protect human rights have proliferated in Canada, culminating in the 1982 entrenchment of the Charter of Rights in the Constitution. Especially since the advent of the Charter, many Canadians have claimed that particular benefits they desire are a matter of human rights and must be provided.

Indeed, the claim that the desired benefit is a human right is often meant to undercut any opposition as unprincipled or even immoral. Lost in much of the discussion is any justification for the high moral grounded occupied by human rights. Most political activists and commentators are content just to look at the United Nations' ever-growing body of human rights agreements as proof that these rights exist universally and therefore have to be respected by everyone.

Domestic human rights legislation represents the local implementation of internationally-recognized rights that are universal and inalienable. Unfortunately, human rights are far more complicated phenomena than that. Any enquiry into the origin, nature, and content of human rights reveals tremendous conceptual hurdles that need to be overcome before one can accept their pre-eminent authority. Indeed, many argue that the problems encountered in this analysis demonstrate that human "rights" are a misnomer, and that the rhetoric of human rights is really a description of ideals-and a controversial set of ideals at that.

A DISCURSIVE APPROACH TO HUMAN RIGHTS

Many of the issues and debates about human rights will be discussed in later stages, and their applicability to social work practice will be identified. At the outset, however, it is important to make a clear statement about the approach to human rights adopted in this book. This is an approach that rejects a positivist notion of rights, implying that human rights somehow 'exist' in an objective form and can be identified, 'discovered', and empirically measured or verified.

The idea of rights existing somehow independently of human agency is characteristic of the positivist world-view of the social sciences, which regards social phenomena as existing independently and objectively, and sees the task of the social scientist as objective empirical enquiry into the laws that govern how social phenomena interact. The positivist view has been the object of sustained critique in the social science literature and the position of this book is one that rejects such a paradigm. Rather than regarding rights as'existing' in some way, hence able to be uncovered through objective scientific enquiry, the arguments in later stages see human rights as essentially discursive, in other words rights are constructed through human interaction and through an ongoing dialogue about what should constitute a common or shared humanity. Hence human rights are not static but will vary over time and in different cultures and political contexts.

The best-known statement of human rights, the Universal Declaration of Human Rights, though representing perhaps one of the more remarkable human achievements of the twentieth century, should not therefore be reified and seen as expressing a universal and unchanging truth. Rather, the Universal Declaration represents a statement of what was agreed by the leaders of the world's nations in 1948 as a statement of the basic rights of all people. It is an impressive and inspirational statement, with significant radical implications, and it has been used in many ways since to further many important causes in the name of humanity. But it is not holy writ, and it can and should be subject to challenge in different times, as different voices are heard and different issues are given priority.

The same must apply to any other statement of human rights: what constitutes the basic rights of all human beings will be a matter for ongoing debate and redefinition and should always be open to challenge. The Universal Declaration has been criticised because of the dominance of western political leaders in the forum from which it was derived, leading to a perceived western bias. This, however, is an argument not for the rejection of the idea of such a universal statement but rather for its continual reformulation in the light of different voices being validated and heard. The Enlightenment view of human rights, as argued by Locke, talks about'natural' rights, namely the idea that the very nature of human beings implies that they have certain rights, as a consequence of their very humanity.

By simply talking about 'human beings' we imply human rights arising from some notion of a common or shared humanity which requires that people be treated in a certain way. At birth we are all equal and therefore we'naturally' acquire equal rights. The idea of rights existing'naturally' might at first sight sound like a positivist framing of human rights, but the idea of'natural' rights in this sense is not necessarily inconsistent with the view of human rights as discursive. It is simply an affirmation of the view that our human rights are the consequence of our common or shared humanity, but it is nevertheless quite consistent to talk about a discursive construction of how we understand those'natural' rights.

The idea of human rights, by its very nature, implies the search for universal principles that apply to all humans, whatever their cultural background, belief system, age, sex, ability or circumstances. Such universality has been absent from many of the more traditional understandings of human rights, simply because not everybody has been thought of as'human'. The discourse of the 'rights of man' and traditional views of patriarchal philosophers such as Locke have distanced women from the definition of'human' and therefore from an understanding of what'human rights' imply. Thomas Jefferson presumably saw no conflict between his advocacy of rights and freedoms and his ownership of slaves. The perpetrators of the Holocaust, while celebrating the high achievements of German civilization, were able to justify their actions by effectively defining Jews as subhuman, and the same can be said of the Apartheid regime in South Africa, the Indonesian occupying army in East Timor, the Serb forces in Bosnia, and so on. Oppressors can justify their actions by effectively removing their victims from their understanding of'human' and thereby avoiding the necessity of recognising their human rights.

HUMAN RIGHTS IN A GLOBALISED WORLD

The idea of human rights is one of the most powerful in contemporary social and political discourse. It is readily endorsed by people from many different cultural and ideological backgrounds and it is used rhetorically in support of a large number of different and sometimes conflicting causes. Because of its strong appeal and its rhetorical power, it is often used loosely and can have different meanings in different contexts, although those who use the idea so readily seldom stop to ponder its various meanings and its contradictions.

This combination of its strong appeal and its contradictions makes the idea of human rights worth closer consideration, especially for social workers and those in other human service professions. This book is concerned with what a human rights perspective means for social workers. Framing social work as a human rights profession has certain consequences for the way in which social work is conceptualised and practised.

In many instances such a perspective reinforces and validates the traditional understandings and practices of social work, while in other cases it challenges some of the assumptions of the social work profession. The position of this book is that a human rights perspective can strengthen social work and that it provides a strong basis for an assertive practice that seeks to realise the social justice goals of social workers, in whatever setting. Human rights, however, are also contested and problematic. To develop a human rights basis for social work requires that the idea of human rights, and the problems and criticisms associated with it, be carefully examined. In this and following stages some of the issues and problems raised by human rights will be discussed, and the implications of these discussions for social work will be highlighted.

Many authors suggest that the idea of human rights is largely a product of Enlightenment thinking and is therefore inevitably contextualised within an essentially western and modernist framework. This has led to the criticism that human rights thinking and rhetoric are simply another manifestation of colonialist western domination, and to the suggestion that the concept of human rights should not be used. While it is true that much of the contemporary understanding of human rights has been shaped by western Enlightenment thinking, the same can be said of many other concepts that are frequently used in political debate, such as democracy, justice, freedom, equality and human dignity.

To stop using such words simply because of their western Enlightenment associations would be to deny their power and importance across cultures and would lead to sterile and limited political debate. The task rather is to loosen them from the shackles of western modernity and to reconstruct them in more dynamic, inclusive and cross-cultural terms. That is the approach taken, though of course cultural issues and the question of cultural relativism are critically important. There is a stronger reason, however, to resist the argument that the idea of human rights should be rejected because of its western connotations.

This is because it is simply not true to say that human rights is an exclusively western concept. Notions of human rights are embedded in all the major religious traditions and can be found in many different cultural forms, though the term'human rights' may not always be used. Ideas of human dignity and worth, ideas that all people should be treated just as to certain basic standards, ideas that people should be protected from what is frequently termed'human rights abuse', and ideas of respect for the rights of others are not confined to the western intellectual tradition. To assume that they are is to devalue those other religious and cultural traditions that such critics often claim to be supporting. Nor is it true, as is commonly suggested, that human rights are a recent concept emerging only in the last two centuries, with their origins in Enlightenment thinking.

Although the Enlightenment was crucial in the construction of the modern western framing of human rights, the idea of human rights has been reflected in writings from much earlier ages, even though the term it self may not always have been used. Human rights, indeed, represent a powerful discourse that seeks to overcome divisiveness and sectarianism and to unite people of different cultural and religious traditions in a single movement asserting human values and the universality of humanity, at a time when such values are seen to be under threat from the forces of economic globalisation. The idea of human rights, by its very appeal to universally applicable ideas of the values of humanity, seems to resonate across cultures and traditions and represents an important rallying cry for those seeking to bring about a more just, peaceful and sustainable world.

As well as the criticism of cultural bias, two other criticisms are commonly made of a human rights perspective. One is that claims of human rights can be frivolous or selfish: people will claim something as a'human right' when in fact they are simply expressing a simple selfish'want'; for example people might claim the right to own a car, the right to take a luxury cruise, the right to smoke in a restaurant, the right to watch a video on an aircraft. Thus human rights become nothing more than a new language for consumerism and self-indulgence.

The other criticism is that claims of human rights can conflict with each other and therefore one is left with the problem of reconciling competing claims, for example the right of freedom of expression as opposed to the right to protection from libel or slander. A human rights perspective needs to show how it will overcome those criticisms, and this will be undertaken in this and subsequent stages. Much of the academic debate about human rights remains at the theoretical level; less has been written about the practice of human rights. The important exception to this has been the legal profession, which has developed a significant specialisation in human rights law.

While lawyers have played a very important role in the promotion and safeguarding of human rights, an exclusively legal framing of human rights practice has limited the applicability of human rights in other professions and occupations. The reasons for this, and its consequences. Other professions, such as medicine, social work, teaching and nursing, are also concerned with human rights issues, and their practice can be seen as very much about the promotion of human rights in ways that extend beyond the more constrained practice of the law. The literature of these professions, however, while acknowledging that ideas of human rights are important for professional practice, does not for the most part define either theory or practice within a specific human rights framework. There is little articulation of what it means in practice for professionals to claim that their work is based on human rights, and so human rights remain a'nice idea' rather than a solid foundation for the development of practice theories and methodologies.

This book represents an attempt to fill this gap by examining what a human rights perspective means for the practice of human service professions such as social work. It identifies some of the important theoretical and conceptual issues about human rights and looks at how they might be applied to practice in a way that can identify a social worker more clearly as a human rights worker.

In general use, the term'human rights worker' applies either to lawyers with a human rights specialisation or to activists working for organisations such as Amnesty International. This book seeks to locate social workers also as human rights workers and to identify some key issues that emerge when social work is reframed as human rights work.

ADEQUATE HOUSING

"The human right to adequate housing is the right of every woman, man, youth and child to gain and sustain a safe and secure home and community in which to live in peace and dignity". This definition is in line with the core elements of the right to adequate housing as defined by General Comment No. 4 of the United Nations Committee on Economic, Social and Cultural Rights. The Committee, while adequacy is determined in part by social, economic, cultural, climatic, ecological and other factors, it is nevertheless possible to identify certain aspects of the right that must be taken into account for this purpose in any particular context.

They include the following:

- Legal security of tenure;
- Availability of services, materials, facilities and infrastructure;
- Affordability;
- Habitability;
- Accessibility;
- Location; and
- Cultural adequacy.

Bibliography

A. K. Patel and M. V. Dubey: *Methods Of Social Work*, Crescent Pub, 2010.

M A Khan: *Social Work and Social Policy : Concepts and Methods*, Book Enclave, 2007.

P.R. Gautam and R.S. Singh: *Social Work and Social Policy : Concepts and Methods*, Centrum Press, 2011.

Sushil Mittal and Gene Thursby: *Studying Hinduism: Key Concepts and Methods*, Manohar, 2007.

B.C. Acharya: *A Handbook of Social Work*, Wisdom Press, 2012.

Brian Sheldon and Geraldine Macdonald: *A Textbook of Social Work*, Routledge, 2010.

Suresh Sachdev: *A Textbook of Social Work*, Dominant Publishers, 2012.

Barbra Teater: *An Introduction to Applying Social Work Theories and Methods*, Rawat Pub, 2011.

Krishna Kant Singh and Ram Shankar Singh: *An Introduction to Social Work*, ABD Pub., 2011.

Jainendra Kumar Jha: *An Introduction to Social Work*, Anmol, 2002.

Suresh Sachdev: *An Introduction to Social Work*, Dominant Pub, 2012.

Prakash Soni: *Applied Psychology for Social Work*, Prateeksha Publications, 2011.

Debotosh Sinha: *Aspects of Industry and Occupational Social Work*, Abhijeet Pub, 2007.

Gurusamy Gandhi: *Career in Social Work*, Jnanada Prakashan, 2012.

Shilpa Jamkhedkar: *Careers in Social Work*, Vision Books,2006.

Sandhya Joshi: *Child Survival Health and Social Work Intervention*, Concept, 1996.

Premanand Choudhary: *Child Survival, Health and Social Work Intervention*, ABD Pub, 2008.

Dinesh Singh: *Communication and Interpersonal Skills for Social Work*, Prateeksha Publications, 2011.

Ratna Guha: *Communication in Social Work*, Centrum Press, 2011.

Mohd. Dilshad: *Communication Organisation and Social Work*, Anmol, 2012.

Farzana Begum: *Concepts of Social Work Practice*, Rajat Publications, 2010.

John Pierson and Martin Thomas: *Dictionary of Social Work*, Rawat Pub, 2011.

Joseph Walsh: *Direct Social Work Practice : Theoretical Perspectives*, Rawat Pub, 2010.

Sanjeev Sarkar: *Direct Social Work Practice : Theory And Skills*, Yking Books, 2011.

Roger Smith: *Doing Social Work Research*, Rawat, 2013.

Robert Brown: *Effective Writing Skills for Social Work*, Prateeksha Publications, 2011.

Anand Sirohi: *Encyclopaedia of Social Welfare : Modern Perspective on Social Work*, Dominant, 2005.

C.P. Yadav: *Encyclopaedia of Social Work and Community Organisation*, Anmol, 2007.

Ashok Walekar: *Encyclopaedia of Sociology and Social Work*, ABD Publishers, 2012.

Chandrashekhar J.:*Essays in Contemporary Social Work*, Cyber Tech Pub, 2012.

Charles H. Zastrow: *Evaluating Social Work Practice*, Rawat, 2010.

Ratna Guha: *Field Instruction in Social Work*, Centrum Press, 2011.

Sanjoy Roy: *Fieldwork in Social Work*, Rawat Publications, 2012.

I.S. Subhedar: *Fieldwork Training in Social Work*, Rawat, 2009.

Mujawar. W.R and Sardar. N.K: *Fieldwork Training in Social Work*, Manglam Pub, 2009.

Tanuja Trivedi and Samitha Rani Natarajan: *Future of Social Work*, Jnanada Prakashan, 2014.

K. D. Gangrade: *Gandhian Approach to Development and Social Work*, Concept, 2005.

K.D. Gangrade: *Gandhian Perspective on Global Interdependence, Peace and Role of Professional Social Work*, Authorspress, 2008.

Sarat C. Joshi: *Gandhian Social Work*, Akansha, 2009.

Tanuja Trivedi: *Gandhian Social Work*, Jnanada Prakashan, 2012.

Sudhir Varma: *Gender, HIV and Social Work*, Rawat, 2010.

Murli Desai and Siva Raju: *Gerontological Social Work in India : Some Issues and Perspectives*, B.R., 2000.

M.L. Janagambika: *Handbook of Practice Education in Social Work*, Manglam Publications, 2010.

Index